The Journey

PAT MARQUIS

Contents

Dedication

I'd like to dedicate this book to two parties that have had a major impact in my life and have recently departed.

Rodney K. Logan

Loving Father to Rhonda and my Dad for the past 45 years.
We will miss you!

Cheyenne
My buddy and a mainstay of our herd
for the past 18 years. What a ride!

Meet the Team!

What you are about to read is my rendition of a series of events that I found to be worthy of reporting and transmitting to friends and family over a six-month period in the year of 2015. However, since this "journey" is personalized by being my individual perspectives of the events that took place, I thought it prudent to bring to you some background and history that led to and predated the actual event. Such as this may allow, you might be able to bring it all into some sort of context and be able to visualize who we are and what we are doing. Or maybe not. But hopefully, you will be able to enjoy reading the text as much as I enjoyed presenting it.

Hi, my name is Pat. I am seventy years young and getting younger all the time, or so I wish. For those of you who have passed this milestone, you should understand of what I speak, and for the rest of you . . . you'll get there. Believe me, you will get there. Nearly forty-five years ago, I was lucky enough to meet a young lass with a lot of Alaska pluck, having been born and raised in Anchorage; and at the ripe old age of eighteen, she was out experiencing life alone but for her beloved companion, a German shepherd named Kohoutek. For those of you who were around at that time, that was the name of a comet that had passed in close proximity to our planet Earth, just a little older than the rest of us, having last appeared in the Earth's sky some 150,000 years prior. Kohoutek, the dog, is the one that accidentally brought us together, that is Rhonda and myself, and we have been together, more or less for the entire forty-two years.

While Rhonda is a born and raised Alaskan, I was something of a vagabond at that time, having been exorcised from the military during the Vietnam conflict a year earlier (1972, to save you the math) and full of travel excitement. The military let me out of my commitments and paid my way to travel from Florida, my base of residence, to return to Northern California, where I was born and raised. They (the US Air Force) didn't say just how long I could (or should) be on the road, so I visited thirty states over the next seven months before returning to the wine country of Sonoma County in Northern California. Those seven months have inspired me and were probably the precursor to my being part of *the journey* as I walked and fished in the Everglades, paddled my canoe in the Okefenokee Swamp, sailed in Chesapeake Bay with friends, endured zero-degree weather in the Pocono Mountains of Pennsylvania, and was robbed in New York City. I generally traversed up and down the area east of the Mississippi before heading towards New Orleans for a breath of warm air—air that I neither saw nor felt as I was notified that my father was very ill and I should return to California in haste.

If my travels were the precursor to later escapades, then my father can be held accountable for another relationship that continues to this day, my love of and fondness for the outdoors and our equine friend, the horse. I was born in San Mateo, California, which is just south of San Francisco, and hardly a place for keeping stock but probably a good place to raise children. However, I would hardly know because my first memories were of a row house and school on Twin Peaks in The City, where my father successfully managed a small business. So where did the horses come from? Well, I have memories of Golden Gate Park and a remembrance of pictures showing me in my father's arms astride a horse in the park. Unfortunately, those pictures were lost when we lost our father, me being the fourth of five children. I had been an absentee son ever since leaving for college and the military some nine years earlier. I'm not even sure when the horses left the family confines of our rural home and twenty acres in Rincon Valley just outside Santa Rosa, California, but gone they were. But what a splendid place to grow up, amid twenty acres of grassland, a prune and walnut orchard, and just about every imaginable fruit tree and bush that could be nourished at this latitude. With a barn and other outbuildings, we just had to have a horse (or horses) along with a cow or two, chickens, and even some pigs and steers my brothers raised in 4H and FFA. My two brothers, my younger sister, and I grew up riding horses and tending to all the critters.

We had moved here from The City in time for me to attend first grade, and here we stayed until after I left home. I can't even attest to what promulgated such a move other than my father's adventuresome spirit to hunt, fish, and generally travel across the western states. A rural lifestyle seemed to fit. He was an avid hunter and fisherman, with many of my fondest memories being of the times we spent in the woods hunting deer, in the rice paddies and sloughs of the Sacramento valley hunting ducks and geese, the grasslands of the area hunting pheasant, and the juniper forests hunting dove. Fishing took us everywhere from the Pacific Ocean to the lakes of Northern California and the streams cascading out of the Coast, Trinity, and Sierra Nevada mountains. And the horses got us to many of these places as we rode on daily excursions to find game or packed into remote regions to fish, hunt, or just explore.

I remember one such excursion to the hills above the Eel River drainage in Northern California where we spent a week, just the two of us (father and son), in a deer hunt that went somewhat awry. My father, like many men of his generation (and even today), did back-breaking labor in his choice of work, and he paid the price. On one of our trips into the edges of the wilderness, we had ridden out in separate directions to look for deer, only he did not come back that afternoon or evening. With nightfall, I was at a loss of what to do but hunker down and wait the night out.

I later learned that in the late hours of the previous day, my dad had been riding along the top of a stream bank of a dry creek bed when the bank had suddenly given way. Horse and rider had tumbled down until coming to rest with the horse atop my dad. The horse was cast with his legs on the uphill side, unable to get up. It took Dad several hours to calm the horse, hand dig enough of the stream bed to get out of his predicament, and then roll the horse over to allow him to rise and stand.

Luckily for Dad, nothing was broken for either party; but by this time, it was too late to head back to camp, with dusk and darkness rapidly approaching. He fashioned a trail camp with the horse blanket for cover and spent the night out while I fretted on what to do back at camp. At twelve years old, I at least had the notion that everything would be all right and that there was nothing I could do in the dark. Deer hunting in Northern California took place in late summer, so there was no risk of hypothermia or weather that could lead to more problems. The following morning, hours would tell the story, and patience would be the order of the day.

Dad showed up the following morning, sore and hungry and in need of rest and recuperation. His back pain had nearly immobilized him, so we made as comfortable a place for him as possible in such a backwoods fashion, and he lay there waiting for things to get better. Only they didn't get better. For several days at his prodding, I would get him settled into a prone position with food and water available, and then I would head into the hills, riding and hunting all day, coming back in time to fix the evening meal. *Hunting* is the right term, because I never shot at anything, only got shot at.

One morning while sitting on a promontory just below the saddle in the ridgeline, I spotted a small herd of deer approaching from below. I kept glassing them and staying as motionless as possible to avoid sending them asunder so that I could determine if any bucks were amongst the crowd. About the time that I determined that they were all does and fawns, bullets started screaming around me as some hunters at the bottom of the slope supposedly saw what I couldn't— horns . . . or maybe not! It was sometimes custom in those early years that hunters would kill camp meat, and to them, the sex didn't matter much. They obviously didn't see me, so I did the only thing that I could think of to stop the fusillade. Shoot back, but way high and into the hillside across the way. I didn't hear another sound all day, but what a wondrous day and week as I continued to ride out each day. While Dad got better and we made it safely home, the remembrance is strong, and it still is a wondrous feeling to be one with your horse, meandering through wooded hills and valleys and across meadows and streams, returning at day's end to the campfire and a healthy meal. Thank you, Dad, for taking me there.

For the past forty years, Rhonda and I have lived a lifestyle that has allowed me to continue the adventures and lessons learned as a youngster growing up on acreage. We have been adventurous throughout as demonstrated by our first few months together. Only a month after my dad passed away, Rhonda and I met in Anchorage during the winter of 1973 while I was working for the Bureau of Land Management as a land surveyor—a profession I have toiled at and enjoyed my entire life. The previous summer, I had worked on an airborne control survey crew that visited five outlying areas of the state as we began surveying the boundaries between state and federal lands in conformance to the state of Alaska's Statehood Act as the forty-ninth state.

But in the spring of 1974, I decided to embark on another adventure as I became the first surveyor to work construction on the Southern Terminus of the Trans-Alaska Pipeline located across Valdez Bay from the small town of Valdez, Alaska. And an adventure it truly was, as indicated by our first day of work, when we took a truck to the boat harbor, then stepped upon a six-pack Uniflite boat that would cruise across the bay and drop us off onto a floating pier. We off-loaded our survey gear and loaded it onto a small twelve-foot row boat, and thence, we rowed ashore to start our first day of work. Adventure indeed! In those early days, before the hordes of workers arrived, I had the joyous opportunity to encounter black and brown bears that frequented those slopes. There were also otters playing and cavorting in the local streams, and culminating during one particular lunch hour when as we rested upon the shores of a small cove, a killer whale exploded from the water while feeding on the herring that was a trademark of Valdez Bay before the oil spill. This was marine land in real life!

My summer was only going to get better as Rhonda had decided to join me in Valdez. We set up living quarters in a small tent alongside Mineral Creek, just westerly of the town. Rhonda had brought her Econoline van with everything I think she owned, which I suppose at the tender age of eighteen was not a ton of stuff. She and I, with our three dogs (two German shepherds and a collie), lived out the summer months together in this fashion, me leaving for work every morning and her keeping the home fires burning. The dogs seemed to keep the bears and moose away, and we just enjoyed our time together—that is, until the fall rains came and the swollen creek had us move out in a hurry.

By this time, Rhonda had also gotten employment on the Flour-Alaska staff as a telephone operator and administrative assistant. Thus, when the rains came, moving was easier than you might envision, with our belongings going into the van and our personal belongings being lodged in the camp provided for construction workers. We would eat and sleep every night in camp and maybe watch a movie, and then embark for work every day on the terminal site. The dogs lived in doghouses on the edge of the parking lot.

Did I mention the fall rains? Well, forget rain as Valdez is known for some of the heaviest snowfall accumulations in all of Alaska, and winter would not be far behind. About this time, I was notified that my father's estate was being settled, allowing us to purchase his motorhome and bring it to Alaska and thus allow Rhonda and me to once again have a life together. The motorhome would be parked in the camp's parking lot, but at least we would have each other, just us and our dogs. Meals and entertainment were still had at the camp, and nights were spent in the home. This young lass had certainly proved her mettle and shown me what Alaskan women were about, taking life in stride and always finding a way to make do. As we formed a life together, albeit haphazard and spur of the moment, I felt it was time to think and gaze into the future. And so it was that in this very same parking lot that I proposed to Rhonda, and she accepted. Thus began our forty-four years together as a married couple.

Two years later, with the pipeline work a distant memory and Rhonda and I now a married couple, we chose to settle on the Kenai Peninsula near a small berg, Anchor Point, known as the most westerly point on the North American highway system. Just fifteen miles north of Homer, we were about to settle on ten acres of wilderness or virtually so. Many years later and living in Oregon, Rhonda would smile when people would talk about visiting the wilderness, a statute designation for government land set aside to protect it from the ever reaching hand of progress. To us, during that time of making a home and raising a family in Alaska, it was a term to describe the area on the other side of the Anchor River, which was adjacent to our northerly property boundary. Bear tracks in the sand and moose feeding on the willows in the river bottom were a normal occurrence, distracting and beautiful at the same time. We eventually moved "outside" to Oregon, and when Rhonda saw the sign alongside the trail that designated the Three Sisters Wilderness boundary, she exclaimed, "Oh! It's a park!"

Our Alaska home was to be in keeping with the times and locale as we decided to erect a log cabin in the middle of the property, overlooking the North Fork of the Anchor River, with a year-round spring not too far distant. Rather than building with trees off our property, which we hoped to preserve for aesthetics, privacy, and our solitude, we purchased logs from a local mill and had them delivered.

Now, how would we get them to the building site since we had decided to keep the building site free of vehicle traffic?

The next step would change our lives forever because in answer to that question, I suggested a horse, of course! Oklahoma Beth thus entered our lives and was to remain a member of our extended family for the next twenty-five years, leaving us only after the kids were adults and living their own lives away from the homestead. She was a treasure, towing logs to our cabin site and in the following years, allowing Rhonda and the kids an adventure as they learned to ride. And she allowed me to return to an earlier stage in my life, riding in the wilderness and packing my first load of moose meat out of the Caribou Hills northeast of where we lived. Beth was the first of many horses we would come to own through the ensuing forty plus years, and while not the best trained or most comfortable ride, she was ever dependable, sure-footed, and safe. We couldn't have asked for more. The vision of Beth leading a procession of equines in our stable was not something I gave any thought to at that time, nor was the inevitable allure of the horse to Rhonda a thoughtful consideration. But I am now thankful for all that has transpired since creating an enduring relationship to our equine pals and to our partnership in marriage.

My chosen profession as a professional land surveyor took me to the far reaches of Alaska and, in later years, to many outreaches of the western US. I spent time on the North Slope of Alaska, surveying and walking from Prudhoe Bay to the Yukon River and crossing the Brooks Range in the process. I've seen wolves in their den and surrounds, caribou in lines many miles long on their pilgrimage to winter grazing, musk ox on the coastal flats along the Chukchi Sea, a polar bear visiting a remote Alaskan village, and brown and black bears in so many encounters I have lost count. Alaska, for me, was truly the last frontier as I spent many a day in the woods or along the water boundaries in the course of earning a living as a surveyor or while hunting and sport fishing. In the nearly sixteen years of being a resident of Alaska, I reveled in each day and the adventure it might bring around the next bend in the road.

The cabin eventually became a bigger cabin, what with a child on the way, and then it became a home of substantial size as the family grew. And we incorporated more conveniences, like water piped in and septic and electricity and telephone. As the family grew, so did the business grow, for now I was an entrepreneur with a professional license and a business license. Dad's three sons all became businessmen in their own right, with me being the youngest and last to tackle one's own enterprise. It allowed an independence that I could not have otherwise been able to achieve, and it provided sufficient income to do those things we desired, like getting more horses. By now, Rhonda was an accomplished equestrian, having ridden all the trails we could find and some areas where trails were nonexistent. And along came Charlie, a gelding of mild manner and with an excellent stride, making for an excellent ride. Rhonda was forever hooked.

As our children, Nicole and Colin, reached the appropriate age, they were introduced to the horses and began the trek through 4-H to learn and demonstrate what they had learned. While the horses were seen by me to be a means to accomplish things that I couldn't do myself, like hauling logs to the cabin site or carrying me to where the moose were or carrying moose meat out of the woods, the family reminded me of my beginnings. Horses could be fun. Horses were great companions, and horses could settle your personal space by just being there. So when the economy of Alaska tanked in the later 1980s, I came home one evening and told Rhonda that I had just finished my last contracted job for that summer and had no new opportunities on the horizon.

We needed to consider our options, all our options, in order to survive and create a life worth living. There was work in Anchorage and most likely leading to remote work as well. And there was contracted work on the Alaska Peninsula, but it would mean my being away for months at a time. We didn't want to go back to the city life, and I didn't want to be an absent dad for months at a time. And then came the kicker as Rhonda explained that she would like to ride Charlie more than three to four months out of the year. After a lot of soul-searching, we decided that a major paradigm shift was in order, and a major move to the Lower 48 was planned and executed in a short two months.

We settled in Oregon, where the economy was on the upswing and Rhonda's mom and stepdad were currently living, having moved from Alaska several years prior. We enjoy family relationships, and the move would also put us within driving distance to my extended family residing in Northern California. And lastly but most importantly, the move to Oregon would allow us to pursue many of the same type exploits we had so enjoyed in Alaska. The Northwest has an abundance of federal and state lands left virtually untrammeled and ready for their exploration by a young family. I had visions of fishing the rivers and lakes and hunting in the mountains of the Coast, Cascade, and Blue Mountains. But I think most importantly, the Northwest is the land of the horse. The Indians had incorporated horses into their culture hundreds of years ago. The settlers that crossed the plains and travelled the Oregon Trail brought horses as well. It is a land that has nurtured the equestrian spirit and held the horse in high regard, and we wanted to be a part of that culture.

Our move out of Alaska began by the four of us piling as many wanted items as possible into our ¾-ton king cab pickup and making the long trek down the Alcan Highway in the early part of December 1988. We would initially settle in Southern Oregon at Rhonda's mom and stepdad's home, thus allowing the kids to settle and get back in school. I began the search for employment in the metropolitan area of Portland and surrounds, where we would later settle after school let out in the summer. The job part came easy, but how were we going to get our belongings, household goods, and most importantly, two horses and three cats out of Alaska and down to Oregon?

That May, I was to find out and see the strength, determination, and spirit of Rhonda as she formulated a plan to do just that. We purchased a new vehicle to make it happen, and Rhonda enlisted her brother to fly down from Alaska and help her drive nonstop back to our home in Anchor Point. Enlisting our many friends as helpers, they loaded a shipping container with all our household goods and then some. In short order, it was on its way by ship to the Port of Portland, where it would be off-loaded and brought to the rental property and acreage I had located near Gresham, Oregon. Rhonda then hitched up our stock trailer, loaded all the horsey gear, including the two horses, Beth and Charlie, and was on her way. Oh yeah, don't forget the cats, the recliner to sleep in during the trip back down the Alcan, and enough horse food to assure all would make it without starving.

Her brother had to get back to work, so this trip was made solo, with horses and cats as company. And to think that she did all this without a cell phone, a computer, or Google Maps. What a gal!

The past thirty years have just been more of the same, living the country life on a small farm just outside the Portland metro area and, once the kids were out of school and entering their working life and careers, a move to Central Oregon and more acreage. We now live in the High Desert country with sage brush, grasslands, and juniper trees surrounding our rural home. Next to us are federal lands managed by the Bureau of Land Management. This provides us an opportunity to ride any day of the year right off our property. But not far away are the magnets of the Cascade Mountains of Central Oregon and the Ochoco Mountains farther east, where riding opportunities abound. This is where you will find us most any summer day, cruising the trails and living out of our living quarter's trailer. Every day can now be an adventure, a test of skill, and an opportunity to enjoy the partnership with our friends, our equine buddies that are now Liz and Cheyenne, in our pasture.

It is my hope that you, the reader, now have a sense of who we are. I hope you have gained a feel for the adventure we will share with you and an appreciation of our relationship with each other and with our equine friends. Thank you for listening.

Pat (PCT trail name: the Wrangler) and Rhonda (trail name: Horse-n-Around)

Prologue

It's Tuesday, March 17, and St. Patrick's Day . . . Departure Day! Wow! The day is finally here, and we are actually going to leave, or at least we are going to attempt to leave. Knowing us, that may be more of a challenge than I am prepared for, but we are both so energized, waking in the predawn hours and rising with the sun. Not Rhonda's forte, but I'm sure the excitement and release this day brings, a culmination of many months and maybe years of heavy mental lifting, shall have made sleep nearly impossible. Me, I'm almost always up with the sun and ready to get on with the day. Anyway, how could one sleep when you are about to take a physical step into an unknown future that is looming with the morning sun?

And sunny it is, and thankfully so because there is much to do. You would think that after months of planning, we would be able to rise and shine, eat and pack a lunch, load the critters, and be off on our grand adventure. I wish. I picked St. Patrick's Day as a good omen for a trip well-travelled, my name being Patrick and all. Actually, any day would have done, but it needed to allow time for us to get to the Mexican border by Rhonda's start date of April 7. We also must provide time for acclimating our critters to the Southern California desert clime and provide for time to desensitize the horses with us being on their backs once again. It will be a long trailer ride, albeit broken up into many short jaunts while we visit relatives along the way and scout resupply locations. We will take it slow one day at a time.

I still marvel at the fact that we are actually going! For nearly two years, Rhonda has been absorbed by the mystique of riding the Pacific Crest Trail, the PCT, as us Westerners refer to it. I don't know how many books she has read, tales of the derring-do of those that have traversed the high country of California, Oregon, and Washington; but it has been many. A year or more ago, when she first mentioned this ride to me, I didn't give it much thought. Fairly new to my retirement, I had many things on my mind, mostly fun things like golf and fishing, and hunting, and yes, some horseback riding to far-off places was in there someplace.

Rhonda had previously done a 150-mile ride with friends while I was still behind a desk at work, meeting and riding with her and the group on weekends. That trip was roughly a two-week journey, with a number of "0" days and travel time looped in. So I figured that a ride of the Oregon PCT would be an interesting journey and encouraged her to keep her sights on the goal while I worked towards retirement. She was back to working also, but the company was a forgiving one, and a two month sabbatical would likely work for them. Yeah, right.

It wasn't until spring of 2014 that Rhonda finally let the cat out of the bag. "I want to ride the Pacific Crest Trail."

"Fine!" I said, thinking of the PCT in Oregon. We have friends that made the journey to celebrate the millennium and moving into the twenty-first century. We had listened to their stories and were intrigued by the adventure. "Four hundred fifty miles should only take about forty-five days, with travel and '0' days all wrapped into one trip. I might consider going along, if you would concede me that opportunity."

"No!" she said. "I want to ride from Mexico to Canada!"

"Oh!" I said. "Are you kidding me?" And thus The Journey was borne.

Rhonda didn't ask me if I wanted to go along, riding the trail with her. Maybe she already knew the answer, because it didn't take long for me, a fraidy-cat of heights, to figure out that this trail was not for me. She just asked for my help, and I didn't answer. In fact, I didn't answer for months, during which time she didn't falter in her quest of information and facts and even some supplies. I asked her a few pointed questions during the summer of 2014, but mostly, I attended to chores around our 4.5-acre spread, tuned up my game of golf, and travelled with our granddaughter, Carissa and son, Colin, to our old Alaskan haunts to fish and visit old friends and family. It was a marvelous two-week journey that got me to thinking.

Why wouldn't I help Rhonda accomplish the unthinkable, monster of a trip, and a dream of a lifetime. So what if it wasn't my dream? We are a pretty good team and have proven so many times over during our forty years of being together, but can I handle her being in charge and determining the order of the day? It really wasn't that difficult of a decision, I just needed to wrap my mind around it and consider what I might be doing for six months without her. And lastly, 2015 is our year of celebration, celebrating my seventieth year, her sixtieth year and our fortieth anniversary, and I can't think of a better way to celebrate. Reminds me of the ancient tune by the rock band Rare Earth and another day of living!

So in the fall of this past year, it was time for me to catch up. Rhonda had been planning for six months or more and mentally considering it for well over a year. It was staggering to find out the PCT is 2,650 miles long and then looking at the map, it was easy to see why, as it meandered over 1,700 miles through the state of California, alone. Oh boy, what did I get myself into? Hehe, not only get into, but it was time to bury myself in it. If Rhonda could average fifteen miles per day, it would take 177 days to complete the ride, and that is an average. What about "0" days (days of rest and recuperation) and just the logistics of being on the road for six months, feeding horses and ourselves, caring for the truck and trailer, finding camping spots, and the list went on and on. And these were just my concerns! What about all that Rhonda had to consider, such as water along the trail, grazing opportunities, pack trips and camping spots, trail conditions and countless other issues as you came around each bend in the trail. And to do it alone!

Needless to say, we spent the next four months poring over maps and books each evening and sometimes on weekends, developing a plan and approach by which we believed we could achieve the goal. Thank goodness for the PCT "Data Book", which listed all the PCT sections with mile points of geographic landmarks and points of interest such as road crossings, trail intersections, creek crossings, springs, and camp spots while listing trail gradients between each and elevations for each.

We coupled the book with half-mile maps, which are topographic maps with aerial photo overlay at a scale of 1 inch =

½ mile, depicting the trail and marked at half-mile intervals on catalogued 8½ × 11 inch sheets of paper. With these tools, we were able to strategize our movements along the entire corridor.

We then purchased maps of each state in book form, the atlas, published at a scale of 1 inch = 5,000 feet, and then walked our way through the book and maps, laying out each day's travel and established our plan for the trip. To be there for Rhonda, I had to know how to drive to every road crossing the trail intersected. We actually did this twice, refining our plan and developing strategy as we went. We argued, cajoled, and pondered, and eventually arrived at consensus, knowing full well that this was just a plan and that reality may need a whole new plan.

For my part in this whole medley, it was time to review the logistical nightmare that was fast approaching. If we were to carry three horses in the Hilton, hmm? You haven't been introduced to the Hilton, which is really a horse trailer—and a really nice horse trailer at that. Back in the year 2006, we had been using a horse trailer we had dubbed Ol' Blue because it was painted robin's-egg blue and was a thirty-year-old living-quarters horse trailer produced by McQuery of Los Angeles. We had purchased it for a nickel and a dime and felt quite lucky to have done so. It got us out of a tent when travelling with our horses, and that alone would have been worth triple the costs. All it lacked was a shower and a little more headroom, as the ceiling height was only six feet and I am six-two, but we got along for many years. Until finally economics and a sore noggin got me to thinking and asking myself what we were waiting for. There were living-quarters horse trailers of every shape and dimension, not to mention the accoutrements they are adorned with. They were everywhere!

We looked online at new and used ones from Florida to California and north to our region of the country. We began to develop insight into what they offered and clarified what we wanted. It should be a gooseneck trailer holding three horses (just in case we expanded the herd), with full living quarters, including a queen bed, stove, fridge, potty, shower, and ample storage space. It should have a pass- through door to the horse compartment, a rear tack area, and a rack for hay on top. And lastly, it should be as short as possible because the forest roads we wished to travel on and camp alongside were narrow and winding. It should be all aluminum to resist rusting out in the moderate climate of the Pacific Northwest. Piece of cake, right? Well, not so right!

We must have perused twenty websites, looking at both used and new trailers and still couldn't make up our minds. Most were too long, too expensive, too ornate, or just too far away to go look at. We had friends that owned a Silverlite, which is made in Oregon, and so one winter day when we were totally bored, we decided to go look at the factory lineup and talk to a real person. Kind of get a feel for the industry and what is possibly in our future. Just a little fact gathering, right? The factory also has a sales lot, so we were shepherded around the factory by the sales rep, but we really liked what we saw.

Silverlite trailers are all aluminum, well-constructed, and offered in models that fit our criteria. Oh yeah, as it turned out, the deciding criteria regarding the length had to do with the refrigerator. Can you believe it? Rhonda had determined that the fridge should be a minimum of six cubic feet. Okay by me . . . what do I know? This meant the short wall, to accommodate the fridge would be somewhere around nine to ten feet, shortest dimension. The trailer itself would be around thirty-one to thirty-three feet, depending on make and model, width of horse stalls, tack room, and all the basics.

The salesman just happened to have one on-site that fit all our criteria, or nearly so. I told him we didn't need air conditioning or a microwave since they don't typically have electric service out in the woods. He chuckled and then said these weren't options, at least not at his shop. Damn, and we really liked the trailer. Even had a high ceiling in the bedroom (over the gooseneck) so that I could actually sit up in bed and it was only thirty-one-foot long. Cool! And then he mentioned the price, and luckily, neither one of us had a drink to our lips. Sputtering, we said it was really nice visiting but we should be going. And of course, he said, "Not so fast!" Where there's a will, there just might be a way, and we thought, "NO WAY!" We make decent money, but we are not rich.

It took a while, but he finally got the picture, but he wasn't done. Finally turned us on to a trailer that was on a lot in Spokane, Washington. Having been delivered up there the year before, it had been sitting on the lot ever since because the buyer couldn't come up with adequate funds. Another victim of the banking frauds and the Great Recession. He called the lot to check on availability, and lo and behold, we would soon to be new owners of a year old but spanking new trailer. The story goes on from there, and while interesting, I won't bore you with it since I started by mentioning the Hilton.

The factory made arrangements for the trailer to be moved from Spokane to the northern limits of Oregon, where we would pick it up near the Columbia River. But a couple of days before our departure, we found out it was now in Eugene, Oregon. Ugh, the middle of February and we would have to cross over the Cascade Range, sans snow and ice, and tow our trailer back to our High Desert hobby farm in Central Oregon. Well, do we want this thing or not? Of course! We were on the road the following day, excited as a couple of schoolchildren sitting below the Christmas tree.

Money was exchanged for our new home on wheels, and off we went riding a cloud of anticipation and dreaming of years of pleasure riding in them thar hills. We were returning home with the horse trailer in tow and passing over the crest of the Cascade Mountains at Willamette Pass, blissfully thinking of the adventures to come, when I glanced at the dashboard of our pickup. Aghast, I saw that the oil pressure for this Ram Truck read 00000. It took a mile to find a flat enough spot of snow berm to allow us to get partially off the two-lane highway. Flashers going, I ran out to put flares on the roadway, warning other motorists of our inability to move out of their way, all the while discovering a trail of oil leading me right back to the truck and trailer.

Here we were, stuck on the side of the road, daylight rapidly transitioning to darkness, and the nearest small town (Crescent, Oregon) fifteen miles away. Fortunately, having lived and travelled many miles of Alaskan roadways when living there for sixteen years, I travel with a host of emergency supplies, including two gallons of oil on this particular trip. I saw no choice but to refill the truck with oil as I still didn't know the cause of our spill and didn't want to remain a hazard along the highway for any length of time. We pressed on, made it to the one and only service station in Crescent, which was thankfully open, and we reassessed our predicament. Roughly eighty-five miles from home in this small little berg of a place, and we just wanted to get home and into our own beds. Let's add a gallon of oil and make a run for it, LaPine being only sixteen miles up the road and a metropolis compared to Crescent.

Damn, that's as far as we got when I chickened out. Having had my own business for many years, I am used to assessing and taking risks, but this venture was getting entirely too risky, especially since we did have AAA towing service available to us. "Come get us, but be sure to bring a large rig to take our trailer as well!" After all, we were paying for this service year after year. Unfortunately, this night was not to end on such a happy note as the tow truck that showed up could only tow the pickup. Decisions, decisions.

Rhonda went with the tow truck and headed home, where she would deposit the load, pick up our older back-up one-ton pickup, and come back to LaPine to pick up the whole works, including a cold but thankful me. After all, it was barely ten degrees out and no propane in the trailer to run the heater. We finally made it home that night around 2:00 a.m., but by golly, we had our new trailer! What an adventure and an auspicious start to our life with the Hilton.

Oh yeah, I was going to tell you how we arrived at the name the Hilton.

Not long after bringing the trailer home, we wanted to take a maiden voyage and a shakedown cruise with our new digs and assure ourselves it was road-worthy. It so happened that there was an event in Portland that we were planning to attend, and this would be an excellent opportunity to hit the road. No motel this time as we would park in a friend's front yard and bring our room with us. Once the word got around the block, all our local "horsey" friends in the Portland area had to see our purchase. We were one of the first in our group to have such a whim and prayer to go out on such a limb. It was this crowd that coined the name the Hilton, and the moniker stuck. It's not really that posh but compared to Ol' Blue, it is deluxe and a very far cry from a tent.

Through the years, we have done some improvements to embellish our purchase and make it more accommodating. We installed two outriggers for high-tying our horses overnight to the sides of the trailer. Those critters can get the place rocking and rolling, but the convenience to rapidly putting them up for the night overrode those concerns. Then I built a rack, and we installed solar panels on the roof to extend our non-urban stays on the road, which is about every destination we travel to. Our friends Don and Gerry gave us a couple of barrels to carry water, and we had a holding tank scrounged from an old motor home by Rhonda's brother John. That would serve us well for water storage in the hay rack on top. Life was good.

In 2014, we felt as if we were well positioned to make the highway trip of a lifetime. However, I was petrified by the prospect of the logistical nightmare we foresaw of hauling and caring for three horses under tow through the backwaters of Southern California and northwards from there into the high reaches of the Sierra Nevada mountains. After all, it is called the Pacific Crest Trail, not the valley trail or the foothill trail. I had grown up in California and hiked the Sierra Nevada on many occasions. I knew this country, although it was a vague remembrance at this time.

Each horse would need roughly fifteen pounds of hay and ten gallons of water every day when not out on the trail. We hoped that on the trail they would be grazing and getting water wherever it was available. But this was desert country where there was little graze and water stops were far between. Our first stretch of trail, thankfully, would have many intersecting roadways, so Rhonda and the crew would be at the Hilton nearly every night. However, that meant forty to fifty pounds of hay and twenty to thirty gallons of water would be consumed each and every day. How much can I carry on the truck and trailer combined? Only one barrel on the truck (forty gallons) together with the holding tank (forty gallons) and four Gerry jugs at five gallons each would give us one hundred gallons, or five days' worth of water. Hay was another story. Our bales at home are eighty pounds, but their size limits how many I can carry. Three or maybe four in the truck and four in the rack on top the Hilton means roughly six hundred- plus pounds. Turns out I could only get three in each location, meaning I would have closer to five hundred pounds of hay, or ten days' worth. I was not willing to put another layer of hay on top the trailer and risk a low bridge portal or overpass that we could not negotiate.

However, more troubling was that I would have to find a source for like quality and variety of hay every ten days in a part of the country I've only travelled through and never explored. Hit or miss! Not every town is going to have a feed store like we have at home. This wouldn't do! It is absolutely essential that we not change the horses' diet during this entire affair. Certainly, we could not do so without forethought and planning, or we would be inviting trouble in the form of digestive disruption and possibly colic, a life-threatening malady for a horse. We had to have good quality forage (hay) and a high-quality grain to sustain the energy levels each horse would be expending on the trail. Think again.

The computer and the internet are wonderful tools when you need to find out something you know little about. We found a solution to our dilemma, being able to maintain consistency of product and also carry a more substantial volume of hay. Compressed bales of hay from Idaho that are marketed throughout the western states were just the ticket, and a pellet feed was also produced by the same folks to meet our need for a higher-protein grain. The hay bales are compact and weigh around sixty pounds each. In the hay rack, I can carry eight of these where I previously had only three to four regular-sized bales—480 pounds versus 240 pounds on the trailer—and in the truck it would be ten bales or 600 pounds for a total of 1,080 pounds of hay. That will last me somewhere near twenty days before I must resupply. Fortunately, the hay producer also put all their distributers on their website, so I knew which towns were likely to have a supply, and I could call them ahead of time to reserve what we needed. Logistics were finally beginning to look up.

Water shouldn't be an issue, but again, the lack of knowledge of the communities we would be passing through and the likely places we would be camping led to some sleepless nights. Not much we can do about it except deal with every encounter in any imaginable fashion we could muster. No sense overthinking the issue, so we let it rest. We had never had a problem in our travels in Oregon and could only hope for the same on this trip. We always carry a small submersible pump, and if we could find a stream or a lake, we would be able to pump to our delight. But this was Southern California desert country, so good luck with that.

The next item of business was securing the proper travelling papers for the horses, which would necessitate health certificates for each horse. We engaged our local veterinarian and scheduled an exam ten days prior to our departure date. The exam would also assure us that each horse was basically sound and healthy enough to exert the kind of energy this adventure would ask of them. While we had been riding them for a significant time, conditioning them out of the winter doldrums, the vet might catch something we had missed. The exam and blood tests were meant to assure the travelling public that we weren't carrying unhealthy horses with blood-borne pathogens along on this trip. Before leaving, we would have health certificates to show any interested party that we had complied with existing laws and with the proper intent to not spread infectious disease. We waited until the very last minute because the certificates would only be good for six months, and if you remember, the time for us to travel 2,650 miles was estimated to be 177 days, or roughly six months. Another hurdle would be passed!

And shame on me! Here I am talking about our friends, compatriots, and riding buddies as if they are incidental to the journey. Far from it, and an introduction is in order because they will frame everything we do from day 1 through the final day of this adventure. Without them, there is no adventure, at least no equestrian adventure. So who are they? Maybe a little history is in order.

Rhonda and I have had horses in our corral for the entire forty years of marriage, bringing two of them with us during our move from Alaska to Oregon in 1988. Beth, a registered quarter horse mare, was with us for nearly thirty years and Charlie, of unknown breeding, for close to twenty years. They had been the foundation for our pleasure-riding experiences, twelve years in Alaska and their remaining years in the warmth of Oregon. Both horses had reached the ends of their lives and left us due to natural causes. Many other horses have come and gone to new owners during and in the ensuing years, some being mounts for our two children, Nicole and Colin, and others just passing through as we refined our tastes and understood more about the various breeds and our likes and dislikes.

When Beth reached her elder years, we allowed her to rest in the pasture and entertain many youngster friends of our children as we led her around the paddock. It was time for me to find a new ride. Smoke, a registered quarter horse, was my next mount. I don't remember much about his acquisition other than it was the first time either one of us (Rhonda and I) had an opportunity to ride a gaited horse. When we went to the farm to get a test ride on Smoke, Rhonda was given a second horse in their herd to allow her to come along as we went for a short trail ride. Both were quarter horse geldings, but Rhonda's horse, rather than trot, did what is commonly called "single foot", meaning a form of gaited travel, laying a single foot on the ground at a time. This short interval of riding history would change our lives in the many years to come. Needless to say, Smoke went home with us. I enjoyed the ride and willingness to also pack our goods when our son, Colin, and I went on many hunting adventures. Riding in the back country and packing out game on horseback was something we had been doing for all the Alaskan years, and we have continued to do so in Oregon up to the current time.

I had purchased Cheyenne in the year 2000 as a replacement of my ride, Smoke, who had passed as a result of the dreaded colic while Rhonda and I were riding on the Pacific Crest Trail up in the Cascade mountains just west of Bend, Oregon. Smoke had a history of digestive trouble, and this time, we didn't have a veterinarian close by to provide medical advice and treatment. We managed to get him out of the mountains and to our vet, but the damage was done, and we chose to euthanize rather than operate. Evidence found later, when some students performed a necropsy, told us that we had made the right choice. They could not have saved him. The first of our horses entrusted to carry Rhonda onto the PCT came to us shortly afterwards out of need and necessity.

Cheyenne is a Paso Fino by breeding, being a gaited horse whose lineage could likely be traced to an origination in South America. Up until the late 1990s, Rhonda and I had always ridden quarter horses or their type of western American mount. However, when Rhonda's horse Charlie passed away, she wanted a smoother ride as touted by many of the gaited breeds.

Now, *gait* is the term to describe forward motion for a horse. The American quarter horse, the Morgan horse, and many other associated breeds typically walk, trot, canter, and gallop. Those are their gaits. While the gaited horses may do the same, they also have, by virtue of their confirmation and breeding, the ability to have a four- beat rhythm or single-foot action wherein each foot hits the ground independently. This can make for a smoother ride as it mirrors the natural motion of our "human" hips associated with walking, a slight lift and arc of the leg and hip. To get any more technical, you will have to go look it up because, while I can attest to the smoothness of the ride, I never really investigated the science of it.

During the interim of finding a new trail horse, Rhonda rode Nicole's horse Image, a Saddlebred by breeding and a tall, long-legged fellow that would test her riding skills and wear out her body parts each and every outing. It was obvious this entreaty was not going to work out and thus our entry into the "gaited" breeds to find more comfort and stability. She still remembered that single footing quarter horse from years before. The result was a trip to Southern Oregon and a farm near Selma that was breeding Peruvian Paso stock. Rhonda fell in love with a sorrel gelding, five years old and as smooth as glass. Expensive in contrast to our prior purchases, but when it comes to your back and your passion, why not have what you want? Later to be named Harley, for the smooth and unquestioned performance, he was ours. I think I only rode Harley once, but the name fit and the ride was excellent. And so it came to be that we ride gaited horses and are happier for it.

Years later, as I looked for a new horse at the start of the new millennium, I had in the back of my mind a trip we had taken to Whitefish Horse Camp, where I witnessed a fellow traveler riding a gaited Morgan horse. I was mesmerized by the smoothness of the ride, the confirmation of the horse, and the exhilaration of the rider. I wanted one! So the search was started, proved to be exhausting, and finally was aborted because that particular horse was one of a kind, or so it seemed. I was not willing to be without a ride for an extended period of time, so I broadened my search to include other gaited breeds, Paso Fino amongst them. We continued our search throughout the Northwest without much luck until that fortuitous and lucky day arrived. We got word through one of the horse clubs to which we belonged that there was a Paso Fino not far from us, really just down the road, that was being put up for sale.

Cheyenne was eight years old at that time, a registered Paso Fino, gray in color; and while foaled in Montana, he had lived many years on a local ranch in Sherwood. The seller was the third owner, apparently weary of learning horsemanship and trying to keep up with her husband. The prior owner and Paso Fino breeder entered the picture to show the horse, provide a history, and allow me to ride in their facilities. I was truly sold on the purchase when I had the opportunity to take Cheyenne onto the trails of a local park and experience his smoothness, training, and willingness to perform. Soon after, he was moved onto our farm.

He was the first of our trio of horses to enter our stable and become one of three to make this adventurous journey, but fifteen years later and at twenty-three years of age, he would be put to the test. I don't know if you can relate horse years to a human life span, but I would guess that he is upper middle age at the time of our departure. Lizzy, our boss mare and Rhonda's current ride, is only a few years younger, so neither is a spring chicken. Their mettle will be sorely tested in the months to come.

Lizzy, short for Elizabeth, having been named after Liz Taylor, is a registered Tennessee Walker mare with sorrel coloring, a flaxen mane and tail, and is quite taken with herself. She has a sassy walk and a smooth gait that Rhonda has nurtured over the past ten years. I was so glad Rhonda was able to find a suitable friend after our heartbreaking loss of Harley in 2004. Rhonda was devastated when Harley was diagnosed with DSLD (degenerative suspensory ligament desmitis), which is a breakdown of the suspensory ligaments in the lower leg. This is quite likely a genetic trait found in several breeds but especially in the Peruvians. It was a painful experience for all of us and led us to the realization that we couldn't let him suffer any longer. We had to say goodbye.

Rhonda immediately went onto all the websites available, looking for the right horse. We even purchased another Peruvian mare with the hope she would settle and become a partner, but after several months of training, she also showed signs of the dreaded DSLD. We might have considered breeding her but to no avail since the disease is hereditary. As responsible owners, we had to have her euthanized. Having horses is much like any other pet because you are going to outlive nearly all, and as their caretaker and leader, you will have many such painful decisions to make.

So the search continued, like mine, far and wide, spanning Oregon and Washington, but looking most anywhere. To stay in the saddle, Rhonda even purchased a retired Arab endurance horse, but the experience only hastened the search and aggravated her back.

A gaited horse was still the target, but it had to be the special one. I remember that during Rhonda's search, she had come back from a trek to the Columbia River Gorge, wistfully talking about this mare she had ridden but just wasn't sure about. She had poor ground manners, and the opportunity to ride was not very telling. The mare, which immediately got my attention because I had postulated that we didn't want another mare only geldings in our field and she should get a pass. The search went on, but not for long as Rhonda decided that another look-see was in order for this particular mare, and hopefully, a lengthier ride in an open setting on the trail could be arranged. You see, Liz (although she was called by another name by the owner) was a "husband" horse so that not much was asked of her. When Rhonda asked more, she got more and found that Liz was a willing partner but just hadn't been asked to do much. She didn't even know how to gait!

And so it was that Liz (Elizabeth) found her way to our stable to become the ultimate boss mare. She doesn't really know how to be with other horses, at least not without lowering her ears and baring her teeth if there isn't an immediate reaction. After ten years, her ground manners still need a tune-up now and again, but she has been one sturdy mount. And when she has someone on her back, she becomes the sweet, innocent Liz, always giving without a fuss and tooling down the trail as if she were a Cadillac. Rhonda had a new partner. And I had my riding buddy back. We were good to go and did to most anywhere we wanted, hitting the trails of the Ochocos, the Cascades, and the High Desert. Cross-country was no problem as the ponies went where we asked them.

As mentioned earlier, in 2010, Rhonda went with friends on a 150-mile ride on the Metolius-Windigo Trail here in Central Oregon, mostly riding from campsite to campsite but also packing Cheyenne and taking camp with her. We weren't strangers to packing but had not done much as the kids grew through the years, and time always seemed to be short. But the lure of the wilderness and outback areas of Oregon and the western states was pulling us in that direction. We had trekked around the Three Sisters here in Central Oregon on a three-day, sixty-mile ride, carrying all our supplies on Cheyenne and Liz and found it to be a little telling on the critters and ourselves. After all, we had a three-horse capacity in our trailer and retirement was not all that far in the distance. Eventually, our horses would be middle- and old-aged and replacement rides would be appropriate for the long term.

So in 2012, we began to keep our eyes and ears open. We knew it would be another gaited horse and likely and ultimately a replacement for Cheyenne, the oldest in our herd. That was about the only criteria we had because we weren't in a hurry and there was just too much we wanted to do rather than spend all our time surfing the web or Craigslist, looking for the right horse. Cheyenne was still sound and a good ride, so we calmly looked around. We were still in the deep recession, and Rhonda had a few random jobs but couldn't find steady employment in her chosen field. We needed to be patient.

Due to the recession, there were a lot of horses on the market. We even brought a Mustang into the herd for a brief period of time. He was a sturdy, well-muscled animal with solid conformation but unfortunately not gaited. However, we only needed a packhorse, and he was cheap, so why not try him out? We found out why in a very short time when he refused to accept Liz as the boss horse. We had to get him off the property in a hurry before he injured one of the others. This was a lesson we knew but had ignored. The purchase price of a horse should not be a controlling factor in acquisition other than the top line of your budget, because if you get the right horse, you will spend that amount many times over as you enjoy every minute of your togetherness. So the search went on.

It wasn't long after that we got wind of a young two-year-old Paso Fino stallion for sale in the valley. The young lady we visited was in over her head with too many horses for her budget and had put this young bay-colored horse up for the offering. He was small for his age but very well-mannered with some solid ground training and a good disposition and bright, intelligent eye. His confirmation was right-on, and he already had the Corto gait mastered, just naturally in his movement. His size gave us pause, but in the end, I thought we could take the chance. We had owned colts in the past but had never taken one to adulthood or ever worked to train one. This was certainly going to be a challenge.

For years, we had been following the current trend in horse relationships as taught by Clinton Anderson, Ray Hunt, and a host of other nationally known trainers. We felt pretty good about how we had put these teachings to use in everyday horsemanship with Liz and Cheyenne, but now we would be sorely tested. It was time to once again get out the videos and pamphlets and refresh our understandings and the process to get to the riding stage. Rio, as we came to call him, was of small stature, and we wouldn't be getting on his back any time soon. Rhonda took on the training mantle as I was going to work every day. Ground training in and out of the round pen was the first order of business as was leading Rio behind as we rode out from our property onto BLM land. Pouring good quality food into him was also a must so that he would mature in size along with his maturity and trust of our leadership.

In his third year, we merely kept to our routine but eventually brought out the saddle. Not the riding saddle but the pack saddle. Rio's stature was still not solid enough for us to ride, but we could certainly get him accustomed to having weight on his back, a girth around his middle, and a breeching on his backside. He was ponied many more miles, even carrying weight as we took another trip through the wilderness and around the Three Sisters Mountains in Central Oregon. It wasn't until his fourth year that we realized we had better bite the bullet, there being no more excuses or reasons to put it off. We must get him under a riding saddle, but which of us was willing to take the risk of injury or mayhem? At this point, we decided that it was not in our best interest to just climb onto him at our age, so we hired a young lady to be the first. We had leaned on him, laid on him, and continued the round pen and corral activities with a saddle on him, but no rider on the saddle. This brave young lady hopped onto Rio's back and a round penning they did go with nary a flinch from this youngster. Eventually, she was able to take him out of the round pen, moving on to the arena without incident or refusal on Rio's part. We were some proud parents, realizing our trepidation was without merit and that we should possibly have trusted our instincts a little more. But all is well that ends well.

Now Rhonda just couldn't stand it, and we knew that she had to get on Rio. After all, we wanted Rio to know our riding style and signals for movement, how we sat the saddle and the whole gamut of interaction of horse and rider. Rhonda needed to gain his confidence, and she needed to affirm her trust and find his cooperation. By now, we knew where we were headed in the coming year and that Rio would be one of Rhonda's stalwart companions on the trail so we wanted them each to have trust in one another and confidence that their pairing could accomplish most anything. We were extremely proud of our accomplishments in bringing Rio to this point and were so looking forward to the coming year and our triumvirate of riding and packing partners.

So now you know all the players in our performance and odyssey of a journey. All but Tucker, our rescued pup from two years ago, being a mix of who-knows-what. Probably a border collie, with some mini Australian shepherd mixed in, and to finish it off, maybe some kind of spaniel as well. I suggest the last because of his instincts as a hunter and absolutely no propensity to herd our animals, except maybe our cat when trolling the kitchen area. He certainly has the intelligence attributed to the above breeds since he observes and anticipates my every move, knowing what I'm going to do before I know. He has the stature of something smaller than a collie as he is only thirty-five pounds, but the instincts of a coyote on the prowl as he sniffs the rabbit and squirrel tracks with the hope of capture and digs for whatever may be scarfed up behind him. I'm looking forward to our many adventures together as we await the missus coming along the trail, and he will be welcome company when the waiting extends for days.

Time is getting real short. The anxieties of preparation have receded, and I do believe we are ready to head down the road. So let's get to it without delay and boldly go where no man has gone before. Or should I say woman!

Note: What you are about to read is a series of e-mails that I sent to family and friends, rather an afterthought but one that got me engaged in this entire affair as we travelled and rode for six months during the spring and summer of 2015. They are cryptic in some cases and rather drawn out in others, but mostly, they were just fun in bringing others along with us on this grand adventure. I hope you find it entertaining and worthy of being read. Enjoy!

The dining table as we planned this adventure

PART

1

March 28, 2015

Hi, folks,

I have just decided, Why should Rhonda have all the fun? So now you get to hear from me from time to time as we move along the road, or should I say I move on the road while Rhonda is out on the Pacific Crest Trail. Hope I don't bore you too much. Maybe I'm just a little bit bored, but more likely, I am so filled with excitement and wonder that I feel a need to pass along some of the energy to all of you that are willing to listen.

Just to set things straight, Rhonda is talking on her blog (address: https://hrsnarnd.wordpress.com), so look for her comments there. And I believe each of you can comment back if she accepts you. She is keeping a log of her travels each day, spending a bit of time each evening to write things down in a small carry book. But when she will find the time to converse with the outside world is only a guess on my part because each and every day is packed with events that must be attended to.

We've been on the road now for ten wonderful days. Like Europe, we are camping again, only a little more posh now with the Hilton and all. But then we weren't trailing three ponies and a dog. Like then, I'm doing the driving and R's guiding. I'm yelling, and she's screaming, and it's just like home. Ain't life wonderful!

In Europe, the camps had internet, and our phones didn't work, while here it's the opposite. Note: I'm writing on my phone since I can't find secure internet service to send messages with the tablet or computer. In six months, I ought to be an expert in the one-finger peck. How all of you use your thumbs in such a nimble fashion is beyond me. However, when Rhonda is out on the trail it is not like I have an explicit agenda of events to attend to. Time and effort take on a new meaning. In the few towns that we pass through, they just weren't cordial enough to let the critters into the library or into McDonalds to use their WiFi, not to mention that it's not fun to tow a thirty-one-foot trailer thru town. And boy have we seen a few towns.

So back to the journey thing. We left on Tuesday, the seventeenth (hoping St. Patrick's Day would bring us good fortunes). Only we were four hours late on our scheduled departure time and arrived in Klamath Falls at dark-thirty to stay with acquaintances at their farm. Carol is a Back Country Horsemen of Oregon member in the High Desert Trail Riders chapter, with their farm located a few miles southwest of the town. We managed to get there in the waning rays of daylight, getting the truck and trailer parked just in time. Then it was a matter of inspecting the facilities for our crew to assure a safe night and carefree sleep. Trying to settle three horses in a strange paddock, mud, and all in the dark was a trial, but Rhonda persevered. Gee, I'd left my muck boots at home. Damn! There's no muck in California! It's a drought. Well, I guess we were still in Oregon.

Carol had waited dinner for our arrival and had even invited a couple of local gals over for us to share stories and events with. We were entertained by these two gals that had ridden the PCT from Tahoe to the Oregon border (seven hundred trail miles) not many years ago. Their experiences were thrilling and daunting at the same time, giving us momentum to go down the road. We had barely gotten started, and here was the lore of years gone by, raising our level of excitement and also our praise as we understood the magnitude of their adventure. As Rhonda and I settled into the Hilton for the night, we were hard-pressed to find sleep as the thoughts kept rolling through our heads on this first night of a six-month journey.

The following day would be another short journey because we didn't want to stress the horses too much with lengthy travel days. They would see enough of that in the near future and a whole lot more. Red Bluff, California, was our chosen destination, less than two hundred miles away, where the county fairgrounds would open their gates and allow our stay. Outdoor facilities of steel pipe corrals and an electric service for the Hilton, what more could we wish for? After a fast inspection of the corrals to assure they were safe, we had the horses settled with hay nets and a full water trough so that we could sit and enjoy the afternoon sun. Our prior travels through Red Bluff had made it seem like the hottest place on this good earth, but in mid-March, it was just right.

A day later, our nephew Jon and wife Stacey and son Henry welcomed us at their place in Hidden Valley, California. Thank you so much. We saw more family while there, including a trip by me to the old stomping grounds, Santa Rosa. It was a sad but also memorable trip, as brother Jerry and wife, Anna, ferried me to a memorial service for the passing of our sister-in-law's mother. Hey, at the age of ninety- nine, Mildred had lived long and well. It was great to have a few moments with Mike (brother) and his wife, Jacquie, and their extended family. I took a few moments to visit our father's gravesite just down the hill, where he had been placed more than forty years prior. Dad passed just two weeks prior to my meeting Rhonda, future bride, and companion to be for a life of wonder and adventure. It would have been great to sit and languish in the California sun, but the Mexican border was pulling and nagging at us every thoughtful moment.

Leaving Northern California, we have been travelling south, staying wherever they would have us. County fairgrounds are quite friendly in California as we happened another stay in Turlock, hoping to visit with our nephew Jay and wife, Loretta! Unfortunately, their schedule didn't allow it. Only one mishap slowed our trek south. Fifteen miles south of Turlock on old Highway 99, which runs along the east side of the San Juaquin Valley, we blew a tire on the trailer. Most of you that have trailered a vehicle would understand when a passing vehicle honks next to the driver's window, scaring the bejeesus out of you and waving to the side. We managed to get the entire rig off the side of Highway 99 to allow the spare to be mounted. Now what? Can't be towing three horses and a dog in unknown territory without a spare. Only it's Sunday, and what tire shop could be open? We googled several tire shops in the vicinity and even went by one, only to be scared off by some teenage thugs that took a disliking to our presence. Time to move on.

Four hours later and fifteen miles north, we were anchored in the lot of Walmart with new tread and three horses glad to be gone from this grassless veranda of asphalt. Got a fair amount of attention from moms and kids not having such an opportunity to get close to horses in this suburban neighborhood. It wasn't long and we were headed south again, only we weren't going to reach our destination. No time left in the remaining daylight, and settling down three horses in the dark is not on our agenda for this trip. But the internet is so great, and couple that with smartphones, you can make miracles happen. Google "horse boarding," and look and behold, one shows up right down the highway. A phone call later, we had a place to stay at a friendly ranch with oodles of horses and plenty of room for the truck and trailer, and even a plug-in for electricity! What a find! Rhonda is a great navigator! Or so I believed.

But if someone had told me a month ago that I would soon be driving the Grapevine into LA, passing thru Pasadena and by the Rose Bowl and Santa Anita race track, I'd have said they're crazy. But you know what? Where Google takes you . . . you go. Well, maybe not always. Rhonda and I remember camping in the Cascade Mountains when, sitting outside our trailer in the pleasant evening hours and virtually at the end of the road, a couple of gals show up, towing their horses and headed right past us. But luckily for them, they were questioning their chosen route. Seems their computer mapping source directed them to take the pioneer and very primitive road to a horse camp on the other side of the mountains. They would never have made it, especially in the dark. Sorry, gals, but backtrack and go around. And yes, it will be three hours more, but you won't be stuck!

And so it was that after three days we are still camped in McCall Memorial Park, a county horse camp with especially good landscape.

Metal corrals, running water, paved road, and a manure bin that only the two of us are using. Yep, we are the only ones to be camping here in March. But it was perfect as we were scoping out the area, resupplying, and just living. We are in need of more hay, filling our water barrels, and checking out access to the PCT in this area. We are camped at 4,500 feet elevation and have glorious sunshine and no smog. We can see Westerly and nearly to the Pacific Ocean. The PCT is only five miles away but still has snow on it here at eight thousand feet. We visited the District Forest Service office in Idyllwild to get current information and found out there was a fire a couple of years ago and the trail is washed out in several spots. They now have a temporary route we must figure out. Unfortunately, they were not very helpful in that figuring. Seems they didn't have a current map and hadn't been on the route themselves. I've been very busy trying to find someone to lead us in the right direction.

In the meantime, a trip to Norco, California, was in store for me. Before leaving Oregon and embarking on this escapade, we considered how we would supply ourselves with hay and grain for the critters. We settled on supplies from an Idaho firm that distributed compressed hay bales and feed up and down the western US. Not always convenient but consistent products were a must to avoid changing feedstock. So sixty miles later, I was stocking up, and thanks to Rhonda, we could buy extra hay and leave it at an accommodating neighbor to the McCall Camp. Thank you, thank you, as we would be passing through in a few weeks. Using the compressed hay bales, I will be able to carry 1,100 pounds of hay before needing to resupply.

Unfortunately, a second trip to town was required to recover $100. I was shortchanged when I cashed a third-party check at the local bank only thirty miles off, but I have more time than money, so a return was called for, and all's well that ends well. And to think that as the crow flies we are only twenty miles from Palm Springs, which seems like halfway around the world when you look at the surrounding mountains. What a world we live in.

Today we are along the dirt road into Fobes Ranch. I read about it in a book of another lady's venture to ride the trail. Husband beat up his camper, trying and actually getting into the ranch. Too rough for us, though. History tells us this is the place where Timothy Leary brewed his magical potion of LSD and distributed it to who-knows-where. Had help from a lot of surfer bums who would come hang out. Kinda reminds me of a visit I made so many moons ago into Morning Star Ranch near Guerneville, California, Hippieville, USA, or so it seemed. That place was deeded to GOD by Lou Gotlieb, one of three members of the Limeliters. Anyway, a bit of history tainted as it may be by my poor memory. Found the road way too primitive to bring our LQ trailer anywhere near it, but Rhonda would have to ride this way in the very near future. Just another happenstance that we will have to negotiate.

Oh yeah, did I mention that the campground has a shower? Well, it's shower day and my turn, so will catch up at another time. Love you all, and hope you get this.

Pat

(Sent from my US cellular smartphone)

Our first stop on the trip. Dining with friends in Klamath Falls.

Horses high-lined at feeding time while at our nephew's in Middletown, Ca.

The gang in Turlock, Ca. awaiting a new tire on the Hilton

We have arrived in Southern California to make
Mt. Center horse camp our home away from home.

PART

2

March 30, 2015

Hi, all!

Well, they don't get much better than this. The day, that is. We left the Mountain Center area yesterday after I had driven, sans trailer, out to a meeting point (where I will resupply Rhonda). Try driving a jeep trail for eight miles, and you get the picture, passable but barely. Looks to me that many years ago someone went four-wheeling over the desert sage, and many years later, the vegetation is gone, and the basalt under layer is exposed to create a travel way. But a road? Come on!

Had no idea where we would end up last night, so I splurged for lunch at the Paradise Cafe. Truck and Hilton in the parking lot, waiting. Oh, but yum, yum! And then it was down the road with Rhonda saying, "You mean you don't know where we are going?" South, I said. Gotta check out Warner Springs, where you'll have a stopover. The atlas map says there is a Warner Springs Ranch, so I'm hoping for a place to hang my hat and house a couple of horses when we pass through.

Warner Springs isn't much, but they have a community center that straddles the PCT. And wouldn't you just know it, there were a whole bunch of horse trailers in the parking lot with horses in various stages of dressing or undressing. Take your pick. And so STOP we did.

After various and sundry conversations, we managed to find the administrator amidst all the folk. Ever notice how when horse owners go past one another they can't continue without a little chatter going on. Amazing that it takes a half hour to cross a 150-foot lot. But we made it thru the gauntlet. A lot of nice horses and a great bunch of folks. We even met a couple that were totally engaged with the PCT, having ridden many portions and hiked even more. They invited us to stay with them when passing through on our way north. They live in a subdivided ranchette area just north of the Paradise Café and south of the Mountain Center horse camp. Tim and Andrea have a nice place to live and raise a horse or two, or more. Terrific! We have patrons!

And the community center's administrator—Nancy's her name—was so nice in allowing us to park and stay the night, high-lining our one horse to a two-hundred-year-old oak out back while the other two are hitched to the outriggers we installed a few years back. Boy does that oak provide some welcome shade. The idea of a ranch stay was obliterated when I found out the ranch was a development in its infancy, with a proposed restaurant, airfield, and subdivision. Ugh!

So this morning came quietly enough. The PCT rush hasn't started yet but will come soon. This year they expect an abnormal rush up the trail as the movie *Wild* has just surfaced and excited a lot of folks to give the trail a try. It is expected that fifty hikers a day will leave the Mexican border, or so the permit system installed this year tells us. So where are they? We practically have the place to ourselves, with WiFi even, a snack shack for burgers and showers added to a Laundromat. No wonder this place is so popular with the hikers!

We have nearly a week before our departure from the border, so this morning, we rode about five miles up the PCT to Eagle Rock. I'll send a picture when Rhonda gives it to me. The trail meanders along a small creek bed, with little water due to the draught, but with huge oaks providing shade over the trail. We then climbed up and onto a high prairie for a couple of miles and the big rock on a promontory. SO COOL! Amazing how huge basalt rocks can come to rest and look just like our national bird of prey.

Arriving back at Warner Springs, it is now shower time again. Just gotta take advantage of amenities when there. Tomorrow we move farther south, getting ever closer to the border. Going to a high horse camp, our friends, the Jimersons, turned us on to. Don and Gerry used to live in the Norco area and have many years of experience living and riding in this vicinity. Cuyamaca State Park is the place we are looking for, with the hopes that we can put some more miles on our critters and explore the surrounding area. We cannot let their earlier conditioning go to waste as they luxuriate in the Hilton and on high ties.

Rhonda is getting anxious to be on the trail, and I'm getting nervous. Gotta find more horse food, or my name ain't the Wrangler (PCT trail name).

We hope all of you are faring well and enjoying your spring. Send us a line now and then or comment on Rhonda's Blog.

Hopefully, we'll get the internet thing figured out so she can post more often. She has been pretty frustrated that it won't allow her to link up with the phone. I think she is calling a few people today. Ah, enough of our trials. Have a good week, and lotsa love to all of you.

Pat 'n' Rhonda

(Sent from my US cellular smartphone)

Arrival and camp out at the Warner Springs Community Center.

Horse-n-Around and The Wrangler test
drive our gang on the PCT.

A spectacular "Eagle Rock" as they head towards Warner Springs

PART

3

April 4, 2015

Well, hello, everyone!

We hope everything is right in the world for each of you. It is from our end.

And guess what? WOW, we made a giant leap today, waking up at five fifteen I had to wonder what was holding us back. But I went back to bed and reawoke at the normal time of six thirty, dressed and went out to feed the critters. Coffee was on the burner, and everything seemed normal. Rhonda was even awake when I went back in. So I had to pose the question "What are we waiting for?" We had a Santa Anna wind all night, and it was sixty degrees at six thirty. The border is only fourteen miles away. Let's go! Aha, she agreed! Said she had been thinking the same for a day or so, like we are really good at talking and bringin' up the hard stuff. Well, we get there eventually.

So we got an early start and pulled out of the camp spot at 10:30 a.m. Now, I didn't say we were in a hurry, did I? This is leisure riding, at least for the first day. After all, I'm goin' today. In fact, the whole gang was there. I had prearranged for us to park at the local hardware / feed store in Campo, California, leaving the truck and trailer under their care. We saddled up and moved on down the trail—or road that is—because at this point it, the trail, went thru town and

15

then Southerly to the big, bad border. Tucker rode with me as Rhonda (rightfully) was worried for him encountering a rattlesnake. Cheyenne was thrilled. Hopefully, one of the pictures will tell the tale. Rhonda signed her life away on the departure/visitor log, and we started snakin' our way north. Oops, sorry, Tucker.

We managed to go all of two and a half miles and then packed her in for the day. Whew, what a day! Anticlimactic, maybe, but it felt good to get started and refocused after travelling and planning all this time. We are camped out at a horse camp Boulder Oaks at about mile 25 on the trail. The trail runs about twenty feet east of our trailer, with hikers passing by all day and sometimes at night, with the full moon. Tucker sounds the alarm every time. Shhh-sshh!

So how did we end up here? Well, kinda by accident. After Warner Springs, we had to go to the town of Ramona to pick up horse food. Got what we needed but not what we wanted. Such is life. I had called that morning, and they assured me they had what I wanted, but when we got there, no one would fess up and say they hadn't bothered to check. Ah well, what's a fella gonna do but get on down the road. Got enough issues to contend with and don't need to blow up each and every one.

So we headed towards state campground Cuyamaca horse camp. After stopping at several campgrounds and backtracking after getting a look-see at a map, we found nothin'! We had gone back over our own tire tracks more than once, so what gives? It's early in the season. Seventy-five degrees out, and what more could you want? None of the buildings were manned, and we came to find out, finally, that the horse camp had burned up in a forest fire. When they went to rebuild it, they found artifacts, you know . . . arrowheads and the like. Now it belongs to the Native Americans. So here we are along the side of the road when I detect flashing red and blue lights in my mirror. Now what? The local posse was wonderin' what we were doin' driving up and down the same roads. Lost are ye? If we hadn't had three hairy heads pokin' out the windows, he may have wanted to see our cargo. Not that far from the border.

Anyway, Rhonda had espied this little campground in some of her earlier research and found it again on Google Earth. We were on our way, and the sheriff said it was only forty-five minutes down the road. Now it has been home for four days and will be for two more. Tomorrow Rhonda rides for seventeen miles in some rough terrain, with me droppin' her off and pickin' up the remains when she and Liz trudge in. And so the real saga begins. Day number 2 of the journey. Don't know when I'll be able to send this out 'cause the internet doesn't seem to travel in these here woods, and the phone company said we had nearly used up their allotment of time. Just one more thing to figure out. Where's McDonald's when you need them?

So the sun is setting, and the warm winds have stopped. Steak and champagne to celebrate the first day on the trail. Time to go clean up.

Love you, one and all. And—oh yeah—a plea for some of you ladies to send Rhonda a note now and then. I'm not the greatest conversationalist, and I'm sure she would love some female chatter. Mail to hrsnarnd@webformixair.com. Hell, call her even. Gotta go.

Pat and the Horse-n-Around lady, Rhonda

(Sent from Samsung tablet)

Day 1 of The Journey as we take off from the
Campo hardware and Feed store.

Day 1 and the whole gang at the Border Monument...
We are on our way.

Horse-n-Around makes it the first mile.

PART

4

April 9, 2015

Hi, folks!

Do you ever feel like your batteries are running down? Of course, you do, doesn't everyone? Yeah, it's got Rhonda and me talking about a "0" day (that's a rest stop in non-PCT lingo). Doesn't seem like we should need one . . . We just got started. But then we haven't really stopped since we left home. No offense, Jon and Stacey, but we were still adjusting to being on the road. Now, Patrick, quit complaining!

Yesterday, Easter Sunday, was such a cool day. Lizzy was really wasted from her seventeen-mile trek over mountains and valleys with almost all of it on rocky ground. She was so stiff in the morning that I proposed an option to Rhonda. The next section of trail, we had already ridden on one of our warm-up days, so why not ride the baby? Rio knows the trail . . . We know it is not too severe or dangerous. Why not now? So that's what Rhonda did. For eleven miles, that colt performed admirably. Now Rhonda had to be a rider and not a passenger, but the pair came through it all in wonderful fashion.

The side-hill trail. So where is the "Crest".

Rhonda said it was a little daunting on the narrow trail on a steep side slope, but Rio kept his wits about him. Today will be Cheyenne's turn to impress us. I remember that on that first day, as we were leaving camp in the truck and headed towards Campo and the border, I was listening to the Rolling Stones and Mick singing Wild Horses, one of my favorite cuts. I commented that this would be good luck, and so it seems. Rhonda is thirty miles into it, with thirteen to go today. Should end up near Mt. Laguna—a town, not a mountain. (Or maybe it is?) Me? I will finally be leaving Boulder Oak campground, which has been home for over a week, and now the Wrangler must prove his mettle to find such classy amenities. Wish me luck.

Just so you get the flavor of the trail, remember when I said Liz went seventeen miles? Well, when I drove between those two stops, it was seven miles. Now you get a picture of why the trail is 2,660 miles long. Here I am in the Hilton, typing away when there is work to be done, so I will close for the moment. We hope you all had a marvelous Easter Sunday and that peace and love are in your hearts and minds. We love you all.

I'll finish this later. Okay, it's later. We are illegally parked on an FS access road with a locked gate in front of us. This is access to Horse Heaven horse camp, but if you can believe this, it is only open from Memorial Day to Labor Day! What a crock. And what an inhospitable part of our country. Mt. Laguna is basically a closed society on leased forest service land in the only part of the country that has trees. No access roads except to privately leased land, which is closed to all but the lessees. America at its finest. At one point, we pulled into the parking lot of a closed restaurant to load up Cheyenne after Rhonda's ride. Someone came out to run us off, but we said not until the horse is loaded up. He went away.

Can't wait to move on. We got the critters settled on high lines between some solid pines just off the driveway and were settling in for dinner and a movie. Yeah, I wish! Uh-oh! I hear a vehicle approaching in the waning hours of daylight. I go, Rhonda stays, and up drives the local fire chief. I'm not too worried 'cause we left room to get around our rig if a fire should happen, which shouldn't since we are at altitude. And even with the drought, it's cold and unlikely to burn. The chief's a nice-enough guy compared to the rest of the populace. Warns us that if the cops come, it is likely we'll get run off after getting a costly ticket. It's dark now, and I tell him we are out of choices and stay we must. He bids us a good night, and off he goes.

Rhonda will be restless all night, waiting for that knock on the door by some uniformed constable exerting his power over us mere transients. First light, and she will be out of here and on the trail with me right behind on a road, I hope. See what tomorrow brings. Forty-three miles into the USA and still on the move. Hope we meet some nicer people tomorrow.

I guess I should close this for now with the thought that everyone we have met on the trail has been super. Shared our campsite last night with a fifty-something gentleman from the San Diego area. Talked to a couple of men I would say are my age, and they were quite organized and determined. I'm guessing from Germany. Their gear was some of the best I've seen. And gone at daylight. And then there is quite a hodgepodge of young twentysomethings that make up the bulk of hikers. Where did all the hippies go? Why, hikin' the PCT, of course. They are a friendly bunch and amazed that Rhonda is doing this. Sometimes I am too. Don't forget to visit her on the blog.

From my earlier comment on the Stones, you can gather that I am into rock and roll, and boy did we rock and roll last night. We did the sway, we did the shudder, we shook all about, and we even slept a little. "Boy, What a Night" by Lee Morgan is certainly appropriate. You see, Rhonda was so paranoid that the gendarmes would show up that we just had to move, but we didn't. And oh yeah, she was going another eighteen miles today. Just a little thing.

So I set my sights on a place called Sunrise trailhead, which brought to mind the Going-to-the-Sun highway in Glacier Park. Now this has got to be for us. Sure enough, when I got here, the sun was shining brightly, and there are five-pipe stalls for our three critters. Hell, we could play musical stalls. So I settled in for the long wait for my bride and my steed (she's riding Cheyenne). Got the trailer perfectly level. Got all the horse fixin's out and, of course, the horses too! Cleaned the inside of the truck and beat out the Hilton's area rug which we walk on nearly every movement. It might be called the Hilton, but it ain't really that big.

And I settled down in the meadow, awaiting while the two horses grazed a bit. Now this was a sunny day, but that doesn't mean it was warm. After all, we are now camped at five thousand feet in the Laguna Mountains and within the Anzo-Borrego Desert State Park. Temp was a measly fifty degrees. Rider due in about 5:00 p.m. Slight breeze that started to escalate about 4:00 p.m. and I got out my chaps to wrap up my legs. Oh yeah, that's better. Wind keeps picking up when Rhonda calls and asks if she should be able to see the trailer. Like I should know? I've never been on the trail. But I don't say that. I merely state that there is a feeder trail that cuts off the PCT and should be obvious since a half dozen hikers had visited with me this afternoon.

Wind is still picking up. But I volunteer to walk out to the trail and check it out.

Now, walking has not been easy the past few days as the other night I tripped over one of those tele poles cut at knee height to channel traffic around the horse camp. I think you all know what I'm talkin' about. Well, ever since then, I can feel my groin with every step and also my glute in the derriére. And then the colt stepped on my boot heel as I was walking him on lead, and I went to my knees and can really feel my muscles now. Top that off, and I lost a filling yesterday morn, so what's a little wind? Rhonda and I texted each other, and she found her way, and went right past me with a little shiver. She could see the trailer now and the warmth inside.

Now the trailer is level and all that but sits in a saddle in the ridge line and is perpendicular to the thrust of the wind as it tunnels up into the saddle. It was time to feed and go hibernate, and that we did. San Diego County had a storm goin' on. Did you ever go to sleep wondering if you would wake up when the trailer flipped over sideways? Yeah, it was that bad! Now if I had put down the outriggers (jacks) used to take the trailer off the truck, we would have been stable. But I hadn't so the truck was now our anchor, with the Hilton swaying in the wind. Then I wondered where the truck key was and if I could find it in the dark while standing on our bay window. And would the door open upwards?

But alas, I am able to tell this story and think about the day ahead. The sun is shining, and it is supposed to for the next five days, hooray! Definitely a down day as there is less than a bale of hay, laundry to the gunnels, and provisions to be had. We are at mile 59 on the trail, and it can wait a day. There will be another long day tomorrow with no water on the trail, so I must find a way in and stash five gallons. And then there is tomorrow night's camp spot to figure out.

But alas, the scouting is fruitful. Picked up a hitchhiker who told me the water tank about halfway down tomorrow's trail has water aplenty. Gee, that was easy scouting. And then I find an old gravel pit near the pickup spot for tomorrow. Wouldn't have found that on the map. And then I pick up another hiker, and he confirms the water, but oh, what a stench. I wish the town well with that one until he finds a shower.

So now I am in the town of Ramona and ready to roll up my sleeves and do laundry. Oh boy! Tucker is overjoyed to sit in the hot truck for hours. And then shopping. But McDonald's is next door, so I should be able to send this off. So love you one and all. This is the Wrangler signing off.

Good night, sleep tight.

Pat

(Sent from Samsung tablet)

Rio gets his first ride on a short 10 mile day.

Now it is Cheyenne's turn as they climb to Mt. Laguna.

Hikers rest stop on the PCT to take in the natural splendor!

Liz and Rio get to graze at the Sunrise Trailhead
while we await Horse-n-Around.

PART

5

April 12, 2015

Wow, yesterday Rhonda had what may be her longest day ride of this entire venture. She left San Felipe Creek at Scissors Crossing at 9:00 a.m. and climbed for a half hour, with the first mile being a series of switchbacks and climbing 1,200 feet, then on sidehill and ridgetops for another twenty-two miles while climbing another one thousand feet, and finally dropping down two thousand feet to our meeting point at Barrel Spring—23.5 miles total. So how would that make your day?

And so I say good morning to all. The babies are resting in the morning sun, and we are hovered over our electronic contraptions, typing our notes, journals, and missives. The reason Rhonda went so far is that there were no access points and no water available near the trail. This is desert country, no trees and a lot of rocks. Just wasn't suitable for an overnight stay. She took two horses, the boys as we call them, and packed one with ten gallons of water and a snack of hay for each. A rest stop at mile 14 took care of the seventy pounds of water and five pounds of hay, and Rhonda switched riding ponies and came into camp just before dusk. Then my work began.

We camp near Scissors Crossing at a gravel pit as Cheyenne
and Rio get ready for a 24 mile day.

My typical day has been to pack up camp as I wave bye to Horse-n-
Around, as Rhonda is known on the trail, load up the critters and
vamoose to the next meeting point or thereabouts. We are currently
housed at a trailhead (parking area for the nonhikers, bikers, riders)
along what is a much-busier two-lane highway than I would have
imagined. Where is everyone going on a magnificent Saturday morning?

Like us, I guess they are all on a mission. No wonder we are such road warriors. I digress.

The night before, we were at an abandoned gravel pit, and tonight we will be at the Warner Springs community center. Before you feel sorry for us, the center serves breakfast and late lunches, has showers and laundry, and allows us to park for free on their property with our three ponies. What a deal! And I previously mentioned the Hilton, which isn't too shabby, just a little confining. A living quarters horse trailer which packs room for three horses, all their gear, a shower and commode, hot water, kitchen facilities and dining area and a queen-sized bed, all in eight-by-thirty feet. It does, however, spook ya when you are travelling on these country highways that have signage "Vehicles towing over thirty feet are not recommended." We have made it just fine.

These roads are narrow as state highways go. Edge of pavement is next to the white stripe. There is no safety zone, with trees and rocks out of the bluff within two feet of pavement, but we've made it this far. You see, that's part of my job . . . to see if the roads ahead are ones we can or could use. Like today, I will drive up Indian Flats Road to a campground to see if the trailer can make it. If not, then I will leave a water and hay stash, and Rhonda might just have her first camp out tomorrow evening. With resources, but still alone. That's gonna be a tough one for both of us. What a way to spend our anniversary—yup, forty years and still counting. A few years ago, Rhonda and I were riding around the Three Sisters Mountains and happened to be on the PCT trail. We met a young couple that was hiking the PCT on their honeymoon. Don't know if they completed it, but I figure if they can hike two thousand miles together, they could handle almost anything. Except maybe a little boredom. Our best wishes went with them. As they do for all of you.

Now, a few interesting facts, especially for those at home. Yesterday I pulled into a small grocery in Rancherita to buy avocadoes. In season, right? Well, they didn't have any, and the fruit stand next door was closed. But they would have been only two bits apiece (that's $0.25 for you young 'uns). Anyway, the gal in the store asked if I was the one with the big trailer. I said yes, and she retorted to her friend that I was the rich one. Wow! Never been called that before. Almost offended.

I explained that it isn't how much you have but how you manage to spend it. She questioned how I could have horses and still manage my money. I didn't have an answer. It's a lifestyle thing and that after forty years you just roll with the punches. Yeah, we've had horses all that time. So how do you become a millionaire with horses? You start out with 2 million dollars.

Oh yeah, I was talking about facts. Well, diesel fuel around here is $0.20 less than regular gas. Hamburger is $6.00 plus per pound. A bale of hay costs anywhere from $18.00 for alfalfa to $23.00 for Timothy grass. No wonder all the horse trailers are small and ratty-lookin'. Gatorade costs $1.89. And people live in the most gawd-awful places you can imagine. Out in the desert, on a hillside with a view, of what I'm not sure, and accessible only with a four-wheel drive on a dirt road. Each to his own, I guess. It's like, "Honey, could you go to the store and get some milk and avocadoes?" Okay, see you tomorrow.

How can 30 million people live in one state and still have all this open land where there is not a road for 23.5 miles? Incredible! Don't ya just love America! I think with that I will sign off for the day. Hope you are having a glorious weekend as I'm sure we will.

Love you all,
Pat 'n' Rhonda

PART

6

April 18, 2015

Howdy, everyone!

> Here I sit broken-hearted
> My sweet lass has just departed
> From where you say?
> Why, from the Hilton, but just for a day.
> We'll meet again along the way
> Off the PCT 'cause a fire burned the trees away
> Down Fobes Ranch Road I'll go and await
> Listening for R's little colt and the familiar gait.

Boy, my poetry really stinks, but what do you expect after living in a trailer with manure a mere ten feet away and showers but occasionally? But yeah, Rhonda is riding the colt Rio once again after a lengthy discussion this morning. Tomorrow she will be riding towards Idyllwild, and there will not be a Hilton waiting for her. And there will be another day after that of camping out as she travels over the mountains and down into the valley, a mere fifteen miles from Palm Springs. All told she will cover nearly fifty miles in three days and pass the two-hundred-mile marker along the way.

It likely will be a "0" day after that as I'm sure she will be zoned out. I know I will be from all the coordinating of feed sources, and then there is the planning we must do to get us over the next hump in the trail. When we left Oregon, we had done a lot of planning, actually coming up with places to meet along the way, where to camp with water, and where to resupply. Unfortunately, there was a lot left unsaid in regard to horses in all the journals and books that Rhonda poured over. Neither one of us has been in this country before.

We hadn't considered things like closed campgrounds or the lack of places to park and the lack of internet in these smaller bergs that roost up in these mountains. One town would not allow motor homes or trailer rigs to stop and park. Takes up too many tourist parking spots.

On the other hand, we have been most fortunate to land with our feet on the ground, encountering generosity and compassion from some of these local folks.

A case in point is our chance meeting up with Tim and Andrea. As you may remember, I earlier mentioned our trip down and seeing horses at Warner Springs. They (Tim and Andrea) were cleaning up (LNT) the parking area when Rhonda struck up a conversation. Tim and Andrea are PCT enthusiasts, walking and hiking and riding many portions we were about to encounter. So they invited us to come share our experiences and stay with them as we ride north and away from the border. And that is exactly what we have been doing for the past three days. At least *I* have, as the stretch from Warner Springs would not allow me to meet up with Rhonda with trailer in tow.

I took water into a couple of places along the first day's route and left hay for the evening and following morning feedings. Rhonda camped out. The next day, I met her at a jeep road x-ing after travelling ten miles on some nasty 4x4 trails. So while this is happening, the "boys" were frolicking around a two-acre paddock, courtesy of Tim and Andrea, with an everlasting supply of hay. Nah, we don't spoil them, only ourselves. Their turn will come. Remember who's in the poem? And the Hilton would be awaiting our return.

Rhonda and I camped out that night, together for a change, albeit in the middle of the road to find a flat spot. Tucker ended up sleeping in the truck 'cause he had loaded up with all kinds of nasty little spiny things while hunting in the desert. I called them stickers, and Tucker learned real quick that my pulling and tugging them out was a good thing. Only we didn't want our new neat little mattresses to be punctured by leftovers. Rhonda really scored when she found these on the net.

Rhonda rode from that campsite down into this very nice and picturesque little valley (Garner Valley) where Tim and Andrea's place nestles in the pines with a whole bunch of other like-minded folks on what I would call ranchettes, with horses all around. This is horse country. And boy was Rhonda excited that we had arrived on Wednesday, and the Paradise Cafe would have their specials going. We had learned on our first pass thru the neighborhood that Wednesday was THE day. So the four of us ventured forth. Tim and Andrea and the two of us to spend a cool evening gorging ourselves. Well, maybe only one of us, as that is the mythology that goes with the trail. All these hikers starve themselves in order to save weight down the trail, and then they order multiple meals when the opportunity arises. We may not be hikers, but we still have to watch our figures, so yeah, it was me who ate ravenous of this football-sized burrito on my plate. And the bottle of wine was half price. What a deal!

Now I am saddened to have to eat my own cooking, but that I must do. Lucky Rhonda will be on the trail and can eat whatever she wants. "Yeah, right," as she would say. And me, I need to get on with my chores, or Rhonda will beat me to the rendezvous spot. What chores, you ask? After all, it is the Hilton! But alas, there are no bellboys, stewards, or maids.

First, I must clean up after the morning coffee and breakfast. That was after I fed the horses upon awakening this morning. That always comes first to make sure Rhonda's ride is full and happy as she or he moves down the trail. Then it would be time to clean up the manure and practice LNT, which for you nonriders is "Leave no trace," with the intent that the next visitors will not be offended or even notice that you stayed there. Now it's time to pack up the hay bags and stow the water and feed buckets. If the truck is unhooked, I must now negotiate the raising of the Hilton and sliding the truck underneath and setting our home into place. This morning, I seem to have a cadre of hay bales strewn about, necessitating some strategy on where they will be stored. Likely I will get our pulley system to haul them onto the roof rack and then wrap them with a tarp to stay dry. Don't feel too sorry for me as I had foreseen this eventuality, and thus, we are using Stand Lee compressed bales that are only fifty to sixty pounds. Today I will try to get four or more up there, allowing us to carry up to a ten-day supply. Boy, isn't this interesting? I better quit before I lose my readership and put you all to sleep. As if that hasn't already happened.

At least I can rest assured you will all have reading material for bedtime. So when I say "Sweet dreams," I really mean it. Now Tucker is starting to gnaw on my ankle. He knows the routine better than I do. Such a smart dog. There are times when one side of the trailer is higher than the other (ground slopes, not the trailer), making it a big step down. On these occasions, we use what we call the back door, or one into the rear of the trailer and out. Oh, don't worry, we practice LNT inside also. Anyway, where was I? Oh yeah, Tucker learned the term *back door* in no time at all. Or maybe it was because he caught a squirrel off guard as we emerged, and the race to the hole was on. What do you think he remembers?

Love you all, and to all, a pleasant good night.

Pat and Rhonda

* * *

Hey, are you ready for another one! Day that is. One keystroke at a time, whew! Transmitted a little tardy, but it's on the air now. Today we travel to the paved part of Fobes Ranch Road to await Rhonda.

Wonder if there is any acid in them thar trees. Nah, I gave that up a long time ago. So I'm off, and we will see you down the road or, more aptly put, "down the trail."

Today is Friday, I think. Funny how they all run together when you are havin' fun. Yesterday was interesting, to say the least. We arose rather slowly. Hmm, I wonder if that half bottle of wine had anything to do with it. Or maybe it was that football I had for dinner. At any rate, Rhonda started out on the trail at eleven o'clock, and those of you that know us will say, "Yeah, that sounds about normal." Eleven miles on the trail, then switchbacks down the hill to a paved road, known as Fobes Ranch Road, where I was waiting. Piece of cake, maybe fifteen miles. You see, we didn't know the mileage because this is a go- around. So what is a *go-around* for you uninitiated? In this case, it was a reroute of the PCT to avoid going thru a burned area that happened in 2013. I saw pictures, and it was a big fire, and now the whole hillside has washed away, including the trail. This reroute is probably twenty-five miles long, with this being just the start.

So Rhonda mounts her trusty steed, Rio, the pup of the litter, and is on her way. Me, I drive off to take back the borrowed trailer to Tim's and complete my chores. (Remember those? I hope so, 'cause I ain't typing them over.) Then it's off to Fobes Ranch Road. All rested up, I perform a little operation on my foot (whole 'nother story), graze the horses and even have a beer and relax. After all, it is only fifteen miles, and with Rio being young and peppy, I could expect Rhonda around four to five. I'm ready!

Little did I know that Rio is being a little, shall I say, *recalcitrant*. Like, "Hey, why is it my turn already? I'm the youngster and only just learning. This doesn't seem fair!" Or maybe he saw Lizzy come in the night before, looking like a lead weight on a string. Let me tell you I had to move her around to get her into this marvelous paddock, and it was like moving a locomotive with one hand tied behind my back. Or maybe Rio remembered the paddock itself where he could run and jump and rear up without any human being weighing him down. Talk about inconsiderate . . . after we had been feeding him alfalfa pellets and all.

So Rhonda had an ordeal and a trying day. At 5:00 p.m., I was getting a little worried. I also knew that there was no way she was going to make it to Fobes, and so I had better get my ass in gear. Grabbed up the six-pack and loaded the horses, and off we went to find this Morris Ranch Road. Not sure why everything has to be a ranch. Like when we were in Warner Springs and kept trying to reach Warner Springs Ranch to see if we could rest a spell on the fringe, you know, like out of the way. When we kept getting busy signals, we figured the boys were out herding cattle. More like they were out chasing little white balls on the new golf course. Shoulda known, bein' a surveyor and all, that the ranch was now a "development" with its own airfield, store, and whatever. Yeah, didn't stay there.

At five thirty, Rhonda texted me to say she had just reached the cutoff trail and was headed down. Oh, crap! This mileage I knew, and it wasn't boding well. Eleven and a half miles in six and a half hours, or 2 mph means there was some trouble along the way. I texted back that I was on Morris Road and headed her way and would find a place to park. I'm sure that relieved the tension a bit but still no word of a problem. I began to relax also. Having reached the end of the road, I texted Rhonda to pass up the spring, and I would have water waiting. She texted back, "What?"

By now, I could see her and Rio (binoculars) and texted back, "Come on down. I can see you, so I know you can see the bus behind me."

"Oh," she texted.

All's well in Garner Valley tonite. Rio, Rhonda explained, just didn't want to go this day. Stopping and refusing to go over a step-over log. He was balking at the littlest things. So Rhonda did a lot of walking rather than fight with the horse. Smart! Hmm, Rhonda walking, now that explains 2 mph. Just kidding, babe.

We stayed the night in the local national forest a short ways off the beaten path. I had scoped this area out the other day, finding these little yellow posts scattered about under the canopy of the pine forest. Some flat areas and even a picnic table or two. Looked really inviting. Come to find out that this is "dispersed camping," California style. In our neck of the woods (national forests), you can camp in a manner called dispersed camping almost anywhere there is a flat spot and room for your rig. Just need to practice "leave no trace" ethics and leave the site with little discernible evidence of your passage. Here in California, they insist that they premark these spots with little yellow posts. And you can't just pull off the road because that means you are leaving an imprint of your passage, so you stay on bare ground, which just might be the road you entered upon. When I asked about high- lining our horses, they said, "No problem there because that is a natural imprint." I guess horses are considered part of the terrain.

And so it was that on this day it was Cheyenne's turn to head into the hills, and in doing so, he leaves behind one stodgy locomotive and one crybaby. Go get 'em big fella. I will be staying at our old hangout, McCall Memorial Horse Park for two days as Rhonda negotiates three long days, two campouts by herself, and finally meeting up on Highway 111 just north of Palm Springs. I should be able to resupply her at the two campouts but won't be able to stay, what with the Hilton and steeds back at McCall unsupervised. Gotta get home to my stove and comfy bed. Play solitaire and any number of exciting things to do.

Sunday I will be off to an all-too-familiar town of Hemet. Remember the lost $100? Yeah, that town. Gonna exchange some rank, mildewed hay for better stuff. Hopefully exchange alfalfa pellets for hay, and do some shopping. Can you believe that our horses won't eat the pellets? Neither can we, but we sure ain't carrying them for ballast, and it's a little late to trade in the horses. Laundry will have to wait ('cause I hate it). Then I go and illegally park once again, or just maybe it will be legal . . . But I have to be at the end of the trail for my lady no matter what.

So that's it, folks. Hope you had a good sleep, and now that it is morning, you can try again. If only I can find a WiFi somewhere to get this sent. Remember a while back I sent one part from my phone. Can't do that again as I had to buy another two gigs for my data plan. Tsk, tsk.

Love you all! Hope you had a good weekend since this is four days late, and guess what? From my phone. Yeah, you got it . . . Typed the whole thing over again, like the tablet wasn't hard enough.

Rhonda, go buy more gigs.

Cheers,
Pat

(Sent from my US cellular smartphone)

I drove to the trailhead at Fuller ridge, but where is the team?

PART

7

April 20, 2015

Hi, everyone!

If you are getting this for the first time, it is because I am now using my phone to send. In the process, I updated my list, and YOU are now on it. If you missed prior parts, let me know, and I will try to send them.

The following is a copy of an e-mail I sent to a dear friend, and it seemed poignant to The Journey. Enjoy, and **part 6** should be read in front of this when I figure out how to get it off my tablet.

* * *

Wayne,

I heard you had written and inquired, so I'm here to say that all is well in the fun and sun land of Southern California. We are now in Riverside County but still in the mountains.

Rhonda is ever pressing forward, and I'm galloping alongside like a good ol' boy. Still haven't seen a river, so I think the county musta moved. She is camped out in the woods high above me while I luxuriate in the confines of the Hilton.

As to our absence from the airwaves, you can blame the locals for not providing adequate intervals of WiFi. Yesterday I went to the local library only to find out their service was down. But alas, the pizza place a few doors down had WiFi. I think it was a "come on" as I was feeling guilty and so ordered up a small pizza to take to Rhonda for din-din. Twenty-one dollars later, my e-mail attempt at sending . . . failed. I think they turned it off, hoping I would buy another pizza.

I was able to reach Rhonda only after some trying times. She had ridden up from the valley to park at a local trailhead at the end of a jeep road. This is a very primitive road with steep inclines. You ever go on FS road 370 from Three Creeks to Todd Lake. Well, think of the worst part and then add 10 to 15 percent slope. Not your Sunday pleasure drive.

So when I get up there, I find this large flat table top ridge with a plethora of roads that look like someone spilled their spaghetti. Not a sign could be seen, so where's the trailhead? And where's Rhonda, assuming she is on the same ridge?

We texted, 'cause now we are on top of the world and have five bars on our cells. I felt like a Martian with little antennae out of my ears. But we still didn't know where we were, or I should say I didn't know 'cause Rhonda had a sign in front of her. Now if I could only find the sign. Felt like I was in a comedy, like, "Where's my sign?"

Okay, I'm a surveyor, right. We each have GPS receivers, so let's trade post positions by texting one another. Of course, Rhonda's settings are different from mine, so I have to change my settings.

All the while, Rhonda is looking at Google Maps and trying to give me instructions on which roads to take to get up the hill. She's not getting it that "I'M ALREADY UP THE DAMN HILL, I just can't find you!"

Finally, I figure out the coordinates and realize that I am south of her position and so I drive north, right? Yeah, right . . . and guess what? I find this road about two hundred feet away that juts to the left off the main entry and goes up the hill even farther. Why am I leaving when there's a perfectly flat ridge, with picnic tables and fire rings and grass and big pine trees for shade? Why would I want to leave? Ahh, but to find my honey!

Another two hundred feet, and there's the sign! Hooray, but where is Rhonda at this postage stamp parking area perched on the side of the hill? I park, and Tucker and I get out. All right, she has a horse and a tent, and where the hell is she? We take five strides when out of the trees comes this bloodcurdling shriek as Cheyenne whinnies, hoping Liz has come to the rescue. Sorry, good buddy.

Still no Rhonda! She has gone down the roadway, looking for me/us/truck, which had been driven by this time farther down the ridge to find *the sign*, of course. We crisscrossed paths along the way. Remember my comment about spaghetti? So now I text her and ask the perennial question: "Where the hell are you?" I tell her I'm at the camp.

YAHOO! And the moral of the story is to put the cell phones away and go "low-tech." If I had honked my horn upon arriving, Rhonda could have walked the hundred yards and led me, sheepishly, to our rendezvous place.

But what kinda story would that have been?

We kissed and made up and then had cold pizza for dinner. I hoped she tucked herself well into her bivy sack and slept a warm and comfy night. Her sleeping bag is only forty years old, but don't feel sorry for her, 'cause it's rated at forty below zero.

I hope all is well for you and that you won't fret about the two of us out here in the wilds where motorcycles and $150,000 sports cars rule the roads. We are well, good, and tired most of the time. Monday will be a "0" day for us (her) to recuperate. Me to plot the next stage of our journey.

Hugs and best wishes for a happy weekend.

P n R.

* * *

Oh yeah, to answer your question. I think we have five e-mail addresses. Use the one this was written on for me. Hrsnarnd for

Rhonda. Then there is Gmail, Hotmail and R's work address. We gave up the RM CAD address.

Have a good day.

Pat

(Sent from my US Cellular smartphone)

Cheyenne is to go from 8,000 feet to 1,100 feet this day.

Camp is anywhere you can find space, especially 11 miles from Palm Springs.

Some spots are a little quieter to camp.

PART

8

April 24, 2015

It's howdy to you from sunny Southern California and the Whitewater River Canyon.

Last night, Eva stopped by for a visit. What a pleasant surprise. She was on her way home after a day's work, volunteering for the Whitewater Preserve, a land set aside by the nonprofit the Wildlands Conservancy. They purchased an old trout farm and have kept that as part of their educational nature tour.

Anyway, Eva was curious about us after having ridden her bike up four and a half miles and seeing our rig, still in a state of slumber this morning on her way to work. Stopping by was on her list as she rode home, and here we were, sipping Margaritas in the backyard after Rhonda had a short ride of ten miles earlier in the day. Eva is a woman of short stature, all bubbly and effervescent, with an adventurous spirit. I hope you all know or have met someone like her because she just seems to light up the room or, in this case, the hearts of those near.

We came to find out that she hails from Connecticut and transplanted herself here in the desert upon retiring. She went to work as a volunteer for the conservancy to find out firsthand all that she could about the desert landscape and ecology. She has used her spare time to hike all the local trails, and her curious spirit led her to us. She suspected what our enterprise was all about but just had to investigate further, and we are glad she did.

She and Rhonda took to each other like two peas in a pod, Rhonda talking about her trail experiences with Eva glued to each word. It made for a most enjoyable evening, having someone care that much about what you are doing and appreciating our short time together. But we had to say our goodbyes, understanding that each of us had to move forward, so with a big hug from Rhonda, Eva was on her way, pedaling down the road.

How fortunate we are to have folks like Eva, Tim and Andrea, Dave, Melissa and Hanna (a riding couple and daughter I met at Mountain Center), Stephanie at the Paradise Cafe, Nancy at Warner Springs, Gene Vick at Campo, and the good folks at Campo Feed along our way to share our experiences and to warm our hearts. That's not to mention all the hikers we have met and remet and rejoiced with for the travels we have done.

Rhonda has gone over 220 miles thus far, and last evening, I had to ask how she was holding up. Some days are just so trying and exhausting, but then there are days like this one to gain back your composure and become stalwart once again. Is she gonna make it all the way? Only time will tell. But she is one tough woman, and if anyone can make it, she can! Her response to my question was a sigh and a thought that she had pondered the same question . . . and that it was the people and the chance encounters, much like our new friend, Eva, that give her strength and the will to continue. After all, what else would she be doing for the next six months? Six months is not all that long in the space of a lifetime, and this opportunity is here, right now, so why not?

So Rhonda is on the trail once again, leaving the desert for a while to hopefully land in a pine forest two days from now. The San Bernardino Forest beckons, and we are anxious to give up some of these rocks, heat, and scratchy things. She will be camped out on her own this evening along Mission Creek, so follow her breadcrumbs on Mapshare (see her blog) and wish her a comfy night.

For me, it will be Travels with Tucker, and Cheyenne and Rio. We have nearly ninety miles to drive around these mountains and meet her. First stopping at the post office to pick up Cheyenne's new boots, as he trashed the old ones. He has had a good rest from the grueling trek over the San Jacinto Range and should be ready for riding when needed. In fact, I may ride him tomorrow just for the exercise (his, not mine).

Well, it's another day and another story. Yesterday afternoon I was on my journey around the mountains, headed west towards Los Angeles on Highway 10 when I heard the chirp signifying a new text. Nearly poised to leave the highway and enter the unknown of a two-lane thru and up into the mountains, I spied a rest area and decided it was time to dump garbage and check my messages.

It was from Rhonda, saying there was an unpassable tree down at MP 236 on the PCT and could I get ahold of the authorities to see if it could be removed. Whoa, this is a new twist, but fortunately, I had excellent cell service and began my quest. I did have one question for her . . . You were supposed to stop at MP 232/233, so did you get mileage wrong? It was a long wait for a reply, but I needed to know because I didn't want someone headed out to the wrong spot.

Eventually, it became clear that this was a tree reported to her by hikers and she wouldn't actually get there until tomorrow. So I had already taken some action and contacted and talked with folks in the USFS Mill Creek District and was told that they don't have summer crews on board yet and that the section of trail was normally cleared by volunteers. On top of that, this MP was outside the forest boundary. The nice lady gave me the number of the local BCHCA party who might be able to help.

Back Country Horsemen representative Val Silver said that this portion of trail was not their chapter's responsibility, but she would give me a name to call that might be able to help. However, she cautioned that this is not likely the only tree in this five-mile stretch that would be a problem. She cautioned that this is a notoriously bad area for blow-down and usually doesn't get cleared until sometime later in the year. She recommended that Rhonda turn around and take the truck around this spot. Since Val spoke from experience, having ridden the PCT from Mexico to Tahoe (one thousand miles), I passed the info on to Rhonda.

And I kept searching for help. The MP is in the San Gorgonio wilderness, and I found a website for Friends of the Wilderness. They had a chat line where I could leave a posting, and I did. I then tried the phone number Val had provided but ended up leaving a message. I also tried the local BLM but couldn't get thru to a real person. It was getting late and decisions had to be made.

Rhonda, of course, would be camping overnight as it was too far back or forward, regardless of the decision. I decided to head back to where I had just come from, thirty miles was shorter than sixty, and I knew what was ahead of me. I hate making camp in the dark at a strange location, especially with this rig. Only one other consideration, and that was to stay where I had cell coverage so Ronda and I could continue to communicate. Found just the right spot, but unfortunately, a storm was passing over, and I (and the horses) would be buffeted by winds all night long. I will be glad when we can move on.

Rhonda decided on the safe exit and go around this stretch so she will be joining me midday tomorrow, I hope. Would be nice to get settled on the other side and get her back on the trail. The decision was hard for her, I'm sure, but the right one. Even if I had reached the right person, it was unlikely they could mobilize that quickly, needing stock animals because they would also have to stay overnight in this remote area, fifteen miles from a trailhead. It's time to move on.

So I'm going to saddle up and take Cheyenne and Rio to go meet Rhonda out on the trail. Wish me luck that I don't get lost. Signing off and hasta la vista.

Patrick

I found mah honey. See you on the morrow.

(Sent from my US Cellular smartphone)

The 1st of many trail hogs in the desert.

What in the world are those?? Giant birds?

Tucker gets to play in the Whitewater river.

And that's where they are going.

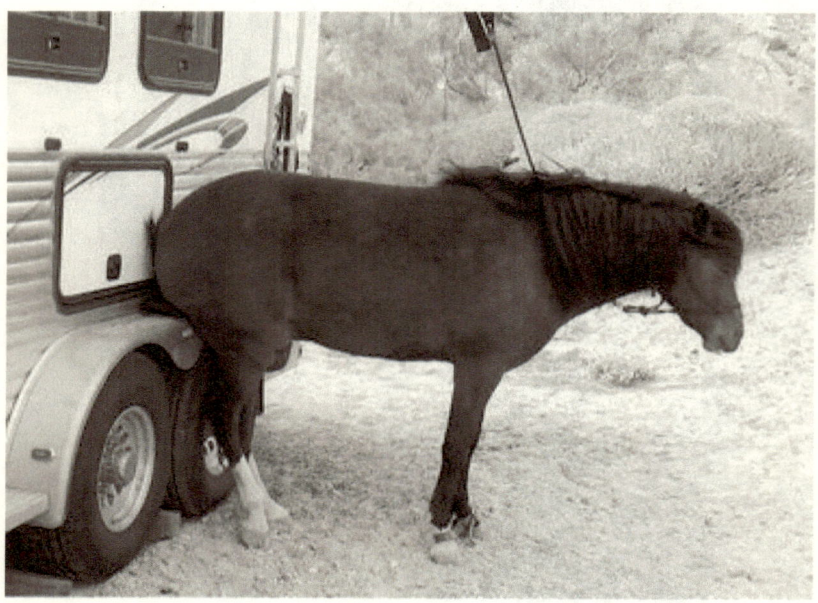

Must be Rio's rest day!

PART

9

April 27, 2015

Good morning, all!

I hope you had a pleasant weekend, nice weather, or maybe rain and snow for those that need it, and are entering upon the coming week with wonder about what it will bring. I know we are. Rhonda is out on the trail this morning, having camped out in her bivy sack on a space no bigger than your couch. I don't know how she does it. Me, I've got to have a tent in most instances, a small one at that, weighing less than five pounds, but some space nevertheless. I hope she slept well. Lizzy was a little farther away this night, and maybe that will help. Lizzy snores! She (Rhonda), or I guess both of them, will have one more night on the trail, and then I will go and retrieve them and bring them back to my Shangri-La. At that point, they will be at milepost 298, Skinner's Cabin near Lake Arrowhead, where it will become decision time as to whether to skip a short portion or venture forth. We'll make that decision together back here under more pleasant conditions. When I say "we," I mean Rhonda will make the decision with my input, which sounds about right to the folks that know us. After all, it is *she* taking the daring leap.

So where is back here? Well, I'm gonna keep you guessing while I fill you in on the intermediary happenings along the way. The last time

I chatted, I had just caught up with Rhonda on the PCT in Whitewater Canyon. Amazing, I didn't get lost! With the horses put away in the backroom, we both climbed into our beautiful new Dodge Ram and looked at each other and exclaimed, "Let's get the hell out of here!" We were sick and tired of the incessant wind, dust, and the smell of failure for having turned around. It was time to go forward, out of the desert and into the woods.

So the evening before I had chosen to park near the mouth of the canyon, as previously mentioned, I would need cell service and a flat place to park. Found one, hooray. Years ago, I mounted what we call "outriggers" onto the sides of the Hilton, up high and on the back end. They consist of a steel and fiber rod that can be swung out from the wall and thereupon have a very strong bungee-type strap attached with the other end attached to the halter of a one-thousand-pound animal. Did I say strong? Ever see a horse stretch its neck out to reach that one last remnant of a green blade of grass? Or better yet, ever see a one-thousand-pound animal pull over a seven-thousand- pound trailer? Feels like that sometimes.

Anyway, I'm about set up for the night, albeit on a wide spot of gravel clearing in the middle of the desert, when I notice a gentleman leaving his aged Cadillac and heading our way. Now, we had seen this very same vehicle the day before parked at a classic and handsome log cabin just up the road. And now I'm imagining that this patch of bare ground is his and I'm having a bad dream of going to look for another campsite at dusk in a countryside that is foreign to me. All right, Patrick, cowboy up and take your medicine, and go meet this guest. So that's what I do.

And Markus (that's the newcomer's name) shouts out above the howling wind, "Can I pet your horses?" And I've just had a heart seizure for nothing. We introduce ourselves, and I find out that Markus is a transplanted Englishman and does indeed own the cabin where the Cadillac resides. But not this little piece of ground. Whew! He has been stateside for many years now and is involved in the film industry, and with LA being so close by, he has this little retreat cabin in the valley to while away his time. He grew up with horses on the island and was overjoyed to see horses in his valley. He wanted to pet them, and that he did. We talked, and all the while, my dinner was burning on the stove. Incredible! And now he is semiretired and has a website dedicated to saving the valley for all time. Apparently, the San Andreas Fault runs under the cabin, which has left caverns and springs near his little oasis, a place where scientists love to come visit and study for its uniqueness. And of course, stay in his little cabin for a paltry $195 per night. Who needs to work when you have a gold mine?

And then Allie and Sarah show up on their matching 1200 CC BMW motorcycles. Have I introduced them yet? Hmmm, can't remember. Allie owns a BMW motorcycle sales and repair shop in Ventura County on the coast. This is their holiday! Yesterday they startled Rhonda by calling out her name when she was coming into the preserve on the tail end of that day's ride. "Now how in hell do two strangers know my name? and why?" she wonders. Little did she know that Allie and Sarah had stopped by the Hilton earlier that day as they hiked up the valley floor, having stayed in Markus's cabin for the previous night. They too had been curious why a horse trailer was parked along the road with no one to their knowledge riding out. Well, while I'm not gregarious and a conversationalist, I do get lonely and albeit starved for conversation. So they got the full lowdown on our trek from you-know-who! Boy, do we get around. Having recognized both Markus's vehicle and my trailer, they decided to stop and say hi, and now my dinner is charcoal.

So now, being the next day, we (Rhonda and I) are leaving the Whitewater Valley for good when who do we see but Markus standing alongside the road. Gotta stop and make introductions, and so a short while later, we are on our way, but in a new direction as Markus has persuaded us to go into the Yucca Valley and see the Joshua trees and have this very picturesque journey up into the high country. An hour and a half later, as we are looking at this dirt trail in front of us, Markus's name is linked to a bunch of expletives, and I begin backing up. Did I state earlier that we were done with go-backs and needed to go forward? Get out the maps, Rhonda, as we set a new course that will take us to the Lucerne Valley and then up into the mountains. A long go-around but better than going back, or so I thought, until I read the sign that "not for rigs with thirty feet from hitch to wheels." Ah,

I'm only at twenty-six feet, piece of cake! And then the sign "Slopes of 10 to 18 percent ahead for sixteen miles." Whew, boy, this new Ram better have some muscle under that pretty new skin 'cause we are nearly twenty-three thousand pounds total weight and hauling another 1,200 pounds. Aha, never a doubt as she performed admirably. But now it is suppertime, and we still haven't landed anywhere. And where might "anywhere" be, by the way?

We knew only one thing, and that was that Rhonda needed to depart from MP 252 tomorrow morning, and so that is where we headed. Right up the mountain, past the lake, stores, the town of Big Bear and all the people to an isolated spot alongside the same highway we were supposed to take before chatting with Markus. Coulda been here three hours earlier, but we did have the delight of seeing thousands of Joshua trees! Here is where we take advantage of the Hilton 'cause all we have to do is find a nearly level spot and put down her roots, and camp is done. Next come the horses who get fed first, blanketed, and on the outriggers for the night. Blanketed because we are at 8,400 feet at Onyx Pass, with a storm rolling in. Dinner and bedtime for us on a trying day.

We awakened to shivers 'cause it was downright cold to get out of that bag and start the coffee. With a skiff of snow on the ground, the onboard heater got its first test that morning, or why else do we have it? Rhonda was out and onto the trail by 10:00 a.m., looking like a cocoon on top of a sorrel mare. But with one thing new . . . Lizzy had on two pair of boots, front and back, which we seldom if ever do. Her shiny green ones on front and Cheyenne's brand-new ones on back. Now, don't be jealous, Cheyenne. You got to break them in yesterday. (Was that just yesterday?)

Packing up, I was on down the road and into town to look for a place to park this carriage and also check with the Forest Service on roads and maps and such. I drove and drove but not finding much but one area back up the hill a bit. It was a stormy day, and I could really feel for Rhonda out on some ridgetop with the wind and mist assailing every body part. I'm so glad she cocooned up for the day.

We met at the highway upon which we had come up the hill (mountain). I first checked it out on foot. A little hike would not hurt

Tucker and me, and I'll be damned if I wanted to go back down an 18 percent grade if there wasn't room to turn around. So Rhonda made record time today as Liz loved her four boots. You know women, always stylin'. And we were off around Baldwin Lake and headed to the place I spotted. On the far side of the lake, oh and by the way, a "dry" lake due to the draught, I pointed out a small area next to the road that I had considered for parking. "STOP!" my honey yelled. "We can fit in there." And by golly, we did, high-lining the horses and settling in for the night, with a whole bunch of long-necked lookie loos travelling by only twenty-five feet away on the pavement. Vittles done and enjoying a restful evening, we were going to turn in early, the horses high-lined out near the fence line, fed, and resting also for the night.

And then out of the darkness of the night came a very stern *rap, rap, rap* on our door. That set off the alarm, and we had to quiet Tucker down before opening up, looking at each other and wondering if it weren't the local gendarmes come to take us away. But no, it was another of the finishes to a long story as we introduced ourselves to a Ms. Becky, who felt sorry for us and our predicament of settling for such a place to camp. Becky lived on acreage less than a half mile away, with stalls and water and electricity and WiFi, and how could we say no to her offer to put us up? But we did, for that night anyway, but graciously accepted for tomorrow night. We really aren't sure how long or how fast we can wear out that welcome, but I'm sitting here and wish to tell you how thankful we are. Or should I say that in the singular since Rhonda is still out on the trail and will be until tomorrow night? I hope to have a "0" day after that for Rhonda to recuperate and me to go find new fodder and where Rhonda can catch up with the electronic business.

So that's my story, and you are stuck with it. It's another glorious day, and time for me to get moving. Rhonda was on the trail two hours ago, so I'd better catch up.

Love you, one and all.

Pat and Rhonda

(Sent from Samsung tablet)

PART

10

May 4, 2015

Hi to all our friends and family!

Today should be a day just like any other day, but somehow it feels different. It's Sunday, May 3, which was my mom's birthday, but that's not it. It's one month since Rhonda started (or we all did) this ride of a lifetime. I guess I'm just starting to realize how momentous this little adventure is, especially when I see Rhonda ride off with two horses, riding Cheyenne with Lizzy in tow.

I am now camped out (in the Hilton) near milepost 347, and the next stretch of trail has little or no water and very little graze. I will be meeting up with m'lady tomorrow late afternoon to provide a water break, but that won't be the end of the ride, having another six-plus miles to go. Then we will camp out together and prepare for the next day, which will actually be a two-day ride with another campout.

So how does one get the gumption to just ride out onto a trail that you've never seen but only read about, and that only in general terms? You'd think I would know, having done it on many occasions myself, mostly on my hunting trips. Having a strong will to succeed, trusting in your own abilities to overcome or think through whatever lies ahead, and a desire that is so strong that you are willing to risk failure in order to succeed. That sounds about right.

Doesn't make it any easier to watch your loved ones take leave of your presence in order to achieve their goal. I'm only too happy to help and be here to marvel at what m'lady is doing, and then stand back and ponder this quest.

Last week, we were staying with our newfound friend, Becky of Big Bear Lake. Becky was kind of awestruck by this whole enterprise and told all her friends, who told their friends, and we almost felt like celebrities. All I can say is that we are forever grateful for her generosity and gracious hospitality. It almost made me feel guilty, but she would have none of that.

Rhonda finally got her zero day, but only after I had delivered a $30.00 hamburger. So how does a hamburger get to be worth $30.00? Meat $2.00; bun $1.50; lettuce, onion, and tomato $2.50; and condiments $1.00; and the fuel to get there . . . $24.00. For the two nights that she was on the trail near Big Bear Lake, I had decided to explore the USFS roadways and take her some water and dinner. I call them roadways 'cause that's what the map says, but the miners must have built them during the gold rush of 1860. Gold's long gone, but the trails/roads remain, I guess for the four-by-four challenge. Too bad I have a four-ton truck that's about a mile long, or I might have enjoyed it.

Becky even went so far as to lend us the use of her smaller horse trailer so I could pick Rhonda up at Lake Arrowhead and bring her back for her zero day in the Hilton and give us time to explore Big Bear Lake. We were surprised to see ski lifts going up the hillside in this Southern California clime, but the summit is at eight thousand feet plus, so I guess it fits. I took her back to the trail and Splinters Cabin the next day, and she was off, heading north toward the Mojave Desert. So much for pine trees and shade. For me, it would be a long drive to go replenish our feed supplies and hightail it around the mountains to meet up with her just south of Victorville at the edge of the San Bernardino Forest.

Rhonda continued to skirt along the northerly edge of the forest, with us meeting back up at Silverwood Lake the following day. There was a campground that was listed for horse camping at the westerly end of the lake. Unfortunately, the resident ranger said the campground was closed this early in the year. You're kidding. It's eighty degrees out! However, a heavy dose of pleading and cajoling got us entry to one site on the fringes, and we could make do. Right on the trail, but we were used to that. The next morning, Rhonda had the joy of introducing me to a young couple she had encountered numerous times along the trail. It's not uncommon for folks to bond with other travelers, hikers, or riders as you experience the wonder and excitement and even the drudgery of being on the trail. Rhonda will be riding Rio to Cajon Pass and above Horse Thief Canyon on her way to meeting me at the McDonald's restaurant at Interstate Highway 15; 340 miles along the trail and we are still within sight of the Pacific Ocean less than fifty miles west of our location.

Rhonda and I have had to make many small and some rather difficult decisions in the weeks of her being on the trail. All the puddle jumping, as I called it, trying to make contact with Rhonda on primitive roads and leaving the horses and trailer behind has not been working out too well. Too much time and energy expended for a short visit, and it also has complicated Rhonda's "get up and go" routine. It forced us to make some tough decisions, one of which was "never again," which leads me back to waving bye-bye to Rhonda with a packhorse in tow. Now she carries her water and fuel for the horses. If we only had reports from horse people on "horse needs" along the trail, such as grazing opportunities, water for stock, and obstacles that could stop a horse but not a hiker, these decisions would have come a bit easier. Someday, maybe I can address that aspect of this effort and help those that may wish to follow in Rhonda's wake. For now, we will do what we believe must be done.

Today we met another couple that intend to do the trail on horseback, albeit in segments, I guess. Rhonda had conversed with this lady by e-mail sometime this past year, as the couple had started a year ago, but she had gotten injured on the trail. They are back to make another go at it, and being local folks, they spotted the Hilton near McDonald's and had to come check us out. Not sure why they are just driving around, but I'm assuming the gentleman is working a day job until they venture forth. Anyway, it was nice to meet someone who could relate to this experience from firsthand knowledge.

This trip has been a most entertaining and an enjoyable opportunity to meet people along the way. The other day, while cleaning up our camping spot after seeing Rhonda off, I met a most interesting man and realized that there is something about trailheads and other visitors that frequent such places, folks with an adventurous spirit, and you just seem to gravitate to one another.

What I learned is that he is a mountaineer (a climber of mountains) and has been most of his adult life. Short in stature and well-muscled, he looked the part. He had climbed all the major mountains in the Sierras and Cascades and had even tackled Mt. Denali in Alaska (yeah, I know it's now McKinley), but I don't agree. Took he and his team twenty-nine days, having been snowed in for four days and climbing for twenty-one and four to get down. I was impressed. Having lived in Alaska for fifteen years, I used to gaze at this twenty-nine- thousand-foot-high peak on many roadside adventures. Even knew a helicopter pilot that had, at that period of time (1970s), made the highest altitude rescue attempt on the mountain.

The reason that he was at this particular trailhead was that he was now in training to accomplish a second trip up Mt. Denali. He had supposedly retired but a group of friends had persuaded him to come along on one last adventure. He had a long history of successful climbing and thought he was done at his advanced age of sixty-two, but these folks still wanted him back. He was out to test his mettle in the coming months to make sure he wouldn't let his team down.

He was now in training to try to return to climbing shape. He told his friends that if he could get in shape he would give them his answer in six months, with the ascent beginning in October. He hiked roughly six miles up the hill and five back down on the PCT trail in a little less than two hours. I think he just might make it. At sixty-nine years of age, I had finally met my first mountain climber.

But then there are those you wish you hadn't met, but they keep coming back, like indigestion. When I made camp on the H&H Ranch property in Whitewater Canyon, way back there twelve days ago, I had just gotten camp set up and was lazing about in the Hilton when I heard voices outside. Tucker barked, and I thought I should check it out.

Three guys in a beater auto, laying out blankets and clothing to air out. Oldest, and I would call him the leader, about thirty-five, and two youngsters in their twenties. I was feeling a little prickly about this time. Like why did they choose this time and this place, of all the wide spots in this four-mile stretch of roadway? I'll never know and really don't want to know 'cause it's nearly two weeks later. Just seemed kind of surreal, like a Stephen King novel.

And a little déjà vu from many, many years before. I was young once—all right, quit your laughing—and was a bit of a hippy or at least trying to play that role, driving my VW camper van across this land, when I was told of my father's ill health. It was time to drive home and forget about Mardi Gras. So I picked up some hitchhikers, hoping to get company and some help driving across Texas. A guy a little older than me, another young adult, and a teen.

Long story short was that the only thing that saved me was that I had a bigger knife than the bad guy, who was hoping to pimp the youngsters in LA after he took all I had and left me to the carrion. I was a fisherman in those travel days and always had my fillet knife at hand. He was a smooth talker and a pretty nice guy, other than the fact that he was evil.

So here I was, sitting in my $48,000 lap of luxury and wondering why these guys had stopped and why were they walking out into the river bottom one at a time. Later that day, I had an opportunity to chat with the local ranger (who carried a sidearm) and asked if he would please check these guys out. He did, and they left. Whew! Seems the area is popular for growing pot, what with the river water and few people. Still can't get the King novel out of my head.

Okay, on the lighter side, I have attached a couple of pictures to this posting. One is rather self-explanatory, with Rhonda riding off into the distant mountains. The second one brings up this question . . . how does an old man with straight white hair get it to lie down on his head? I went out and chatted with our visitors a while ago and then came in to set up camp—you know, get out the beer and chips—when I looked in the mirror. No wonder those folks were looking at me in such a peculiar way. Felt like I was in *Back to the Future*! Oh well, such is my fate.

Okay, now it is time to walk up the road and see if I can get cell coverage. And here I wanted WiFi when now I can't even send from my cell. Life goes on.

Hope yours is a good one. This has turned out to be a grand day. Thanks for joining me.

Love you all,
Patrick

* * *

Egads! I've been on the trail too long, but
who's out there to see me?

So guess what? It's another day! And I was rudely awakened this morning at 5:00 a.m. by the sound of traffic going by at speed. Now, what in the hell? It's dark out, and why would people be going by at speed on a gravel road in the dark? Running from the cops?

Well, guess what, I'm on a gravel thoroughfare, and here it is, six thirty, and they are still coming. From where? I don't know. Haven't seen any burrows big enough for a car! Ain't no town within ten miles. But now that I think of it, there were two motorcyclists yesterday that stopped and wanted directions. Thought the road led to the old Route 66, like I would know. Aha, I've got it, I am in *Back to the Future*, and these guys are on Route 66! That explains my hair!

But wait a minute, these cars are too new. I see Kias, Subarus, and even dually trucks. Guess again, or better yet, get out my trusty old map. No, not from the fifties, just old. And what do I see but a very light, almost indistinguishable, double gray line that goes roughly eight miles to an interchange on Highway 15, just outside San Bernardino. These guys have just cut out about fifteen miles of boring freeway driving and can pretend they are in one of those Baja race buggies at 45 mph thru the desert. Now I see why all the cars look new as they are probably leased and can be turned in for new ones in two years. Just a few rattles. Fit right in with the snakes.

Has Rhonda mentioned her encounters with snakes? She has had quite a number of them. Even stuck around long enough to videotape one until it coiled in striking mode when Rhonda decided that she and Liz had seen enough. I bet Liz was thrilled. After all, they weren't Ronda's legs sticking out there.

They even have classes around here to teach your dog (and I suppose a few owners that are mentally challenged) how to not get bit. You know the mentally challenged guys when you see them trying to ride their skateboard down a steel hand rail. Anyway, they take real rattlesnakes and tape their mouths shut and then put 'em out in the yard and turn your dog loose. Not sure how this works, but the dog is supposed to learn to avoid or stay away from a mad snake. I'm sure Tucker would think this is a real fun game, like, wanna try to take this toy away from me?

So where do I go and park this rig tonight? Where there aren't rattlesnakes or high-flying commuters. Maybe farther from civilization, but then there will be more snakes, right? Under high transmission lines seems to be our favorite, where no one comes around and rousts you out in the middle of the night. There are roads in and out and reasonably flat ground, and there are plenty of them to feed the 10+ million folks in the neighborhood. Hmm, hair standing on end, huh? And who was talking about the mentally challenged?

Whew, sun finally sneaked over the horizon, and the traffic has slowed to almost nil. Almost cold this morning in this little mountain valley, and now it will get blazing hot. Give me Central Oregon, where I wake up to the sun creeping over the horizon just when it's time to do chores. Only five more months to go.

Time to get movin' and go find a cell tower to park under. Have a good day, and don't forget to hug a loved one. Or if you have cell service, call 'em up and give a verbal hug.

I'm on down the road. Hugs and warm wishes to you.

Pat and Rhonda

(Sent from my US cellular smartphone)

Well, the pack fits her and they are on their way.

She is a princess, isn't she.

PART

11

May 8, 2015

Sink or swim?

I think Rhonda is swimming all the way. Damn crazy woman. Those of you that know me should have figured out that I'm not too fond of heights. Actually, I'm scared shitless sometimes. Today was almost one of those days, and I was in the big truck, leaving 6,330-foot elevation to hit the pass at 7,900 feet. Rhonda was climbing switchbacks to the top somewhere above me and then would ride the hog back ridge back down to the Islip Saddle, where I am now parked at 6,650 feet. She is traversing the top of Mt. Baden-Powell, named after the man responsible for starting the Boy Scouts of America, with this being the tallest mountain in the San Gabriel Mountains at 9,399 feet.

I couldn't do it! Just plain and simple, couldn't, could not, won't in one thousand years. Hell, I was having nightmares in the daytime, envisioning losing my brakes and going over the edge. Iron grip on the steering wheel, I can tell you that. And oh yeah, don't look down. Best tunnel vision in the West. I liked Europe because they tunnel under these mountains, so what gives? We are transplanted Europeans, aren't we? Or some of us, maybe.

I sometimes wonder how I got this way. Doesn't seem like I was always afraid, having climbed the mature English walnut trees with the best of my grammar school chums. And we had a fort in the old eucalyptus tree at the end of the corral. So what gives?

Maybe it was the day I toppled (along with the three-legged harvest ladder) from high up at the top while picking pears. I can still picture the ground rising up to meet me. Couldn't have been when I slid off our cabin roof in Alaska while applying tar and paper to the roof. I think I already had the disease by then.

Funny how it didn't seem to bother me when flying with my dad. We went all over Northern California; of course, it wasn't over these mountains. But we did go over the Sierras and they are a damn sight taller. And then I took my own flying lessons and flew solo for thirty- some hours in both California and Alaska. So what's with that?

So I'm back to giving credit where credit is due. Damn, I'm mighty proud of that woman. If she were a man, I could say something about *cajones*, but alas, she's got what it takes. So, ladies, what do you say? She is due in most any time, and soon is not soon enough. It looks like we have weather coming our way, with fog or clouds starting to envelop the mountaintop. Not going to be pleasant up here this night, but that's why we have the Hilton. Gonna be a blanket night for the babies. I think I am presently at 6,500 feet. One of the locals said this is not normal, that it is usually about eighty plus degrees during the May days and fifties at night. Instead, it feels like Central Oregon, so we should be right at home, except for the wind. We have had wind for nearly 75 percent of our time down here. It can wear a fella out.

Time to go look for m'lady. Talk to you later. And by golly, she made it—an hour later than expected, but she made it. Had a little trouble with a log on a steep side slope of shale. Couldn't go up or down, so she tried to get Lizzy to jump it. Yeah right! Lizzy jumps? Come on. She had my trail saw, so she tried to cut a notch but, after some time, realized it would be dark before she finished (twenty-four- to thirty inch tree). Finally figured out if she couldn't make the tree come closer to the ground, then she would just have to raise the ground up towards the tree. So with a few flat boulders, she could manage to raise a platform, and a whole lot of shale later, she was able to get the tired locomotive over the log. Where there's a will there's a way, or should we say that when there's a Rhonda the only choice is forward. Go gettum, girl.

So yeah, the weather is still troublesome, with some rain forecast for Friday. Hope we can get off the tops of these mountains before then, but I'm not sure the other extreme of desert is all that more appealing. Maybe it will be time for another zero day. Just did evening chores, and I froze my you-know-what, but could still crawl into the Hilton only to find my better half under the covers. Why, what a good idea.

See you everyone on the morrow. Good night all!

And so it is the morrow, and the progression down the trail wasn't what it used to be. No, by golly. Remember that gal I mentioned last time . . . saw us from the freeway and decided to come visit. Well, she kept saying she was a BCHCA member, but could Rhonda please make note of any trees she encountered and send her a note so that they could get someone up to cut it? Kinda irks me . . . Why isn't she up here and with her friends to cut these damn trees?

Rhonda had to turn around today and come back to the trailhead. Of course, I was already gone. You know me . . . Mr. Speedy. Yeah, well, this was the second trailhead as she went 4.5 miles this morning and then met me on the road to bypass an area due to an endangered frog. Some sort of mountain frog—now that's a unique moniker, like we can't see the mountains. I had done my chores earlier, at the first trailhead, so this time, it was just, "Load up, boys. Time to go." I tell you these guys have been in and out of that trailer so many times that I almost think I could do that. I did say "almost," didn't I? Haven't taken my hand off the halter, rope, or bridle yet. Oregon is too far to run!

So Rhonda goes down the trail, and me, why, I'm at the next meeting point. Even got tonight's camp spot all picked out so I've got time to spare. Hmmm, what to do?

Beard's gettin' a little long, and you can smell me over the horse flesh I'm towing, so I think I've got it. Heat water, get out the wash pan, towel, and washcloth. (Gawd, has it been that long? I'm forgetting what I need.) Oh yeah . . . SOAP! A little PTA bath as we used to call it.

So remember now that I'm at this wide spot in the two-lane highway, top of the ridge at another "saddle," and I don't want to extend our slider or anything else 'cause Rhonda's gonna be along, and we just want to load Liz and head on down the highway to this neat camp spot I found. So my choice is to pretend I'm real skinny and do this thing in the camper or go enjoy the wonderful sunshine and complete my ablution outdoors. Hehe . . . outdoors, right!

So I'm standing on the pavement, cleanly shaven and workin' on the PTA (or should I say the P of PTA) when two cars decide to come on up the road. No matter, they don't know me, and I sure don't know them. They can chalk it up to the crazy Americans. But wait, one of them stops, and OMG, they are backing up. I'm not that cute, and my abs were gone a long time ago, so what gives? They stopped well short, like do we dare get out with this crazy guy so close? But he did. This really neat old guy with a cane popped out of the car and told me, "This lady back at the campground road was on a horse and waving at us, but we were already by her before realizing she might need help. Can you help her?" like this is two miles later, so I guess the mental synapses weren't clicking right on this particular day, but at least they did click. What we have to look forward to as we age.

Mine were sure clicking about that time, so I thanked the old gentleman, covered my breasts (nah, not really as there's nothing to see there), and started packing up. The boys are getting lotsa practice loading and unloading today, and we were on down the road ten minutes later. I'm sure glad I was prepared for this.

Now it is midafternoon, and by golly, I'm not waitin' for nothin'. Just sitting here conversing with all of you and enjoying an afternoon off. Tomorrow will be another day on the trail, so I better enjoy this one to my heart's content. Rhonda will break the four-hundred-mile barrier tomorrow as we start heading for the lowlands. Gonna be another of those long twenty-miler days, so she will pony one horse and switch midway. Can't afford to wear anyone out. Me, I've got to drive fifty miles to get around the mountains and on down to lower elevations and catch up with her.

So we are gonna catch up with you another day and just maybe find some cell service where I can send this thing off. Been fun talking with you, and hope you enjoy being with us on this sojourn. Until then, happy trails, happy thoughts, and just be happy!

Pat and Rhonda

* * *

And guess what? It's another day, and I lied yesterday. Rhonda didn't pony a horse because we could meet at the last road crossing, five miles down the road, and she could switch horses. Cheyenne would get the honors of finishing this day.

Me, I just had to drive around the mountain (twenty-seven miles it turned out) and find this ranger station that we discussed last night. Right on the money, it was there on the top of this spur ridge with gale-like winds traversing the canyon. Oh boy, I can hardly wait.

I went looking for a more sheltered area and found one about four miles down the canyon. Not wind-free, mind you, but sure a lot better than out in the open. You see, this Arctic air mass had somehow gotten south of the border and was about to wail on us. Shelter has become paramount.

With that taken care of, I went back to the ranger station, as that is where we would meet, and they also had a water spigot for me to refill our tanks. I texted Rhonda that we could meet at the highway and day-use area. I had just unfurled my hose when the ranger showed up as I was sheepishly trying to hide the hose. Not everyone is fond of giving away eighty gallons of water, especially in parched Southern California.

But instead, she had heard that Rhonda was coming through and offered the area behind the station for us to park and camp. How kind, as she said many of the trail workers with horses had come before us and liked the spot. I checked it for wind, and it was as protected as the first site, so I made a command decision and began to set up camp, with water jugs all full. But not before I texted Rhonda of the new plan. Now you folks remember back when and I said low-tech was sometimes a better choice? Well, this is one of those times. You see, the wind is really howling by now, and the temp is down to forty-five degrees, cloudy, and lookin' like rain, per the forecast. Rhonda is back in her cocoon stage, and where do you think the phone is? Not in her hand, that's for sure.

I estimated her time of arrival and stood by the trail at the upper level to greet her as she came off the hill. Two young hiker girls were there and said they had passed her a ways back. Cutting a tree, so she should be along anytime now. After a period of time, I was getting concerned. I asked the girls to keep a lookout while I went and looked at the day camp area. Mind you, now it is cold and windy so that any movement out in the open is unpleasant to say the least. She's not there.

But the girls are back. Radish and Pocahontas are their trail names, and they had just returned from the lower level and trailhead. They had checked it out for a camping spot, but the winds were ferocious, and it was getting colder by the minute. They went so far as to check out the waterless toilet where they could snuggle in, albeit on concrete, but at least out of the wind. Problem was that there were several male hikers already settled in, leaving little room to spare. They had come back because there was another toilet in this vicinity of the ranger building. It seemed like a poor choice to me, but what do I know? I am in the Hilton! But wait! Maybe they could stay in the Hilton too, so I offered, and they accepted even though the space was normally occupied by our three hairy friends. A little sweeping, and they were ready to lay down their sleeping mats.

I go back and check on the girls, the horses on the high-line rope, and then head back to the trail. Now mind you, the trail goes right by the upper rest stop, potty, and parking area. This is where I've been waiting, and it is also the one place I have a cell signal. I'm there a couple of minutes when I get this text, and of course, it must be from Rhonda. (Who else?) Finally, but what do I read? "I'm here. Where the hell are you?" Oh, crap!

Now I run down the hill, and what do I see but a big white horse and a steaming cocoon of a lady in a black rain slicker. OMG, am I in for it? And you know what? I got it, both barrels and a little more.

Remember low-tech? If only I had left a note at the lower day camp area or on the post by the trail as you passed the upper rest stop. You know, the paper plate kind you see all over the woods. What a thought, only a day late and a dollar short. The steam dissipated by the time we got back to the Hilton and there was much work to be done. All our anxieties worked out, and we had a good night's sleep, with two young ladies sleeping in the horse stalls 'cause it was cold and windy and supposed to rain all night.

Didn't rain, or we woulda heard it. Snowed instead! Next morning . . . to go or not to go? Well, we didn't drive four thousand miles (already) to sit around in the camper. That's the spirit!

Rhonda is on the trail again, seventeen miles to the N Fork Ranger Station, where she will camp out this eve. Me, I'm in Agua Dulce, awaiting her arrival tomorrow eve. So once again I sign off and wish everyone the very best. And tomorrow I will find better cell service to send this off.

Love to one and all.

Pat

(Sent from my US cellular smartphone)

Logs like this can be a show stopper.
Rhonda was able to ride around this one.

A look west towards the Pacific Ocean and the
Sheep Mountain Wilderness in between.

Mt. Baden Powell, named after the founder of the Boy Scouts.

The view from the top of Mt. Baden Powell.

Another log got cut.

Mill Creek Ranger Station and one cold night out.

Pocahontas and Radish leaving us after a night together.

PART
12

May 14, 2015

Wow, seventy-five degrees, a bright blue sky and a welcome respite from the mountainous terrain we have been facing for the past month. Not that there aren't any mountains, but these are a lot shorter. Like no snow on them. Who'd have guessed Southern California could get snow in Los Angeles County, in May no less? You might say we have weathered the storm.

So I hope all of you are enjoying this fine Sunday and Mother's Day at that. Happy Mother's Day, Nicole!

Rhonda is on the trail after a slow start up this morn. We had a fine dinner last night to celebrate the weekend and a short day for riding. Boxed-up kung pao shrimp and some Sichuan pork ordered up by yours truly at the local bistro (five miles away) to take back to our trailer. The restaurant was right near the hardware store that had an adaptor, four inches to three inches for our sewer pipe. We are lodged at the KOA after Rhonda had done her magic this day, and it was time to celebrate.

You see, I had been trying for the past two days to find us a place to park the Hilton and six warm bodies but failed to do so. I am still in Agua Dulce, near the trail but had hoped to be nearer. The spot I stayed in last evening, a wide spot just off the road, would not do. Having hearing aids can be a blessing sometimes, 'cause all I have to do is pull them out and then it is "What road noise?" Freeway a quarter mile away and the local spur road less than a hundred feet. Put the hearing aids back in, and it is unbearable. Just think how the horses feel.

All this because a lady, name withheld, had offered her place by commenting on Rhonda's blog a while back. Lived near Agua Dulce and would love to have us stop for a night and talk about our travels. Trouble is she did not leave a contact number and has been oblivious to any of our entreaties. What a fix.

So in my travels, I happen to cross a KOA campground in the river bottom. Gotta stop and check this out, so I ask, "By any chance would you allow horses in the campground?" It was an emphatic no. How about a dump station as the Hilton was about to overflow (not too many dump stations in the mountains)? Yeah, great! I was off to do one of my chores only to find out that they were all three-inch pipes and I have a four-inch hose. Foiled again, and off I went to find my highway repose.

At least Rhonda was all comfy in a bunkhouse at the N Fork Ranger Station. North Fork, now doesn't that sound familiar. For the first twelve years of our marriage, we lived on the North Fork Road in Anchor Point, Alaska. Some very sweet times, with Nicole and Colin coming into our lives and many friends we hold dear today. But I digress, nah, not me.

Tomorrow would be another day, with Rhonda riding into the very same KOA, as the trail goes right through it. I would do laundry down the road apiece and then rush to meet Rhonda for lunch and a sendoff for the next ten miler into Agua Dulce. The town is rather unique because the PCT goes right through it, although not the only one of its kind. Remember Campo and Mt. Laguna? Rhonda will be riding on some of the local roadways as we manage to get to the northerly side of the community, then it's back onto the real trail.

This day, everything seems to go right, as Rhonda texts me that she has arrived and sitting under the huge oak trees near the manager's and commissary of the KOA, and I am only a few miles away and in transit, still looking at every wide spot I see for the possibility it just might house us for the night. I drive into this all-too-familiar site, the

KOA, when I see Rhonda just where she said she would be. Yeaaaaah! High-tech wins one for a change!

I jump out of the Ram and ask, "Do you want to switch horses or ride Liz all the way into town?"

"Neither," she says.

Uh-oh. "Honey, I still haven't found a place to stay."

"No problem," she says. "They offered to let us stay here, and I'm tired, so let's camp out."

Oh heaven's joy, and I ain't askin' no questions and don't expect any answers. But I'm sure not going into the office and expose my face to the young lady that turned me down yesterday. So Rhonda's a magician amongst her many other talents, and she got a little respite off the trail. We have a camping spot on the grounds of the KOA, just not where there are any utilities or hookups. Okay by me because the Hilton is made for just such a rest and repose. It's warm, it's flat, and the maintenance crew has even brought us a wagon to load the manure into before we leave.

Today is another day, and I better get with it if I'm to meet her in town.

Talk to you later.

Agua Dulce turns out to be not much of a town proper, but more like a commuter village, being only a few miles from Highway 14 and a fast trip into the metropolis. How do I know fast? Well, remember where I said I was parked that first night in this community? Yeah, now you get the picture. Zoom, zoom!

Once again, lots of horses and mini hobby farms, but no way to get to know anyone. Drat, it would be interesting to chat with some of these folks. Guess I'm just not the gregarious type to walk up to anyone and start a conversation. Usually, when I mention Rhonda and the PCT, they have to ask what that is, and then they kinda shrug, like what'd she want to do that for? I can see now how the hikers, angels, and these two misfits with horses kind of create your own community of common purpose and goals. Rhonda is building relationships as the travels continue, and I hope she can nurture and hold on to some of them.

Tomorrow she starts segment E, as they have broken the whole trail into approximately one-hundred-mile segments, with each given a letter of the alphabet from start to finish. *E* will start at MP 454. Makes it easier to set goals and talk about certain portions. Me, I think of the terrain we have covered. We or more accurately Rhonda has been over or thru the Laguna Mountains, the Volcan Mountains, the San Felipe Hills, the Santa Rosa, the San Jacinto, the San Bernardino and the San Gabriel Mountains and is about to cross the Tehachapi Mountains before entering the Sierra Nevada. Who woulda thought that Southern California had such a collection of mountains? Not what you see on TV!

She has crossed San Diego, Riverside, San Bernardino, Los Angeles, and soon to enter Kern County, California. She has entered into or crossed the Hauser Wilderness, the San Jacinto Wilderness, the San Gorgonio Wilderness, and the Sheep Mountain Wilderness. She has crossed Highways 8, 10, 14, and 15 of our national interstate highway system. She has entered into and crossed a small portion of the Anzo-Borrego Desert and will soon enter along the northern border of the Mohave Desert. And she hasn't yet completed 20 percent of the trail! So far, the lowest point was in the desert at the crossing of Highway 10 just north of Palm Springs at 1,195 feet, and the highest was on Mt. Baden-Powell at 9,245 feet in the Angeles Forest. That was when she had to rebuild the trail to get over a downed tree. How's that for a numbers guy?

Rhonda has also been into and through portions of the Cleveland National Forest, the San Bernardino NF, and the Angeles NF and is soon to enter the Sequoia NF. And lastly, the Santa Rosa and San Jacinto Mountains National Monument. Seems like a lot, but all of you Oregonians can relate 'cause if you rode for more than five hundred miles, think of all the forests in Oregon that you might enter into or cross.

So today is Wednesday, May 13, and I'm sitting here in the rig waitin' along San Francisquito Canyon Road in the fringes of the Angeles Forest for m'lady to show up from a twelve-mile ride. Sort of an easy day as mileage goes. Yesterday was a zero day because I had to do a major resupply and also wanted to see if I could get service on the

Ram. Four thousand miles in seven weeks, not too shabby. Boy am I glad we made that purchase back in November of last year because this truck has performed beyond all expectations.

While we previously had a three-quarter ton Dodge Ram pickup with a fine diesel engine and running gear that had taken us to many pleasurable locations and rides, I knew there would be a day when it would need to be replaced. We don't figure to quit this lifestyle for many years. Thus, I fidgeted and fussed over this decision to move up to a one-ton truck with a bigger engine and body style and disc brakes all around. This PCT escapade was going to be a momentous adventure, and we didn't want to spoil it with a breakdown or accident because the Wrangler wasn't prepared. Really wasn't a hard decision at all, just had to get a grip on my Libra mentality of weighing all the evidence before taking the plunge. So now I had better hold up my end of the bargain and make sure I took care of its needs. Off to the garage, and glad I did because the oil filter was coming loose. Thank goodness, no leakage yet.

Anyway, resupply meant groceries and feed, the latter being the highest priority. Had to go forty-five miles to get what I wanted, but ya gotta have what you gotta have. For those of you not familiar with horses, you don't want to change up their diet without giving their gut a chance to adjust. This means NO changes, or if you must, you make it a very gradual change. This trip took all that into account, and we are feeding hay produced in Idaho and shipped all over the western US. But of course, not every retailer carries it, so travelling to the retailer is what I have to do.

Then there is the fact that our two main steeds, Liz and Cheyenne, are losing a little weight. Partly a result of their work and partly because they didn't like the alfalfa pellets we originally thought were the end-all solution. And the retailers down here don't know what we are talking about when I mention packer pellets. Way back at the time we were passing Mountain Center, I came upon a small feed store and a young lady that was also a distributor for a grass pellet made in California. Because she was a distributor, we could make arrangements to have the pellets shipped directly to other retailers along our route of travel. I tried a sack of them out on our trusty steeds during my three-day stay at the County Park while waiting for Rhonda to traverse through the mountains. Remember that episode of "Where's my sign?" Now you've got the timing. Well, the horses seemed to like these pellets, gobbling them down at each feeding, so I abandoned the alfalfa pellets and bought all fifteen bags she had in the store and made arrangements for the others to be shipped to the proper locations. So we then upped their ration of alfalfa hay together with Timothy hay and added some rice bran supplement to their new pellet feed, and finally think we have it figured out.

Anything else you want to know about horse feed? Go ask your vet. We are now carrying 900 pounds of hay, 700 pounds of water, 250 pounds of horse feed (grain and supplements), and then we can start adding our own stuff. Now that we are hundreds of miles down the trail from Mountain Center, it is time to pick up more pellets at a little place called Leona Valley.

At least we didn't have to fix dinner last evening. For the past two days, we have been the guests of a very wonderful family that welcomed us onto their small organic farm southerly of Lancaster on the edge of the Mojave Desert. Raising organic pigs? Okay, quit laughing! I know, aren't pigs organic? It's not them, you yokels; it's what you feed them. And then they had two hundred free-range chickens from which she gets and sells forty cartons of eggs a week.

Tucker thought he had died and gone to heaven. Chickens everywhere! First skirmish, and we yelled at him so loud the roof almost came down. Oh, no . . . they weren't in the house, as free range apparently has its limits. This was in the patio. Apparently, their seven dogs were not free range because they were in the house. Lucky for us that we too have occasionally had a passel of critters, and so we got along just fine. I sometimes brag on Tucker and how smart he is, but he did not once go after another roaming chicken. I was proud.

We did keep Tucker on a pretty short verbal leash after hearing of all the rattlesnake encounters these folks put up with. Nearly one every week. Now why would someone want to live here? Apparently, not too different from the area we come from in that a family can't hardly afford to live where they work. The breadwinner of this family is the foreman of a multifaceted construction firm that works all around

Southern California, from Bakersfield to San Diego, so I guess the choice of abode is whatever works. They are happy with it, and that's the important part. Now it is time to move on.

We are camped out this night near milepost 511, where Rhonda will start out tomorrow. Amazing! Rhonda told me she didn't much care for the "0" day, as it was too packed with things to do, and then being dinner guests meant more obligations. Next "0" day will be just that, a time to rest and recuperate and consider the next leg of the journey. I told her, "Welcome to my world!" Another amazing thing . . . we have gone five hundred miles on the trail, and we are still in Southern California! When will it ever end?

On our local visits, we have discovered that the locals think somewhat differently, mostly because of their familiarity with the trail, the terrain, the access points, etc. They want to steer you onto their path and how they would do it, or they want to volunteer their time to make it easier for you. It's unfortunate, but this just doesn't appear in our eyes as a solution but more of a complication. Some of you guys might relate to a project you plan to do and you have all scoped out until your bud shows up to help. Not necessarily what you had in mind, eh?

So anyway, Rhonda and I had this discussion tonight and came away with the marvelous conclusion that we were both tired and that our "0" day had just worn us out. We had better go to bed. No wind tonight, so hopefully, we'll get into the zone of true and restful sleep. We hope you do too.

Until next time, rest easy and give someone a hug 'cause we miss you.

P 'n' R

(Sent from my US cellular smartphone)

PART

13

May 18, 2015

Happy Sunday morning to one and all!

I was just sitting here, thinking life is grand and sometimes quiet. It is 8:00 a.m., and some of us are still in bed. The critters are fed, and breakfast has just been served. The life of RVers ain't all that bad sometimes.

We are nestled into the back (or should I say side) yard of trail angels, Mike and Patty of Tehachapi, California. They are horse people also, with a little acreage (twenty acres, more or less) and with room to spare, fenced paddocks, round pens, electricity, and running water. Wow, what a splendid happening to find these folks, with warm hearts and open arms.

Remember Tim and Andrea from Mountain Center? Well, they are PCTers extraordinaire and came up with a text to me a while back to contact our current hosts. Thank you, thank you! We are reveling in a windless night, warmth, and relaxation.

Rhonda will ride today, but only a short distance of eight miles and then we come right back here. My, what are we gonna do with all this spare time? Well, for one, yours truly fixed a hot breakfast of scrambled (free-range eggs from Christy), some avocado (in season), and a little pepper jack cheese to spice it up. That along with a cheese quesadilla, and we are all set to tackle the day. Well, some of us are. The computer and journal and blog site seem to need a little tackling of their own.

No problem since the critters seem to be still chowing down, or should I say the boys are. Ms. Princess, Liz, is off getting her morning snooze and a little sun tan. That's the female way, I suppose, especially on a lazy Sunday. Well, she has eight miles of work ahead of her, so I can't say that I blame her. She has performed magnificently to date, albeit a little reluctantly at times. Did I tell you that Cheyenne is now the official packhorse? It's just a little embarrassing when towing the princess, or should I say "glowering locomotive," getting your arm yanked out of its socket and only making 1 mph. So she gets what she wants, being boss mare and out in front. Wow, isn't that a surprise?

We still haven't figured out how to get around the herd-bound nature of these animals. Remember Cheyenne's screeching holler at the South Ridge Trail Head when I couldn't find my sign? Well, imagine the same every morning as Rhonda leaves the trailhead. And for miles down the trail! Of course, the shortest distance to the next meeting point is always the way back along the trail to the truck and "let's ride the Hilton to the next spot."

Rhonda says that when they are on switchbacks, the horses always go faster on the portion that is facing the way back. One hell of a compass in that tiny brain of theirs, or maybe they have a gyroscope. The trail is composed of a lot of sidehill that follows the contour of the land, and with all the mountains and small spur ridges, you eventually come to a portion that runs in the direction from which you came. Well, the compass didn't jam, so you had better hold on until headed forward once again. But I tell you that when they spot the Hilton on the other end, Rhonda had better have a tight grip on those reins. Lizzy is so beautiful in full gait mode, head up and ears forward. Then it's time to find your ear plugs, or the banshee yell from Cheyenne will curdle your last meal. Who needs mountain lions, bears, or rattlesnakes when one of our steeds lets loose with that holler? Enough to scare 'em all away.

And guess what? It's Monday, and we took the afternoon off also on Sunday, and then went to a movie *The Avengers*. Yeah, I know, but you tell me where there was a movie house on our itinerary. So it took us a while, and we weren't part of the $222 million spent the first weekend. In fact, it cost us only $12 for the two of us. Wow! Tehachapi is a pretty cool place at the southern tip of the Sierra Nevada Mountains. This seems like a major milestone, headed into the mountains after so much dry countryside. I don't think we will miss the Mojave Desert, but we were lucky it was cool and breezy for us there. "Breezy?" Rhonda asks. "Don't you remember Palm Springs, Sunrise Saddle, and all the damn windmills?" Yeah, yeah . . . Okay, as I recall, fretting over the Hilton lying on its side.

There was one particular day and night that has stuck in Rhonda's craw for weeks. It was back a ways and along the edge of the desert where she had to follow near to the windmills for five continuous days. Whoosh, whoosh, they went for an interminable time, and then to top it off, finally rising off and away onto a ridge where we had planned for her to stay the night, it was necessary for her to spread the tent and lie on it while driving the pegs at each corner to keep it from blowing away. Incessant wind coming at you all the time is a mind-altering experience. No wonder Rhonda wanted to relish the peace and quiet of the Hilton this morning.

Rhonda is now into her last week of riding before we split for home and the Saddle Up for St. Jude's ride. For many years, we have been stewards/coordinators for this charity event to pass money collected for the cause from the hands of riders and into the hands of the St. Jude's Children's Research Hospital. While it will take ten days off our schedule, we are not ones to sluff off our responsibility or miss this heartwarming event. We kind of happened into the role of coordinators many years ago as we volunteered to assist another pair of individuals from our riding group, Oregon Equestrian Trails. During the ensuing years, we have tried to make this a lasting memory for our participant riders, one they won't forget and hopefully will tell their riding buddies. We have groomed the trail to incorporate a pleasant ride through the ponderosa pine forests of Central Oregon, up into the foothills of the Cascade Mountains, along a meandering creek; and as it descends back into the valley floor, we get a panoramic view of the snow covered Cascade Mountains known as the Three Sisters. It is truly a memorable ten-mile ride. Consider this an invite to come join us some day on the first Saturday of June each year.

But we are not gone yet, and there is still more riding to do. Rhonda will ride out and camp along the trail tonight, and then I hopefully will be able to meet her on Tuesday. Then it's back onto the trail and another camp out before we meet at a small trailhead at the junction with Highway 178 on Friday. We will hustle on home from there.

As she leaves the desert today and heads into the Sierras, she will be going into the Sequoia National Forest and on Friday be going through the Sequoia Wilderness. I mentioned this in my last missive and got a note from a buddy from way back. Crazy H, as he has become known, like forever! H was remembering some fond moments of travelling in the Sequoias back in the yesteryears, which naturally led me to reminiscing about my own travels.

We were together in the Air Force, or should I say we were stationed on the same air base. Those were interesting times, what with Tricky Dick using our base to access his Key Biscayne retreat. You might say that H and I were not warmongers, along with a few other associated fellas. Almost got us in trouble, but luckily for me, the AF offered an early out to those officers that were detrimental to the morale of the many. I and three others left early.

Crazy H and Sally (wife) were instrumental in helping me through some troubling days and morose feelings during those last week's in Florida. We built some rather rudimentary fiberglass canoes from a kit we purchased, and while not pretty, they floated pretty well. So come out of it I did, and I set off to crisscross the US for as long as it took to reach California in my VW camper, with an agreement to meet midcontinent when H would eventually have served out his time the following summer. I canoed in swamps, streams, and lakes along the way, looking every bit the fisherman in my Volkswagen camper.

Now, if you are an astute reader and haven't obliterated your memory banks before now, you will remember that I traveled after release from USAF and then hustled home to see Dad. Well, Dad was sick, but there wasn't much any of us could do, so when the subject came up for me to go back to travelling, he said I should go. Footloose and fancy-free, I didn't need any more prodding than that. I was to meet Crazy H and Sal of sound mind somewhere near the Tetons that summer.

Since I had some time to burn, why not go to all the national parks in the West? So I made the circuit, heading towards Fresno, California, and Yosemite first then the Sequoias and on to the Canyon until one night I found myself out in the Arizona desert. Now a friend recently inquired of Rhonda if she, during her ride, had sung while riding thru the desert. Well, she's not much for song, but a great dancer as she listens. But me, hell yeah, especially when in the desert where no one will listen to my tone-deaf tributes as I sang along to Neil Young's "I've been through the desert on a horse with no name, it felt good to be out of the rain," and I can tell you that if she didn't, I most certainly did.

That night so long ago was spectacular, made even more so by whatever drug I happened to ingest that evening. So once again, I digress.

Of course, I went to Zion and, what's its name, oh yeah, Bryce Canyon, before going into the Colorado Rockies. And then my time was up, and I forged on into Jackson Hole. Boy did H and Sal and I have a grand time that night. H plays the harmonica, and I still remember hammering my boots into the boardwalk and having the grandest of times dancing to his tunes. Memories, aren't they just great! Days after, we paddled our canoes across one of the lakes and climbed the scree slopes on the other side. Ever paddle a canoe across a large lake when the wind is buffeting you from the other side? That little jaunt took forever, but the trip back was a piece of cake. I trust all of you can reminisce some too, and if not, then go do something you can tell your grandchildren, like riding the Pacific Crest Trail.

Man is Rhonda gonna have some stories. She's been pretty religious about keeping up with her journal. Can't wait to read it someday. Me, I'm a day-by-day guy, and you get whatever comes out. At least I hope it keeps comin' out. Been fun, y'all, but I better get moseying on to the next story in my life and be there for m'lady.

See ya on down the trail. This is being sent without proofread 'cause there probably won't be service where I'm goin'. Ooh, that sounds sinister. Nah, good night, all.

Love,
Patrick

(Sent from US cellular smartphone.)

Camping in the Mojave Desert.

Rhonda on Liz with Cheyenne packing for a two night sleep over.

Looking back at the desert.

Liz and Rio finish up the desert ride into Tehachapi.

PART

14

May 23, 2015

Hey, here I am again! I just won't go away now, will I? Here's wishing you all a fine day at work or whatever you may be doing. I remember Jack B., who would respond whenever asked "How ya doin?" by "I've never felt better!" Well, that's kinda how I feel right now, so I'll drag all of you along with me.

And oh yeah, try typing that paragraph on your smartphone.

So here I am, all settled into a cow pasture at the entry into Jawbone Canyon. I'll bet the cows just love that name. I'm looking at a map printed by "The Friends of Jawbone Canyon, Off Highway Vehicle Riding Area and Trails." Well, I gotta tell you, folks, that I won't ever badmouth the OHV community again. This map is super, and I would be lost in Kelso Valley if it hadn't been for a young lady putting up Off Limits signs as I was coming into the area. She just handed me the map when I stammered, "Where am I?" Whew, saved my bacon, I can tell you that.

See, I'm supposed to meet Rhonda up on the mountaintop at the head of Jawbone Canyon, but once again, there are a myriad of dirt roads to follow and just where is this Jawbone anyway? Now you can just imagine Rhonda's consternation if I'm not there after she has just ridden nineteen miles after camping out along the trail last eve. Horse food's all gone, clean clothes ain't clean anymore, and where the hell is my dinner? Now you get the picture. Why they couldn't put the crest trail down here in the valley, I'll never know, and neither would the rest of America. Sure would have made my job a lot simpler, and Rhonda a lot warmer, thus in better spirits, if I were to be a little late. But life is what it is now, ain't it? And we don't want it too easy, or it just might get boring. And jeez, what would I write about?

This day has not been boring, having started out at the Walker Pass camp ground where many PCT hikers congregate and look for rides into Lake Isabella. I decided to join the group instead of hiding out in the Hilton and took along some breakfast cereals that I won't need in four more days. They gratefully took me up on the offer, and the cereal was gone in no time, all except the granola. What's the matter with this generation? Don't they know that stuff is good for you? You, young parents, have got to mind-warp these young'uns to eat what's good for them, like spinach and carrots and granola!

Actually, I am surprised any of it was eaten when I found out a trail angel in the motor home next door was fixing tortillas filled with scrambled eggs. Ahem, here's my order! So I'm healthier this afternoon, not having eaten all that cholesterol.

Next to the motor home was another angel who introduced herself as Muggs and has come to be known as Aunt Muggsy. Later in our conversation she lamented that her given name was Margarite, and why couldn't she have been called Maggi or Margie or a host of other by names being short for Margarite. Ah well, she might not have been remembered quite as well by all these hikers. Came to find out that she was drawn over to me by the horse, having had horses herself for many years. Just had to find out what was happening. It seems that a lot of horse folks are envious of m'lady and the adventure she has set upon, wishing that they also could venture forth.

Muggsy is now headed back to Wyoming to gather up the last bit of her things and move back down to the desert town of Ridgecrest right smack in the Mohave Desert. She offered her place for us to stay upon our return in three weeks, but I did not have the heart to just say no. Can you imagine what the temp will be the second week in June? Not like it is today, that's for sure.

The lament on the trail is about the wind, and won't it ever stop? Well, yes, it could, but then it would be ninety-five degrees on the trail. Pick your poison, and I think most find the wind more acceptable under those terms. Me, I'm a born and raised Californian and think I could take the heat. Course, when the wind takes our front door off the trailer, I may be looking for another choice. As it is, the door now needs fixin' after having been blown out of our hands so many times. Oh my, life on the road does have its trials.

Like after talking to Muggsy, I was ready to pull out and so made a last check around the trailer. Oh boy, don't ever forget that last check. Driving down the road with one of our outriggers still poking at traffic or knocking the hats off hitchhikers would not be a good thing. So this day, I notice the rear tire on the trailer looks low. Being a well-prepared motorist, I get my little whatchamacallit, and sure enough, all are at eighty pounds, and this one's at twenty. How far is town? I know Lake Isabella is waiting for me at thirty-four miles, so I am off down the road ever so slowly. Sorry, folks behind me, but I got a low tire, and I'm too damned lazy to put the spare on.

So motoring on down the highway (two-lane), I come to a town. Weldon it's called, and by golly, there's a garage in town. Looks like two young fellas just opened up and lie in wait for tourists like yours truly. "Sure, we can fix it," they say. Who am I to quibble? So off comes the tire and into the bath. Now it's cleaner than I am! Oh well, I don't think the cows in Jawbone Canyon will mind. So what do they find but a cracked aluminum wheel. Only a small crack though! After all, the tire is not flat!

So they propose to me, "We'll pull the tire, mend the wheel with JB Weld, and put 'er back together, and then test the air pressure." Boy, to say I'm dubious is just a little off the mark, but what the hey! We got this far, and they're gonna put the spare on for safety. Okay, I go for it. They do all the above while Tucker and me go for a walk. Come back, and the trailer's back on all fours, and I ask if they take credit cards, 'cause these boys have been at it for at least an hour, dropped everything to help little old me, and I'm ready to be held up. "How much?" I shudder, and the response is . . . thirty dollars. OMG, pay 'em quick! Actually, I tipped them another ten dollars and sailed off into the sunset. What a deal. Of course, I'll have to replace the wheel at the first opportunity, but it sure beats driving to Bakersfield and being late for my rendezvous.

Speaking of which, it's time to go. Talk to you later. Well, it's later, and as rendezvous go, this one could have been better. I'm not sure what gets the missus so riled. Maybe it's the nineteen miles she just travelled or the recalcitrant darling Liz or maybe there's a sticker where one never should be. It can't be li'l ol' me.

I told her I'd be late because I didn't want to leave Rio in the trailer all lonesome and forlorn for too awfully long. Getting up that hill was no easy chore either, having to back up in four-wheel drive when halfway around several bends in the granite dirt path. Tight little switchbacks they were. So I arise, and no one is there. Well, I'm a good little soldier, and the last e-mail I got was "I got going later than I thought. Love you."

So being a good scout, I figure I'll go intercept her back a mile or so . . . save her some effort. Park the truck and walk down to the trail, and what do I see but little bootie prints in the loose basalt. Oh heck, to my chagrin, she's already gone by! What to do, what to do?

Well, surely she will go to Robin Bird Spring to get water for the ponies, and I got that covered 'cause there was a guy there just twenty minutes ago, and I asked him to let Rhonda know I would be right back. See, I was going to leave a low-tech message on the trail. Oh, what to do, what to do? Why, back to the spring, of course, where Rhonda will be waiting for yours truly. Only Rhonda doesn't go to the spring. Only two hundred yards off the trail, but she doesn't go there. How do I know? 'Cause Tucker runs up the trail. And to validate that fact, I see bootie prints in the trail. Oh hell, oh hell! She's going to where the trail crosses the road! Now, why didn't I think of that!

Rhonda gets riled over the simplest things, like a little time thing or a slight miscommunication. Makes no difference who miscommunicated now, does it? What's the theory of relativity? Well, Einstein never spoke to Rhonda. There is only one "real," and guess where that is. So time heals all wounds, or so they say, and I help Rhonda get set up and give her the resupply modules. But Rio is still waiting patiently (I hope) in the trailer. You see, I had locked him in, believing that he was just too pretty to leave tied to the side of the trailer for hours and hours. Someone might take a fancy to him. I eventually would meander down the hill in the dark, backing up on the curves because I can't see over the hood and have ground in sight. Unnerving. Forty some minutes to go five miles. Now didn't I say something previously about the folly? Ah, never mind.

Still a great day, long at that but quite enervating. Hmm, maybe I should look that word up. Anyone want to help? 'Cause I've moved to Kelso Valley and there still ain't no internet.

I remember living in Anchor Point and resisting the temptation to get a phone. I didn't want to be at anyone's beck and call. After all, we didn't have electricity and were getting along fine. Running water was running to the spring to get a bucket of water to fill up the igloo on the kitchen counter. Boy, where did those days go? I now have more conveniences in the Hilton than I had in our cabin, including internet sometimes. What is this world coming to? The simple life still has its draw and beckons me from time to time. Maybe that's why I trek back to Alaska from time to time, or could be the draw that keeps me out there hunting every year even though my success really stinks. Not the meat. But the lack of it.

Hmm, must be getting late or my eyelids are feeling the effects of some wine I had hoped to share with the missus but drank alone instead. At any rate, I will sign off and say goodnight, all. Have pleasant slumbers.

Your friend and for some a relative,

Patrick

* * *

And now it is Friday, and Rhonda should be in to Walker Pass campground sometime late this afternoon. I left her back at Kelso Valley Road yesterday morning, with thirty-five miles to cover in two days. Tough miles at that until the last six, which the hikers tell me is a gradual descent into the camp. I hope so, but I'll bet it's a long six miles at this stage of the trip. I am at mile point 652 on the trail at a trailhead built for hikers and campers but not the Hilton. However someone built corrals, reportedly BCHCA, but they are several hundred feet up the hill, and I'll need to schlep water and fixin's at mealtime. We'll manage just fine. In the meantime, I will do some trail angel stuff because Muggsy is gone and the pickings are slim.

Tomorrow we plan to leave the trail and head home, what with the Saddle Up for St. Jude event coming and our commitments to it. Got some things to take care of also, like a new wheel for the trailer, see if we can fix our door, more boots for the horses, get the truck checked out 'cause a hundred miles or so back we picked up a transient passenger of the pestilence kind, and before he could do too much damage, I put poison under the hood. Figured he would drop out along the way and not poison Tucker! Hope he's gone, which I think he is, but still need to make sure the wires and all are still intact.

I remember one fella that had gone elk hunting in the snow country of NE Oregon. When they were getting ready to leave, he discovered a pack rat had nested and chewed up all his wiring. Towing and repairs amounted to $900+. Some of these places I've been . . . that would have been catastrophic! Poison is still under the hood, just in case.

Reminds me of a few weeks back, in warmer days, Rhonda had picked up a few hitchhikers along the way. When we quit counting, we had eight ticks removed from her hair and neck, yuck.

This is the country for critters. Not much water, so you have to be cautious whenever you get near to springs. Rhonda is finishing up Segment F along the trail, and I've been told it is one of the most difficult because of the lack of water. She took ten gallons with her on Cheyenne, the packer, plus some hay and grain to make it into Walker TH. Glad of it too as I visited with some hikers this morning, and the only water was a mile and a half off trail and was out of a sump with a rat floating in it. I cannot imagine, but these guys sure trust their treatment bottles or filters. I've had Giardia a couple of times, and that would be the least of my worries from a dead rat. So Rhonda is spared this misery, and the horses too. And a couple three girls I gave water to the day before. They trucked right on past the side trail, knowing they had good, plentiful water. Remember the gals that slept in our trailer back at Mill Creek? Yeah, same girls. They know better than pass up on a good offer. Guys all refused it, like they are tough or something.

All except Dave, whom Rhonda has been shadowing for a week or so. Smart!

So this afternoon, I get the shower ready, have dinner figured out, and with three-horse stalls on the grounds, we are covered. I'm sure Rhonda will be ready for a cozy night in the Hilton. And I will be happy having m'lady back, safe and sound. Tomorrow's another day, and a big day of travels, just a different mode. For those of you in the Bend area, see you soon, like the OET meeting. Everyone else, see you when we see you! Don't think we are anticipating any further travels other than to get home, get warm, hug the cat and one another. Looking forward to it. And all of you!

Have a great weekend, and remember to be happy, 'cause what else is there?

Love to you all,
Pat and Rhonda

(Sent from my US cellular smartphone)

The team heads out for another overnighter.

Lunch on the trail.

Headed home for the St. Jude ride.

PART

15

June 14, 2015

And now the rest of the story.

So an enthusiastic "Hi!" to one and all. Like howdy, brethren and sisters! We are on the road again. And back in familiar territory and the Tehama County fairgrounds, only this time it is 103 degrees. Rhonda is melting.

Hard to believe I grew up in weather like this, working on the ranch or at the wrecking yard. Brings back memories of sucking down five or six Coca-Colas in a day. Yeah, no wonder I have high cholesterol. But I still love my Cokes even if they are zero calories these days. I digress.

Where were we? Well, we headed back to Central Oregon after completing 651 miles of the 2,660 total. That is, Rhonda completed the miles while I watched from the sidelines. Oh, I had to work so hard! My hands are still recovering, not from the work but from the dry dust and hay that led to rough skin and cracks at every fingertip. Poor me.

But we were glad to be heading back because the Arctic storm had just dumped many feet of snow on the Sierras. A white mantel covered them as we headed north toward an eventual landing at home. Never mind that the snow was above eight thousand feet, Rhonda's ride would take her up to ten thousand and beyond, so it was a good time for a break. So three days on Highway 395, 31, and 97 got us back to the homestead.

One of our friends asked if we were having trouble and had to leave our quest, but nothing could be further from our minds. This was all part of the plan. I'm sending along a picture of our dining room table, and hush . . . it does not always look like that. This was the planning table, and we spent many an evening right here, planning every day and every stop along the way. That's how I knew we would have 145 days on the trail, plus many zero days.

I remember encountering a hiker at one of our layovers, and he was asked, "What was the secret to his success thus far?" His answer was "Planning!" He had been planning for two years. Fit right in with us. Rhonda is detail-oriented, maybe to a fault, and I am organized and always have a plan and a list in front of me—i.e., I have a list of projects to do around the property that spans three years and is updated every year. Course, this year, I had to kiss it goodbye. Oh, lordy, lordy. How does one do that?

So we planned to be at Highway 178 in mid to late May and would head back home from there. And that is exactly what we did. Of course, you have all been along for the ride and know that it wasn't necessarily that simple, with a few twists and turns that hadn't been planned. So now we are headed back to the trail, but the twists keep coming at us, and hopefully we are making the right turns to get us back in the saddle and headed north.

But before I get into that, let's talk about yesterday and the weeks before that. One of our friends asked if we were excited to be back home. Funny thing that, but my answer was that it was rather anticlimax and maybe just a bit boring. I mean, how do you step back into a routine when nothing will be routine? And TV? Where are our favorite shows? And who wants to watch it after two months of absolutely no TV!

First off, the trailer needed repairs, like a new wheel, a new tire, and a couple of doors repaired from when the wind whipped them out of our hands. The slide and the jacks needed maintenance, and the vent had to be replaced. And what about the rat in the belfry? (Actually, the engine compartment of our wonder worker Dodge truck.) I think he departed weeks ago, voluntary or not, I don't care.

And that's not to speak of all the neglected items we noted on return. The weeds are overrunning the place, just when I thought the drought would take its toll. We had an inside pane of glass shattered on our Thermopane French door into the bedroom. How does that happen? And it appears we may have had an intruder.

And then there is the one thing that we came to town for . . . OET's Saddle Up for St. Jude trail ride, which Rhonda and I have ramrodded for nearly ten years. Of course, it has not been without the tireless help of our dear friends, the Jimersons, and many other OETers.

Once again, it was a smashing success, with seventy-one riders raising $6,500 and having a good old-fashioned "good time" while doing so. Rhonda, with her food handler's permit, assured that all takers went home full and happy.

Having developed portions of the trail system that these folks ride out on, Rhonda and I are always thrilled to hear the good reports of a marvelous trail and fun ride. That, along with the help we give to the children of St. Jude, keeps us coming back year after year. This year was no different. We spent two days riding the trail ourselves, once to check for downed trees or other obstacles and once to flag it before the day of the ride. After the ride, it was all accounting and number crunching, but we left yesterday knowing all was accounted for and on its way to St. Jude's.

Among the other things we set out to do while home was to thoroughly clean and ransack the Hilton. Having just lived in it for the past sixty-plus days, I can truly say that scaling down our lifestyle would work for me. Like all the rest of you, we have STUFF! Well, unneeded stuff or unused stuff is staying home this trip. I'm tired of picking up the same thing day after day because it is in the way of something I really need. Like, why do we keep something that does not work or barely so? We have a tool to remove the cork from our wine bottle. So even though we drink two buck chuck, you still have to open it. Who said the opener had to be two buck crap? Guess we've just had too many years drinking our wine from a box. Well, we don't have room for a box!

So our holiday away from the trail was to be eventful in resupply, especially horse feeds and anything else they needed. More boots! Remember me talking about planning? Well, the old proverb of the best-made plans holds true here because the manufactures lay in wait to foil even the best of plans. I ordered more compressed hay three weeks ago, needing weed-free certified hay because we are going into some very special forests that require it. Well, after two weeks of phone calls to the manufacturer and the local dealer, I was finally told the day before last that they didn't have any. But trying to have a backup plan, I had called ahead and found some in Yreka, California. So instead of heading towards Reno, we headed into California, only to find out that the hay (they assured me twice over the phone) they had saved for me was NOT certified. But they did have four bales in another corner that would do for me. Coupled with bales, I had squirreled away months ago we would make it for a few weeks.

To top that off, all the arrangements we had thought were made to have our sack feed delivered to places we could stop and pick it up fell through. So today we were shopping at the local feed stores for substitutes. Just what we had planned to avoid all these months. I am totally, totally flabbergasted by the lackadaisical attitude of makers, deliverers, and dealers in this industry. They are so used to people coming in and plunking down cold hard cash on their counter that they don't believe in customer satisfaction or in making an effort to make it so.

Boy, can I bellyache! Is anything going right? Well, yeah . . . we'll be in South Lake Tahoe tomorrow, and the ride goes on. Rhonda decided to skip over a section of trail and do Northern California next and when that's done, we'll go back to Walker Pass, and she'll ride through the Sierras. Gotta let that infernal snow melt away to a safer trail.

And I gotta go feed the horses their evening ration of hay. See ya. Wow, three days go by fast. We arrived at South Lake Tahoe on Friday, and after fueling up at Meyers, we immediately left town for Carson Pass. Beautiful country but we aren't here for sightseeing, so it was a drive about (as opposed to a walk about) last evening as we searched for a place to park the Hilton. Got here late because of a stop at Costco and Home Depot at some village east of Placerville. Ever try to park a fifty-two-foot-long rig in Costco's parking lot? I didn't think so. Whew, what fun! Home Depot provided us the makings of new closet shelves as the old ones collapsed the evening before. Finally, back in Carson Pass, Rhonda talks me into going up the drive entry to the

Caltrans maintenance station. I'm really skeptical, having worked for ODOT and knowing these stations are well fenced. Lo and behold, we drive through the station (no fence?) and intersect a USFS gravel road with a pullout and perfect spot for the Hilton. We are blessed as sis would say. This was one of the most pleasant spots we have camped at during this entire journey and all because Rhonda had a "feeling."

Saturday, Rhonda saddled up and made her first ride of her return to trail. This would be a reasonably easy ride of twelve miles to get a feel for new terrain and weather. Eighty degrees plus as compared to snow when we were leaving Walker Pass just three weeks ago. When home we discarded our winter duds and prepared for a long summer, and here it is. I caught up with Rhonda at Echo Summit after fifty miles of drive time compared to her twelve.

And then we had another one of our senior moments as I was at the pass with trailer in tow and m'lady was down the trail a mile at the highway crossing. Fortunately, both of us had sufficient cell coverage to text our position and meet up with smiles and cheers. Yahoo, we are on our way again. Sobering as that might be.

Now why did I say that? Well, today Rhonda left for a four-day ride with three campouts. She has two horses, Cheyenne being the packhorse. I will next see her at Donner Pass and Highway 80 on Wednesday. This time, we have some handheld radios to help find each other, so keep your fingers crossed. In the meantime, I know what Rhonda will be doing, but what am I gonna do? We left the colt at home as he is just too green for this arduous and technically challenging ride. Just Tucker and me to while away the time, maybe do some fishing, golfing, or whatever pleases me (or Tucker).

But first, I have to Wrangle and earn my trail name of Wrangler. We have horse boots to be reworked with a little fiberglass, as the rocks have been tougher and thus have worn holes in the toes. Put up our new shelves today, so that's all done. But my main focus will be finding out the trail conditions up ahead of us. What we have seen on the Yahoo conversation sites is all related to hiker needs and not equestrian, so that's my focus. What blowdown should we be prepared for, and is it passable? What fire damage is there, such as burned-out bridges, and are there fjords Rhonda can use? The list goes on and on and on. It's all part of the game.

Speaking of games, the Warriors just won. Whoopee! After all these years, I'm still a Bay Area fan vs. anything east of the Sierras.

It's time to call it a night and wish you all a good sleep. Rhonda has the horses, so I'm mellow and content to hang out. I could say, "I wish you were here!" but there's no room. Good night, all, and pleasant dreams.

Patrick

(Sent from my US cellular smartphone)

Upper Echo Lake

PART
16

June 15, 2015

Hi, everyone!

You will find below the emergency note that I sent to our kids on the late evening of June 15 after having texted them earlier that day. The rest would follow:

-------- Original message --------

From: pnr
Date: 06/15/2015, 11:17 PM (GMT–08:00)
To: John and Nicole
Subject: Rhonda and Cheyenne's ordeal

Well, sorry if I scared any of you, but it was the quickest way to get the word out. It appears that both should be all right with some time to heal the bruises.

Cheyenne was being led as a packhorse with panniers and top pack. The top got hung up on a tree branch, and Cheyenne, being the sensitive guy that he is, backed up to take the pressure off. Unfortunately, he backed right off the trail and went over backwards, tumbling down the slope.

He came to rest upside down with his head down the slope, as we horse folks would say. He was cast against some brush. Some of the pack contents were strewn about, and the rest of the pack was still bound around him. Rhonda went down the hill, pulled the ropes and pack off, and then had to loop the rope over his legs and pull him onto his side. It worked even with little room to maneuver. He got up. She was able to get him up the slope, but when they reached the trail, Cheyenne shoved her facedown against some rock, bruising her upper chest and right shoulder.

We are just now getting out of the emergency room, assured that nothing is broken. Now time to heal.

Cheyenne, on the other hand, is severely bruised on his right hind leg, scraped up on the right side of his muzzle, and has at least a dozen other scrapes and cuts. We didn't get out of the woods until nearly 6:00 p.m. and the nearest vet is in Nevada, so tomorrow we'll trailer him down if he is mobile enough to get in and out of the trailer.

We were able to locate a paddock for him at an old packing station, now called Richardson Ranch, and he was taking water and eating grass hay, both very positive signs. We still need to see good color in his urine to know we have escaped major problems. Tomorrow morning will be telling.

So that's it, and it is time to go hit the hay, climb into the sack, or have a cool one. We'll keep you posted.

Love to all,
Pat and Rhonda and our entourage

(Sent from my US cellular smartphone)

* * *

To everyone else:

Well, before you can read thru this, I want to tell you that we had a mishap today. Cheyenne fell off the trail, but we believe he is bruised but okay. Rhonda was banged up, trying to get him upright and back onto the trail. She now has a hiker helping her out of the woods on a feeder trail, taking them to Fallen Leaf Lake. Five miles to go to a trailhead.

She is taking the shortest route to get off the trail and get everyone checked out. I'm going to meet her at the closest rendezvous spot, but the roads are too narrow, and the Hilton won't make it. I'll leave it at a wide spot and wait for her at the trailhead.

I'm amazed as they come walking out of the woods. Cheyenne is limping but still carrying his pack. And Rhonda is . . . *Dazed* is the best word I can come up with. Bruised but mobile and really patient because all I can do is take the pack and gear off the horses, but she and the ponies will need to be ridden another two miles to where the Hilton is waiting.

From there, we go to a local packers and riding stable (tourist trap) where I have arranged an outdoor stall for the horses. We get them settled in with feed and grain and watch Cheyenne to see if we need to stay longer, but he's eating and moving about so we are on our way. We can't stay there because of insurance concerns of the owners, so it is off to the hospital to see that Rhonda is taken care of, and I will find a trailer park where we can spend the night.

Can you believe it, a trailer camping spot just around the corner from the hospital? Only fifty dollars a night. Glad we are only staying one night.

So don't fret, but keep us in your thoughts. No messages back to us right now as we will keep you posted on what's happening.

Thank you! Love you all,
Patrick

(Sent from my US cellular smartphone)

PART

17

June 20, 2015

Hi, everyone!

Rhonda and Cheyenne are both on the mend, with bruising and soft tissue damage. While Cheyenne has numerous cuts, they are all small and just thru the skin (not deep).

However, his swelling on the right rear is significant, and until that goes down, we are stuck. We do not believe anything is broken because we don't see any flinching when walking (he walked out five miles), just discomfort and dragging the leg a little. He is perky, eating and drinking and pooping normally.

Rhonda has put a note and pics on the blog. She, on the other hand, is sore from the right shoulder down to the breast line. Still taking multiple drugs, but nothing appears broken. Bruised ribs and soft tissue, most likely. At least the doctors said so.

We are camped out while the horses are in large paddocks at a nearby stable. We are doing what we can to improve everyone's condition with the expectation that the ride will continue. Just don't know when.

Will probably take all of us out to the forest after another day and camp out. Too expensive to do otherwise.

This is not the way I would have wished to see Tahoe once again, but I'm sure getting to know the town (South Lake Tahoe). We will definitely be in the forest by Friday and likely not have cell phone coverage, so this will be my last message for a while.

We miss everyone but don't want to return until done.

Hugs,
Pat

(Copied from an earlier, Wednesday, note to a friend)

* * *

Happy Saturday to everyone!

It is remarkable how one day and one event can change your future and your outlook. Of course, we have all been there, mostly with good things, but occasionally, with bad and worse. Marriage proposals and pregnancies have an astounding impact. Accidents, on the other hand, can be mind-bending and have horrific consequences.

Throughout Rhonda's and my planning for this travel and journey, we had always known that there was risk of bad things happening. It was unspoken most of the time because who wants to think the worst? But Rhonda and I have always dealt reasonably well with adversity. Although we have been blessed with just minor events thus far in our lives or the inevitable.

So how does this latest happening stack up against all the rest? I guess that depends on the prognosis of recovery for the injured, and even then, we can deal with it. Rhonda's injury was not minor but not earth-shattering either. As the tissues mend, she can find new movement in her arm and shoulder almost every day (and it's only been five days). The bruising color will go away with time.

Cheyenne, on the other hand, will be a day-by-day evaluation, and it could take months for full recovery. If there is such a thing as full recovery. We just don't know how much damage was done and where exactly and what was damaged. But he is up on all fours and eating and drinking and doing all the normal things in a normal fashion, EXCEPT walking. What would you expect after taking a tumble down a mountainside? He is a gamer, and we are expecting a full recovery while fearing the worst.

For these reasons, we are now back home after assessing Cheyenne's ability to withstand the trip and then jetting back here yesterday from South Lake Tahoe. I haven't done that much driving in one stint in a very long time. We made it without any further issues as we stopped twice to let the horses rest and us to eat. We couldn't risk taking Cheyenne out of the trailer, so you can imagine the mess that awaits us. His injury has particularly made his "backing up" difficult because the swelling won't allow much movement of joints in his right rear. At least that is what we are hoping is the cause, but also the reason we have a vet coming Monday to help us with an assessment. For now, he will see limited activity and lots of attention. He has been such a trooper through all this; it has endeared him to us even more.

It became obvious to us after treating Cheyenne with morning and evening cold water baths on the swelled area, coupled with Banamine paste administered twice daily, that the damage to his musculature would take a lot of time to heal. And as mentioned, we are not sure there aren't other things wrong, and we are only seeing the surface. Now he is home in a comfortable environment and can rest and recuperate.

Rhonda is also resting and recuperating, but the drive in that woman is going to take her back out onto the trail, probably sooner than should be. It will be hers and her body's decision as to when she can lift a saddle and lift packed panniers onto a horse. Thank goodness, Liz and Rio are short and easy to reach. But this decision can't be taken lightly because she can't risk further injury by pushing too much too soon. I guess that's where I come in, trying to level the field and put reason above emotion and drive. But I understand the drive. We often have heated discussions but come out the other side with well- thought-out direction and motivated action. We will press on.

Now, Rio is going to have to grow up fast, as we are down to two horses. Don't remember if we told you that we had left him home this past trip out, with a neighbor caring for him along with Turtle, the cat. Rhonda (that's our neighbor's name also) has been a dear heart and allowed us our adventures by being here for us. We owe her our gratitude and so much more, the hugs and conversations, and occasional chore trades don't hardly seem sufficient. I hope she won't hesitate to let us know when it is her turn to adventure forth and leave us to tend for her.

So now it will be Liz carrying the boss lady and Rio bringing up the rear with all the gear. In the meantime, which is probably the next three to four days, Rhonda and I will have to revisit all our planning and decide if some changes are indicated. Does she start back up where she just left off, or do we travel to another section of the trail? What gear do we take with us? What are the trail conditions in various sections of the trail? What weather can we expect? So much to do and think about in such a short period of time. At least now the hay I ordered here locally may actually be here. Gotta think positive, right! Hard to do sometimes when things are not going as planned.

During our hiatus from the trail, Rhonda has been trying to get info from the Back Country Horsemen of California regarding trail conditions, clearing activities, and just general lay of the land. It is quite a challenge to wake up each morning, saddle and gear up your pony, and start moving down the trail without the faintest idea of what you might encounter this day. It's not like you have been here before (been there, done that), so around every curve is a new adventure or trial or just a boring section of trail.

The PCTA (Pacific Crest Trail Association) has books, a website, and numerous ways to get informed and stay abreast of current conditions along the trail. But all that information is geared to the pedestrian, hiker, or day user and not typically all that useful to the equestrian community—i.e., a water source might provide a cup of water every minute. What are you going to do when you need two gallons for each horse? Or a fire last year burned out a bridge over a creek. Has it been rebuilt? Is there a fjord? Can a horse even get down the embankment to cross the creek? Something a hiker can do, like, climb over big boulders, but is impossible to do on a horse. It can prove to be an insurmountable obstacle.

Rhonda and I clear twelve miles of a local trail and along that route is an old burn area that has fallen trees that look like a field of pick-up sticks. If a big tree comes down across the trail it makes it nearly impossible to get by and the slope of the land won't let you go around without extreme danger. What can you do but go back or take another route that is also questionable. So we have been trying to find out what conditions are like on the remaining portions of trail in California.

The responses have been a mixed bag and not all that helpful. Not their fault as there just isn't enough manpower to do all that is needed, and these guys and gals are like me . . . no spring chicken! Yesterday one leader said they will not touch or even see the section of PCT trail he is responsible for because there are other "higher" priorities in the trail system. And where does that leave Rhonda? She is in a quandary and supposes that there will be an imaginative solution to every problem. We can't change it, so she just has to deal with it. It's a wonder that any equestrians make it thru this gauntlet.

One thing she has learned from this recent and most unfortunate event is that every decision, large or small, has its plus and minus sides to it. We are hopeful that we dodged a bullet and that Cheyenne will recover to his old self, because anything else is just unthinkable right now. I think back to my youth and you may remember my mentioning the fall from a ladder while picking pears. Maybe I shouldn't have reached for that last pear. Or when tarring our cabin's roof, maybe I should have taken the time to tie a rope to avoid falling off the roof. How many of us fasten our seat belts? In the blink of an eye, disaster can be waiting.

For Rhonda, there could be danger around every corner, but that is also part of the attraction, or is it? You will have to ask her, but I think not, but I do think the adventure is a magnet that draws us to it. Seeing that sunset that no one else in the world will see but you. Or the flowers or the game. Or just conquering the day in order to settle into your bag and tent, knowing you had a day to remember.

With that, I will say peace and goodwill to all of you. May your day be a happy occasion of good cheer and of wonder, experiencing one more day of life.

We love you all,
Pat and Rhonda

(Sent from my US cellular smartphone)

Back on the trail at Hwy 178.
Only 2 horses available now, Liz and Rio.

Return to the Sierra Nevada Mtns. and
the Sequoia National Forest.

Passing the 700 mile stones.

PART

18

June 28, 2015

Howdy, pardners!

Well, it has been an eventful week and a half, don't you think? We are on the road again with only 7,000 miles expended since this journey started. So let me see who has the most hours in the saddle; 7,000 vehicle miles at, let me see, let's say 50 mph, would put it at roughly 140 hours of driving time for me. Whoa! Is that all?

While Rhonda has approximately 48 riding days, averaging 15 miles per day at 2.8 miles per hour, would give her—oh hell, where's that calculator again?—257 hours of riding the horse time. She beat me! What else is new? Hey, it's a team effort, right?

Well, one of our team members is stricken and shall not likely return. We got home early Saturday morning, like almost on Friday, and had to unload the horses in the dark. Cheyenne, of course, was not in good shape to back out of the trailer, so we had to find a sloped part of our hillside to back up towards so that the drop off would be lessened. Okay, get out your geometry books and figure it out!

So we turn on all the lights we can find and a flashlight or two and then coax him to move. Actually, it was more like get the hell out of my way! Ever been in a trailer for fifteen hours, being fed and watered through the window and not having a toilet handy? I'd say he was ready to move. And so were we. It was a successful extrication as he did not fall down. Yeaaaaah! Now this is familiar territory, so let's just lead the pair (Lizzy too) over to the paddock. Uh, where is the paddock? It is pitch dark and no moon. All we can hear is this banshee kid (Rio) galloping and snorting on the other side of the fence. Yeah, this makes sense . . . turn an injured horse over to the kid. I don't think so.

So Rhonda takes Liz into the paddock because if anyone can handle the kid, it is Liz. Hey, no more galloping. In the meantime, I try to sneak into the upper paddock during the turmoil of "LIZ MEETS RIO," and once more, our sound judgement and a little guesswork wins out. Thank goodness, maybe we can still get to bed tonight. A little feed (hay) and the critters are set for the night. We watch for a while, trying to see if we should be concerned or troubled by the way Cheyenne reacts to the patch of familiar territory, but there is nothing to worry about. Ahh, bedtime is cometh, and we disappear under the covers.

The rest of the weekend is uneventful, unless you want to hear about the mess two horses can make in fifteen hours. Yeah, I didn't think so. Two people can make quite a mess as well, so it is clean up the trailer time; only Rhonda has one bad wing so the duty falls where it may. Actually, I felt pretty lazy on Saturday and probably watched more golfing than any other chore. The fridge was still cold, meaning plenty of cold beer, and we still had dip available. And could you believe it? Rhonda made some of her world-famous clam dip for me to savor during all those hours of doing nothing. Oh, manna from heaven.

We kept an eye on Cheyenne all weekend, having stopped the doping and triage to see how he reacted . . . in pain, discomfort, or what? Mostly, it was about mobility with one leg about half again bigger than normal, but not with wincing pain. We were hopeful for a confirming prognosis when our vet was scheduled to arrive Monday morning. And that is what we got! Cassie, our family vet (no not for us, you dummies, for the extended family of dog, cat, and three equines), confirmed that she didn't think anything was broken, just distressed from soft tissue and muscle damage from the tumble. Thank goodness! But it would likely be months for a full recovery, so a pasture pet is what he is slated to be until this venture is nearly over.

Rio, ol' buddy, how do you feel about? Yeah, that's the story, like, what choices do we have? Say none? I knew there was a reason we put up with his shenanigans. Actually, that's not fair. Rio is a treat and quite a wonderful horse for us. We started packing him one and a half years ago, and then Rhonda started riding him last summer. He's been a dream come true, just a young buck who has more energy than two oldsters, Rhonda and I, not Liz and Cheyenne. They have horse language, which we are still trying to learn, so the communication is straight and true between them. You know . . . ears back, snarl, mean look, kick, and finally bite. Rio pretty much toes the line until Rhonda or I get into the mix. Then we are a mile behind, but eventually, we do catch up. As I've heard said, make what you want a horse to do . . . the easiest thing on his limited horizon. Like most animals, they think in the present only. Not ten minutes from now or five minutes ago, just now. A horse is basically a lazy animal, so if he has to work, then that is less preferable to sitting still. Making him work allows him to appreciate the time when he doesn't have to work, and thus, your preferred direction. And then, of course, is the hierarchy of the herd where each one has his rung on the ladder but is always trying to go higher, and we humans have to help them understand that we are at the top and thus must be respected accordingly. Is this animal science or what? Aren't I supposed to be talking about a trip or something? Oh yeah.

Yesterday we drove from sunup to sunset, or so it seemed to the driver, now with eight thousand miles and counting. But we made it, and thank goodness for a half-moon because at Walker Pass campground the corrals are about a hundred-yard walk up the hill. Horses, then grain, then water for the night (4 gallons each), and finally, hay. Did I mention that I have a pulled groin muscle and a strained hamstring? Now don't you feel sorry for me. Didn't think so. Tucker sure liked it, though, after being cooped up in the truck for twelve hours; and actually, I kinda did too for the very same reason.

My other maladies took care of themselves while we were home. The doctor confirmed I had just pulled some muscles and not torn my repaired hernia apart, so one visit to the physical therapist and I was set to go. The dentist repaired my lost filling and broken tooth. The optometrist took back my new glasses to set the proper prescription, so I'll keep wearing the old ones for a while longer. And finally, the audiologist thoroughly cleaned my hearing aid so that Rhonda doesn't have to shout all the time. I can see why kids text each other from the front seat to the back. Screwy, but I understand.

So now that I am all fixed up and ready to rock 'n' roll, there's no one here and nothing to do! Our brave warrior of the PCT (Rhonda) is once again going about her business, having departed from Walker Pass this morning on a three-day jaunt to Kennedy Meadows, meaning she is packing Rio and planning to have two nights on the trail. These will be long days riding in order to cover the fifty miles between. If we are lucky, I will be able to resupply her about midway, providing another day's rations and some horse feed. Since there is a campground at the end of the road I am proposing to enter upon, we are assuming it is passable. I'll leave the trailer here. These kinds of situations are why I didn't want a third horse along for this part of the journey. Complicates things.

We came all the way back to Walker Pass because it is now time to finish this trek up to Tahoe. It is HOT, being in the midnineties most of yesterday. While we are at a much higher elevation, it is still hot, especially for Rhonda and two working horses. So it is time to press onwards, with the snow concerns mostly gone and being replaced by concerns for adequate water along the route. Can't dillydally. We have lost nearly a month with the trek home for St. Jude's and now the injured horse, so the finale may just be held in the snow. But as always, we have a plan. Finish the damn thing, that's my plan.

Those that wanted to join us in Oregon may not think so highly of our plan when they are riding in the rain and sleet of October! We are just saving the best for last. Come the final day, we'll probably be like a bunch of cockroaches when you turn on the light head for cover and your hidey-hole. Boy, will we ever appreciate home by then. But I'm gettin' way ahead of myself because there are only one-hundred-plus days to go. OMG!

So it's time to think of others besides Rhonda and me, as we just got word that Brother Rick, good buddy from my college days, just got a pacemaker installed. We wish him and Jackie the very best and all our love. Hugs to the both of you. Big brother Mike (real brother) is going in for hip surgery in July, so everyone wish him well. Although it is difficult to feel too sorry for him since he, his son Jeff, and granddaughter Harper just went to see the Golden State Warriors whup up on the Cleveland b-ball team. Good strokes for good folks.

And I just heard that cousin Sandy just had a birthday on the twenty- third. Sandy is on Rhonda's side of the family, and she and her hubby, Ralph, run a B and B in Soldotna, Alaska. I've stayed with her on numerous occasions and can vouch for a most pleasant experience. Sterling Needle B and B if you are in the neighborhood. Red salmon fishing in July is my favorite.

And I could go on for quite a spell, but this is supposed to be about the journey and maybe a little commentary along the way. So for the time being, I'll close with the thought that tomorrow will bring another day and a whole new set of trials and experiences as m'lady heads on down (or is it up, like up north?) the trail.

Love and hugs to everyone,
Patrick

* * *

Boy, did Rhonda ever have the trials yesterday and this morning. Can I call it or what? She left yesterday morning a little later than we had hoped, but not surprising since everything was packed away for travelling and not readily available. As I mentioned, she was all primed to get this fifty miles done in three days.

So her first stop was to be at Joshua tree spring where she would gas up the horses, but lo and behold, the spring was dry. So after a thirteen-mile jaunt, the horses are really thirsty, and Rhonda decides that forward is the only way to go, onward. A small creek lay awaiting just five miles ahead, and still time to make it there. Five miles ain't so bad a trek on known trail and cool mountain air, but she had neither. Or should I say the horses had to trudge along, trusting the lead human to do them well. After having to cut a few trees with her saddle saw and coax the princess between two logs (actually had to lift and place

Lizzy's feet) to get along the trail. Water they did find, and after digging a trench, them critters sucked and sucked to their hearts' content.

But the day was not done yet, as there was not a campsite to be found anywhere near this creek. Onward! And I think Rhonda stopped counting miles and footfalls and just hoped she could find a place before dark. Keep in mind that the temps are still in the upper eighties well into dusk. A flat spot at last and none too soon. Off came the packs, horses tied up, and the neat little air mattress pumped, and Rhonda climbed between the folds of a tarp and grabbed what sleep she could. Horses wouldn't eat without more water, so feeding time was short.

All this time, Rhonda had been texting me using the Delorme InReach Explorer but to no avail since I didn't have cell service. I merrily awoke to a cool morning and more sunshine. Performed my morning ablution and went to visit with another couple we met seven weeks ago that are also on horseback and headed the same way Rhonda went. Course, I didn't know then what I know now, such as springs being dry.

Today I was to meet Rhonda at a campground about thirty miles up the trail. Per our plan, she would have about twelve miles of riding to get there, and with her normal get up-time and morning preparations, I figured noon would be a good time for me to show up. But knowing I didn't have cell service, I decided it would be best if I first went into the nearest town where I would likely be able to catch all the messages awaiting me on the airwaves. Ever think about it? Where do they wait while trying to find you and deliver their message?

Ah, another time, as this time they all found me at once, six texts to cipher through. The first one put me on alert—no water at the spring. The next one was relieving as water was found. The next added stress as I was informed that there were no campsites. You realize that I am getting all these in the past tense as it is 10:00 a.m., but I'm sweaty and anxious as if I'm there. Rhonda says she is pushing on 'cause she doesn't see any options. I agree in past tense, but going all the way to the campground, no way! That's nearly a thirty-mile day, with a late start. Finally, at 9:30 p.m., which is in the dark, she says she has found a spot and crashed. I'm thankful, knowing all will be real, real thirsty but okay in the morning.

And the last text is sent at 6:00 a.m. as she is breaking camp and back onto the trail. Me, I'm goin' OMG, she's gonna be at the campground way before me, so I'd better high-tail it myself. As it turns out, we arrive at almost the same moment. Thank goodness, this forest road was halfway decent, and I made good time. Hugs and kisses later, I realize that Rhonda and the horses are spent, but certain things have got to be done. First is water to the horses, then to ourselves, and then the work begins. Rhonda considers her options for going forward as it is only 11:00 a.m., but the decision is to stay for the night. They have tons of water, and I brought hay and grain, and they are all spent. I agree. Tomorrow will be a twenty-one-mile day, but with the rest and plenty of energy, it should be manageable. So, Kennedy Meadows, here we come.

Me, I'm back at the Hilton and putting my finger on the keyboard for all of you. Still the one-finger press on the screen. The airwaves should have a spot for me on the morrow to lay this out there for all of you. I hope you are having your own adventures this weekend and enjoying every one of them. Nicole, John, and extended family and friends are enjoying our place in the sun back at the Ranch, so I at least know some are smiling.

Hugs to Rick and Sandy and best wishes to the rest of you.

Pat and Rhonda

PS. Rhonda says I missed part 15! Did I? If so, let me know. If not, send me a copy. Tsk, whoops, I don't need thirty copies. John and Nicole, you are on the hook, please.

(Sent from my US cellular smartphone)

Kennedy Meadows camp site with all at rest.

Prepared for 2 nights out, rising 3,000 feet to meet at Horseshoe
Meadow Campground at 10,500 feet.

PART

19

June 30, 2015

Hi to one and all, family and friends,

Today was a move day for me, moving from one destination or jump off spot to another. I left Walker Pass with the intent of being at Kennedy Meadows to catch Rhonda as she rode in. Now don't get your underthings in an uproar because everything went just as planned. Well, sorta.

You see, when I get free time, uh? Like time that has no other commitments, and I am free to cruise around and catch a glimpse of this and that. No! Time is not free. So today I came off the mountain and cruised through Inyokern and kept right on going to Ridgecrest, where I ran right smack dab into the gate for China Lake Naval Weapons and Testing Center. No, they did not let me in, remembering my antiwar stance of forty-five years ago. Just kidding as I did not try. Too many other things on my agenda. Like buying milk for breakfast. Lordy, lordy, I must have my milk for the granola!

But seeing this place was kind of a wonder to just happen across it. I keep thinking that this was where *Top Gun* was filmed, but I'm probably wrong. This place is 1,100,000 acres large and has over 2,200 buildings on it. Its annual budget is nearly $3,000,000,000. (Can you count that high?) Doesn't matter; just think big. Shared by Edwards

AFB and the Marines at San Diego, it must have one heck of a lot of ordnance on it. Anyway, it was a kick to behold such a place.

Got my milk and a whole bunch of other stuff to keep us alive for a while. Actually, I should restate that as keeping me alive. Rhonda is entering the phase of trail along the PCT, where we will see each other less and less. Tomorrow she leaves for three days and two nights, with me catching up on the third night. After that, it is even more nights out and all alone along the trail. So she has magically discovered, thanks to our dear friend Rhonda, freeze-dried foods by someone else other than Mountain House. We have even dined together on freeze-dried, and I didn't wilt up and blow away, such good fodder it was. How come it takes one seventy years to find these things out? Ah, don't answer that! Anyway, Rhonda is going to eat hearty and well. That is if she has enough energy at the end of the day to boil water, and of course, there has to be some water.

We are a bit worried about the latter. And if there is a dearth of water, where do we expect the animals to graze? Doesn't your going to work sound so much better after listening to me bellyache? Work, stop at Costco, pick up a pizza. See how easy life is, not a care in the world. Ever eat chocolate chip cookies after they have been in your saddlebag for four hours? Nah, we all have it pretty easy, cookies in a cup.

Makes you wonder how our ancestors (or maybe yours, 'cause mine took the train) got their butts across the plains, the Rockies, the desert, and finally the Sierras. It truly amazes me. The other day, when we were trucking down Highway 395, we stopped at Devil's Gate Summit to get the critters out of the trailer and eating some grass. They stay healthier that way, and the mess ain't quite so overpowering. Anyway, I take a mind to read one of these placards set in a stone monument along the route. This one tells of one General Fremont and his exploration of the area to find an easier crossing of the Sierras. He is of a mind that he should be able to follow the local river up to its headwaters and merely cross over the divide and descend down a similar drainage on the other side to Fort Sutter. Now, get this. He does this in the late fall and early winter. Now I don't know when the Donner Party was lost, but this fella ought to get a clue.

The story went on to say that when the snow got too deep, they had to abandon the 1,500 pound howitzer cannon they were carrying and trudge on without it. What about the bears? How're they gonna kill ol' Smokey? Man, has the military gotten any brighter? Of course, I can envision the good general getting up in the morning after the private has delivered his coffee, started the stove in the tent that he shares with no one, and brushed and curried his mount. What's the big deal about crossing over all these mountains? In the winter, no less. They made it to Fort Sutter only to turn around in the spring and do a forced march to St. Louis. Wow!

Now you historian buffs can correct me if I'm wrong, but I believe this is the same General Fremont that our forest is named after in Central Oregon. Seems he also did some reconnoitering there. I seem to remember that in late fall, he left the Columbia River near The Dalles, traversed the countryside to come along Squaw Creek and near to Sisters, Oregon, and then towards Bend and along the Deschutes River. He left the river and crossed desert to end up in the higher regions of what is now the Fremont Forest. From there, with winter dead ahead, he once again staged a forced march to cross the Cascade Mountains and press on to San Francisco. What a guy. Just who I'd want to work for. But it is pretty amazing that they travelled far and wide without a Hilton or Dodge Ram. I should have it so tough. Here I am scared to death to pull the Hilton, while sitting in an air conditioned cab, up a 10 percent grade for twelve miles. Such is life in the twenty-first century.

Rhonda is reliving the nineteenth century, only with a down sleeping bag and a tent from North Face. She makes me proud to be associated. Maybe that's how that private felt when he brought the coffee. The Allman Brothers' "Ramblin' On." Gotta go to bed. Good night, all!

Well, my mind is not workin' a whole lot better this morning. Sleep deprivation thinkin' about having to get up and make the coffee in the morning, feed and curry the horses, and . . . ? There isn't anything else to do. It's so hot that we have all the windows and doors open, so there is no fire to start. Darn it, I wanted to flip that thermostat switch. Just call me Private Pat, and I'm here to do all your chores. Nah, Wrangler sounds better with no military connotation. But the incessant heat and lack of water startled me into another revelation.

Maybe old General Fremont wasn't so crazy or calloused as I thought. After all, the late fall and early winter would definitely be cooler. Likely there would even be some fall rains to keep the dust down. Course, they didn't have gravel or dirt roads to travel on. Just imagine Missus Fremont hollering to the general, "What you up to now?" and him answering, "Oh, just makin' trail, Ma, just makin' trail!" 'Cept when the snows hit. But it would still be a damn site cooler for the ponies who by now are growing winter coat. And there is water in snow, so you don't have to go lookin' for it because it is right underfoot. Of course, if he were really smart, he would have made friends with the indigenous natives. We call them Native Americans, and they could have shown him the way.

But alas, Rhonda has a trail to follow, and wouldn't General Fremont raise an eyebrow or two to find out that these folks are going 2,660 miles for the fun of it? Or the experience? Just to say I did it? No destination in mind and no real purpose, like opening up a new trade route or access to a lush green valley. In fact, this trail crosses a valley only to reach the ridge (crest) on the other side. Kinda like the chicken. I wonder how many American veterans of the Afghanistan war are trudging up the PCT. Not like they have anything to prove, having been there and done that.

So today is a zero day for Rhonda and the critters. Yesterday was twenty-two miles, and the colt is fresh out of the paddock. He needs to refresh himself with rest, and they both need to know there is some respite to the endless grind. As does m'lady. I will see Rhonda one night over the next two weeks, so we do this with a plan, reviewing the maps and our earlier thinking to the realities of what we now know and what we don't know. Water has become the number-one issue. We are camped next to the South Fork of the Kern River, and it is dry except for a few puddles here and there. Not many times do we get to camp in a picturesque valley and have the peace and quiet we have here, so here we stay.

Time to give water to the horses, so catch up with you later.

And later it is, with me sitting beside the Hilton in a BLM campground just five miles West of Lone Pine, California. And when I look back behind me, I can nearly see to the west Mount Whitney, the highest peak in the continental US. Yeah, I'm at the base of it and looking east. Gotta be in the shade of the Hilton at 5:00 p.m. and it being 105 degrees out there. There's a breeze blowing, and it feels like it may become a gale before long. This is LIGHTNING weather, and I'm hoping the best for m'lady.

Looking to the southeast, if only I were Superman, one could see Death Valley some 130 miles distant. Makes you wonder how come the lowest point on the continent is so close to the highest point. Whoops, not continent but continental USA. Folks at the last campground left at 3:00 a.m. to go desert touring and not burn up in their car. Some twenty years ago and about this time of year, Rhonda and our daughter Nicole, fresh out of high school, went touring the southwest by car, and I believe crossed Death Valley. Now I get to see parts of what they saw. Cool!

Well, jeez, I get to reminisce once in a while. But back to the journey.

Rhonda is about forty-six miles southwest of me and, per her recent text, is camping at mile point 717 along the trail, with good graze and water. Thank goodness as we have really been stressed out about the water and then the graze. She took along one meal in the form of hay, just in case. She has three meals a day for each horse in the form of grain (pellets). This is the third time we have switched grain (grass pellets) for the horses because the suppliers could not deliver on their promises. We think we hit the jackpot because this maker is into marketing and has his product all over the place. Plus, without the third horse, we have more room to store it. And the horses like it! That along with fat supplements, and we seem to be able to keep the weight on our ponies. After all, without them we go nowhere.

Speaking of going, Rhonda left Kennedy Meadows (MP 702) this morning and will be on the trail for three days and two nights, with us sleeping together, sans Hilton on the third night. I'm not sure I can get that low to climb into a tent, but it will be worth the effort. The road to get up to our meeting place will not accommodate the Hilton, thus the reason I'm in a campground. Someplace I can leave the Hilton and feel reasonably secure about doing so. Plus, it's cheap—$2.50 a night with a Golden Age card. What's a Golden Age card, you say? Grow up and you will find out.

The following morning, Rhonda will leave on what may prove to be her greatest adventure of the entire trip. Ten days and nine nights on the trail without support of any kind. She will be carrying her own food and that of the horses (grain), and all the rest will depend on her wits, fortitude, and grit. We have set up new emergency contact protocols for the occasion as I may not be anywhere near cell service to receive info. The InReach Explorer was purchased just for this situation. But you know, I am confident that Rhonda is going to do this without a hitch.

There will be challenges, that's for sure, as she must navigate thru Forester Pass, which is the highest point on the trail at well over thirteen thousand feet, and then not long after must cross a ninety-foot suspension bridge. Now you see why I'm not up there with her. Gutless wonder, that's me! I'm gonna drive thru over and around the mountains in order to deliver horse feed via a ferry boat on Lake Thomas Edison in two weeks. All I have to do is worry and fret and come unglued until then.

Whoops, Tucker just barked at our neighbors when they came back to camp. He's been here an hour and thinks he owns the place. Since we have been travelling, he has understood that the Hilton is his "house," and by gawd, I think he would protect it and me to the death. We don't lock our doors at night because of his "watchdog" talents.

But just maybe, this was his way of telling me that it is dinnertime. Come to think of it, it's my dinnertime too. Thanks, Tucker! Now his meal is easy, the same every night, and we wonder why our pets beg at the table or under it. So the thought of food got my juices going, but what do you fix when it is ninety degrees out and a hundred degrees in the trailer? Well, a little rummaging around in the fridge, and I glommed onto just the solution, a whole and fresh avocado cut in half and smothered in ketchup, with a side dish of cottage cheese with a freshly sliced tomato on top, a stick of string cheese, and a glass of ice water. Couldn't have been better. That trip to the grocery the other day really paid off.

Boy, the shade comes early when you are in the shadow of the highest mountain. I'm thankful, just as I'm thankful to all of you for following along these past few months. I just realized that Rhonda has traversed (that's surveyor lingo) 25 percent of the trail. Just think of how many more months you'll have to listen to my jabber. Thank you for coming along. With that, I'm going to say, "Goodnight, all," and get this missive onto the airwaves.

Have a good night, and we will come visiting again soon.

Sweet dreams,
Pat, Rhonda, Tucker, and the ponies

(Sent from my US cellular smartphone)

I drive around to the Owens Valley, with a view of the high Mountains.

My camp site in the valley with a view of Mt. Whitney

PART
20

July 5, 2015

Well, it's a howdy and good morning to you all.

It's the fifth of July, and Rhonda has departed for the hinterlands. It wasn't the smoothest send-off we could have accomplished, but we got 'er done. Actually, it was our second attempt, as we had figured she would leave on Friday, having gotten into the Horseshoe Meadow campground late Thursday afternoon.

But what with wet gear from the downpour of the night before, she literally had to dry out, and the ponies needed a rest. That, all combined with the fact that Lizzy did not eat her evening meal or munch ravenously on her hay, had left us a little worried thru that night. I even got up and checked on them at some ungodly hour of darkness.

All be told, we did try to get 'em going. Lizzy was eating her breakfast, and the colt had lain down during the night to get his beauty rest, so we figured we were good to go. Just slow movers, that's us.

When I had arrived on the previous day, I was a bit anxious to find a place for us to settle for the night. Course, the twenty-mile drive up a steep (more than 10 percent) grade for fifteen miles along a narrow road bed cut out of the side of a basalt mountain with little or no guard rail had nothing to do with my anxiety. I just had to walk around and relax, so my inverted insides could find their right place and order. I had driven into a gorgeous campground that was packed to the gills with horse trailers, horses, and mules and even a couple of donkeys strewn about thru the woods. Now why would this surprise me? After all, it is the Fourth of July weekend, one of the most camped-out weekends of the summer.

Well, it's because Rhonda and I had talked often about all the horses in Southern California but the total neglect and lack of use of some really nice horse camps and grounds. We had been chastising these folks for their lack of protecting their heritage and getting out there to show some usage. So all that, coupled with the fact that I had stopped to talk to the Forest Service folks at the local Information Center, where they told me that taking a trailer up that road was ill advised, led me to believe we would once again have our pick of a campsite. Whoa, guess again, as I walked the loop road looking for a wide spot in the road where I could park the truck (sans trailer due to bad advice) and find a level spot for our tent. Well, I got absolutely nowhere with my walk, as this place was really crowded with horse trailers, motor homes, pickups and even a few tents. Don't these people know that road is dangerous?

My next step was to go to the pack station nearby and inquire if they had any idea of what my options might be. Heh, no one home. A pack station, for those of you unfamiliar, is a location setup to house-working mules and horses, along with their handlers (or wranglers) to provide transportation into the back country, where there are no roads for hundreds (thousands) of square miles. Many were established by the government (USFS, BLM, and the CCC) back in the depression days and before. Actually, it was the CCC, as I don't think the others existed at that time, being a later invention of the bureaucracy. (Wrong!) They supplied all the accouterments of a moving village for the workers building trails, cabins, and whatever else was happening in the woods. A lot of that was providing the general public, mostly the rich and famous, an opportunity to experience the great outdoors in a modicum of comfort. While many pack stations were originally government run with government employees, now they have civilian contractors who still service the government work crews and also still outfit those wanting to travel and camp in the backcountry without owning their own stock, like we do.

This particular station has over forty mules and horses to accomplish its mission. Big corrals and a ton of tack and gear to outfit each animal for whatever mission it is chosen for. Unfortunately for me, no one was home. So once more, around the camp ground, but this time, I was more brazen, which isn't my normal mettle but absolutely necessary at this time. Rhonda will be here in a matter of hours.

Once again, good fortune struck us, or maybe all horse people are as accommodating as our newfound acquaintance, Mike, was for us. I approached him with my predicament, explaining that we needed a place for us and our stock. But not knowing the local rules, I was reluctant to head a short ways out into the woods and make ourselves a new home. Mike was occupying an established campsite and was holding one for his friends and wife, who would show up that evening. But he said no one was going to use the tent pad behind his trailer, and while he had set up a high line for his stock, he would not likely use it. (I found out later that he had his horse and mule in the overflow corrals across the parking lot.) I told him thank-you but that I would walk thru the campground one more time to make sure I hadn't missed anything, especially now that I knew we could plant ourselves most anywhere.

Ah, but the choices were few and not to my liking, so it was back to Mike with a resounding "Yes!" It just didn't seem necessary to fight the battle for the overflow corrals when we would just be staying the night. Rhonda found out later that Mike was using the corral because his horse and mule couldn't be trusted to stay out of mischief when high- lined, which meant he would have to sleep out there with them. As it turned out, I decided to set up our own high line to be a little further out and not inconvenience our new host. An added factor was safety as our horses were used to how we set things up, and I wasn't sure how they would react to someone else's setup. Minor details but not insignificant if you are relying on these critters to get you through the next three months without mishap. So Rhonda and I would use the tent pad to set up our little pup tent and the horses their new digs. And Rhonda was due to come in most any time.

Keep in mind that this campground and trailhead is enormous for where it is located, at 10,500-foot elevation. Paved roads and parking areas in at least four different locations with four trails that lead out into the wilderness and at least twenty lakes within hiking distance. It has a regular campground, the horse camp, the pack station, a hiker's trailhead, and the stock trailer trailhead with overflow parking for everyone. That's what I remember, with Rhonda coming in on one of the trails. This is an opportunity for disaster when Rhonda is wandering around, looking for you-know-who!

But alas, with forethought and hindsight when we were home, Rhonda packed our walkie-talkies. Hooray! "Hey, Rhonda, got your ears on?" Nope, but not five minutes later, I hear, "I'm on the road to the horse camp. Are you around here?" Now she has just accomplished a miracle because I drove around for ten minutes before I found it. Never saw a sign directing drivers. But Rhonda accomplished another amazing feat and waltzed right in, or should I say Liz sashayed her way in. Ah, peace at last.

We untacked the horses, checked for sore spots, pulled their boots, and brushed them down for comfort and to disclose any problem wear areas we hadn't noticed in our first look-see. To the high line, they went where their hay nets were waiting. Now it's time to start pulling the packs apart because everything is soaking wet from the storm Rhonda endured the previous night. Tent is hanging off the host's high line; other stuff on trees and bushes and the tarp spread out to set saddles and gear onto. The sun is out, and I think we can take a moment of respite. A premade margarita with ice and a beer for me, jalapeno/avocado dip and crackers, and the day has suddenly turned wonderful. I could finally relax after worrying for m'lady as she sat through the storm last night. Not to mention how Rhonda felt!

During the night, Rhonda did something that is truly amazing. She might put it on her blog when in a week we get back to society where she can indulge herself and lay it out there. During the night storm, she sat in her tent and turned on her phone in video-recording mode, with the result being spectacular. Envision total darkness with a constant roar in the background (rain), and then with a flash of light that lights up the skin of the tent and then the BOOM of the thunder following up with a mighty crescendo. WOW! It was magical and scary all in one flash of a second. I don't think I'll ever forget it, and I wasn't even there.

Eventually that evening, after a dinner of taco salads, we got the tent set up and the critters tucked in for the night. We learned years ago that dogs and pup tents don't go well together, and that was with our greyhound and constant companion Kippy. We didn't figure size would make a whole lot of difference, so Tucker was relegated to the truck. Happiness all around, and we wouldn't be awakened by the ever-present watchdog alarm. Didn't have to worry about that with Kip, unless it was to welcome the critters with "Yeah, sure, there's plenty of room, and these sleeping bags are really cozy." Off to dreamland it was after cramming ourselves into a space made for dogs, not people. Thank gawd for air mattresses.

Only to be awakened at 11:00 p.m. when Mike's wife and friends showed up, parked their trailer (oh, please, miss our truck!), and got settled. Now I don't know if they had to unwind due to the trip up the mountain or if these were longtime friends that had to catch up with all the happenings over the years, but I could hear the fire crackling and the nonstop conversation for some time. Me, I'm lucky, 'cause I can just take my hearing aids out and it suddenly gets peaceful, but for Rhonda, who can hear a pin drop, the night just got longer. Maybe bears in the woods would be better.

The next morning came a little late on Friday, July 3. The routine is pretty much the same for us. Critters get fed first, but hmm, Lizzy isn't devouring hers with gusto. Ate some hay during the night, but only one poop. Definitely out of order, but she does start on the new hay. I watch as I saunter over to the table Mike has set up, and the coffee is hot. Probably my first mistake of the day but certainly not the last. We chat and find out a little about each other, or should I say I find out about Mike, as he is a real chatterbox. Good conversation though, and he keeps me riveted on the history of the area and all the great places to visit from this campground. Oh hell, where's my horse? But alas, I have other duties, which I am shirking at the moment.

Rhonda is still in the tent, awake and getting all her clothes and personal items sorted out for this long pack trip she is about to embark on. Me, coffee's good, conversation is good, and I realize, only now, that we have both been alone for a period of time or just with each other, and maybe a little starved for social chitchat, so the morning moves on. I start preparing my breakfast—granola, of course—when Rhonda asks, "Where's hers?" It dawns on me that I didn't bring any for her, as in normal times I'm up and done with breakfast and don't have the foggiest what she eats regularly. Uh-oh! But Mike comes to my rescue, asking if Rhonda would be interested in chorizo wrapped in a flower tortilla for breakfast. Boy, would she! Oh, thank you, Mike. Thank you. Time to pack.

This morning has been so pleasant that Rhonda and I are both moving in a haze. Things are getting done, mind you, but conversations continue, and the morning stretches on. Horses get saddled, and I finally manage to get the colt's boots on, realizing why I always leave this chore for Rhonda, but she can't do everything. Finally, it is time to put the pack panniers up onto Rio's pack saddle. Each weighs approximately forty pounds but is awkward and difficult for Rhonda to get head high and strapped on. But we have decided that she needs to do this because there will be no Pat out there in the woods. It's a tough battle, with sore shoulder and all, but she gets it done. So as she is getting the box hitch tied to hold all this gear steady and stable on the horse, I go get my camera to get some pictures of m'lady in action. That done, I happen to glance at that time, and oh, shit! How do I break this to Rhonda that she needs to stop and desist, and she won't be going anywhere today? I do so in the gentlest manner I can muster and offer to go down that horrid hill and fetch the Hilton with all the spare time I'll have.

Rhonda nearly broke out in tears and mumbled, "Thank you, thank you," as she gave me a hug. She was so stripped of energy and fortitude, with only guts and grit to keep her going that the release was a welcome respite. We were both reminded that this is a journey and not a race. There will be other days in the future to press ahead and defy our fatigue, but this is not one of those times. Sleep tonight in a comfy bed and give Lizzy a spell to recover her old self, and tomorrow will be another day. I really don't want to make three more trips on that road, but I know I can do it and will be happy for making the effort. In the meantime, Rhonda will take the saddled ponies and go find some grass to eat and discover which of the four trails will get her back onto the PCT. Good idea.

So as I said early on, this is the day after. Things went smoothly on Saturday, although very similar and parallel to our Friday experiences. She should have headed out a lot earlier, but it just didn't happen that way. Rhonda has become sort of a lady hero to the womenfolk we have met along the way, and you guys know women . . . They gotta talk it through over and inside out. Now I'm not saying that was the only reason for a tardy beginning, but it is something to behold, and it pleases me to see the strength these women pass on to Rhonda, wishing her success and good travels.

Yesterday Rhonda had to travel through another stormy day of incessant wind and rain, and having to travel sixteen miles through it all had me very concerned. Yeah, I made it down the hill, with the Hilton pushing me every foot of the way, which I counted throughout the journey. I don't know how many times I had to remind myself to release the grip on the wheel or it won't turn. Thank goodness for our new Ram and a compression brake so that I only had to hit the brakes about every quarter mile, the whole time with visions of the brakes failing and me turning into the hillside to stop the train.

The good weather lasted just long enough for me to get back to my campsite and set up before the winds started buffeting the Hilton, and I had to shut windows and vents to keep out the rain. The whole time worried about travels on top the mountain. The wind and rain kept it up until dark and then subsided to let the stars come out. I could only hope that it was doing something similar on the other side of the crest and that Rhonda could settle in for the night. However, she still hadn't texted me, so the worry continued, and I contacted the kids to find out if they had heard anything. Nope! I dozed and then woke with a start and immediately grabbed for my phone.

There it was, a text from 9:50 p.m. saying she was camped in a grassy spot with water nearby. My heart heaved a sigh of relief. I guess I'm used to being the protector, and this sense of powerlessness is hard to swallow and especially when occupying a splendid home on wheels, protected from the elements, dry and warm. I suppose I've put Rhonda through some of these trials when I've gone off alone to hunt for the elusive elk or deer that always seems to lure me into the woods, come rain or shine. We are an adventure- seeking couple.

So today is sunshine all over but likely to have thunderstorms in the heat of the day, especially in the high country, and Rhonda will be high. She camped last night at 10,500 feet and will have a relatively short jaunt today of ten miles to get to a spot on Wallace Creek, almost due west of Mt. Whitney and along the combined John Muir Trail and the PCT, with the elevation being slightly higher. Tomorrow will be the big push to get up and over Forester Pass, the highest spot on the entire trail. A seventeen-mile trek, so I'm hoping for the best of weather and an early start for m'lady.

Rhonda, our thoughts and prayers, for those so inclined, will be with you.

Hugs to everyone and have a great rest of your Fourth of July weekend.

Pat

(Sent from my US cellular smartphone)

On the trail North towards the infamous Forester Pass

PART

21

July 8, 2015

Friends and family,

I'm lying here on a blanket alongside the Hilton, shaded by a Hawthorne Grove of trees with a small running brook not ten feet from my other side. While it is ninety-plus degrees, the breeze is stout, and the shade must lower it by ten degrees or more. Comfortable, almost exotic. Even Tucker is lying still, although I think the stillness is his hunting modus operandi, peering from under the truck and daring some critter to try to cross the clearing. Rhonda should be here with us, and then we could truly let the surrounds envelop us and fold us into a peace and quietude the scene deserves.

But no, Rhonda is many miles west and more than a mile higher as she traverses another wilderness and finds her own Shangri-La. It is afternoon, and the storm clouds are brewing their magic and getting ready to light up the mountaintops, sending a crescendo of thunderclaps across the valley. She seems to have weathered it thus far, my hearing no outcry, but it has got to be troublesome at the very least. Two horses to care for and shelter to erect when Mother Nature is displaying her full bag of tricks. Got to be wearing, but in the same note, most spectacular. Feeding the passion and the drive to ascend into another pass in the mountains and to drop into a new vista and drainage on the other side, seeing and doing what few have done.

My thoughts are being laid out there for all of you to see, while Rhonda's go into her journal, private until one day she may show me. The world? Or somewhere in between? We can hope, now, can't we? She has been so stalwart and just plain tough, moving northward nearly each and every day, while I laze about in the afternoon breeze. It's hard not to feel just a bit guilty for not suffering and not helping, even knowing that there is no way unless I am with her, which was decided many months ago. She can do this, I know, and she has entered upon some of the best trail along the entire route. A wide, well-travelled trail kept clear and free of obstructions, with a panorama not matched anywhere, as she is on the famous John Muir Trail, which is one and the same as the PCT in this stretch of the mountains and woods.

Oh! I was just visited by a most beautiful bird, yellowish orange in body, with a black topknot and goatee, with a black cape down the center of his backside that stretches over his wings and tail, with a white lightning strike down each wing on the sides. About the size and shape of a starling. Any of you have a bird book to look him up? My cell service is a little lacking, and I'm not gonna go surfing the web. Uncool in this environment. A rather elegant bird. And speaking of birds, I saw a roadrunner the other day as I was ascending to the peaks of the mountainside on, what else, but a road! So cool!

We (Tucker and I) came to this wayside by virtue of a recommended place to while away the time, a comment from Mike back at the campground named after horseshoes. Said the creek has fish, so I went out and got a temporary license, having brought a pole along for just such an occasion. Mike understood the dilemma of too much time and not enough to do, having finally realized that Rhonda wasn't going out for a day but for weeks. It just took a few days to wear out the sidewalks of Lone Pine and the conversations with fellow campers at the last place, Tuttle Creek.

Not that Lone Pine isn't a cool place and the Alabama Hills alongside are truly spectacular. I know you have all seen them; you just didn't know where they were or what they were called. The Alabama Hills have provided the scenery and backdrop for over eighty movies and a number of TV series, including nearly all the *Hop-along Cassidy* series and *The Lone Ranger* (gotta be elderly). *Rawhide*, *Gunsmoke*, and *Bonanza* also filmed there at times. Gene Autry, Roy Rogers, and the Lone Ranger all have rocks named after them. It started way back when, in the silent movie days, with Tom Mix and others, and the movie lust just kept on due to its close location to Hollywood, the acceptance and help of the community, and the magnificent hills with the Sierras in the background. Tucker and I took a few strolls through those rocks, with me scolding him not to dig 'em up to find critters.

And then there is the movie house museum that chronicles all that has gone on in them thar hills over the past one hundred years. Their program was well done, and the displays were colorful and educational. Wish I could have gotten onto the seat of the medicine wagon used in the move *Django*, directed by Quentin Tarantino. He was the one that donated the wagon. They also had a parade saddle loaned for display, the saddle having taken forty-five years to complete. It was so laden down with silver that I would hate to be the one who dropped it trying to get it up onto your ride. All in all, a good museum.

But alas, we are here on the side of Taboose Creek, and I had better get my fishing gear together and relearn all those knots from twenty-plus years ago when I took a fly-fishing course from Clackamas Community College. I wonder if Colin remembers that occasion. He was a dapper young lad, and we tried to take every opportunity to fish just a bit. Amazing that I still have some of the course's paperwork. Glad to see that fishing hasn't left his stable of things to do in the modern age. Guess I did something right, remembering that he caught just as many red salmon as I did last summer. Course, I caught Giardia, and he didn't, so I guess I'm one up on him there.

Guess my age is kinda slipping up on me, considering I brought a pole and reel but left the line lying on the table back home. Sporting goods store in Lone Pine was real happy to see me come in the door. I'm just glad they had some line I could use, which was the last one on the shelf. I'm assuming they stock these little creeks with fish as I can see them (fish, not people) from time to time, but who knows? Interesting how you are travelling northerly on Highway 395, up the valley (Owens Valley), and off to my left and at the base of the Sierra

Nevada mountain range are all these green rivulets leading easterly from the crags and crevices formed in ancient times. Springs or small lakes providing my backdrop of cool running water. Every now and then, you see a farm or ranch that is taking advantage and drawing enough outta the creek to grow something green and luscious, with desert all around.

Now Owens Valley has its own story from yesteryear and continuing on today, as folks do tell. Paralleling Highway 395 and just westerly is the aqueduct which runs some three hundred miles from Bishop along the Owens Valley to Owens Lake (south of Lone Pine) to and around the northerly, westerly, and southerly fringes of the Mohave Desert to seemingly disappear at Lake Silverwood, just north of San Bernadino. Thence into the city of Los Angeles, where it feeds millions of people with cool, clear water from the high Sierras. As I understand the story, there was a time when LA realized that it was going to outstrip the locally available water supply, which would put a severe limit on its growth potential. So some bright young water master developed this concept of the aqueduct carrying water by gravity from the Owens Valley, at 4,500-foot elevation to just easterly of LA at 1,500-foot elevation. The powers that be sent undisclosed and secret buyers to the Owens Valley to buy up all the ranches and their water rights to thus have a stranglehold on the entire region. Who knows if any of this is true, as I am hearing it from the sixth generation of hand-me-down legend, but the animosity does seem to linger a bit. It is rather an engineering marvel that they were able to move this water that far without a pump ONE on the line, or so I'm told. So interesting are the little tidbits you learn if you are willing to sit and listen.

As an aside, I listened to my neighbor at the last rest stop who was about my age, and of course, we had to discuss our purposes for being in such a place at such a time. After hearing of Rhonda's pilgrimage up the PCT (I still say north is UP), he told me a bit about his experiences in the Sierras. Seems that in the early seventies, not long after he and his wife were married and fresh out of Berkley (the University of California), they did a wintertime travel by cross-country skis across the Sierra Nevada along the East-West divide, identified by the Kern River to the south and the King River to the north. I just sat there with an open mouth . . . What did I ever do that could compare? Twenty-plus bear encounters, maybe, but who wants to be bored, listening to all those tales. And they weren't hard to do, where by my own wits and perseverance I survived. No, the bears just left me standing there all alone after they scared the shit out of me. Simple enough!

So no bears came in the night, and this morning, I was up and reading how the fly aficionados tie their flies to the leader, or tippet. Now I've been tying hooks onto leaders for a very long time and think I can remember this one, but if you are going to be an elitist, better do as the elite do. Same ol', same ol'. I'm armed and ready, having attached a little red ant—not a real one, silly. I figured that if I had to kill twenty flying red ants the other evening just to go to bed, and oh yeah . . . wake up and kill some more, then the hatch is on, as they say. Of course, having witnessed a spin caster, using a little red egg the other day was also a good sign. So my ant hit the water in a not very glorious manner since the creek is only six feet wide and my tippet is ten feet long, but I managed. And you know what, a strike on my very first attempt and I reeled in (actually there was no reeling involved), and I lifted a mighty five-inch trout out of the water. After a few pats on my back and a high-five with Tucker, I decided to release this one. I don't think I have a fry pan small enough. Then I looked down, and Tucker was kinda lookin' at me cross-eyed. "You're not gonna hit me with that big stick, are you?" I then thought it was best to discuss with him the facts of life, that meat comes from land AND sea, or its facsimile. I think he understood because boy did he have a good time after that. Or maybe it was after I caught the twelve-incher and let him smell it and the blood and him eyeing me as I put it on the stringer and back in the water. After that, he went swimming and running and chasing and cavorting all around me and another fish I did not see. But who needed another one 'cause I got dinner already. Tucker understood that I was not gonna hit him with the big stick.

That was easier to explain than my rampage throughout the Hilton the other eve as I took vengeance on those twenty flying ants. Man, they were hard to kill. Came out of the air easily but did not perish as flies do. No, they went crawling, and I just had this vision that they would take vengeance once the lights were out. Remember the cockroaches!

So half a box of Kleenex later and the rampage was over, but not for Tucker, as he lay cowering in the corner. Boy, he did not like that swatter. So an evening stroll in the twilight was what he needed and a mad dash for the rabbit that was sneaking across the drive towards water. Try as he might, he couldn't find that cotton tail, but he sure forgot about flying ants. We had a good night's rest after that.

And yet another day goes into the annals of the Marquises' journey. Tucker and I caught two more fish last evening and this morning. These go into the freezer so that m'lady may partake in the bounty of the Wild West. She has just passed through some of the most spectacular fishing spots in the entire nation, where large golden trout and brown trout abound. I know because as a young and carefree youth, we hiked into these mountains in search of just such a group of lakes and the bounty they might provide.

Whoa! Just had an F-16 fighter jet fly over at about three hundred feet off the floor and 300 mph. Could see the pilot's helmet. China Lake, here they come . . . or here they went. Been flying around these valleys and mountains for days but never so low as right now. Reminds me of my days in the Air Force. Had a couple of friends that were pilots, and they'd tell me how they would scare the pants off truck drivers as they flew in low and in attack mode out on the edges of the Everglades. I'll bet it wasn't funny for someone.

So back to my tale about fishing the high mountain lakes. As I recall and as there are none of you to contest this story, we started hiking at about five-thousand-foot elevation, with ten to twelve miles to go and climb to eleven thousand feet to where we would pitch a tent alongside one of these lakes. Now this was way above tree line, or so it seemed, but could not have been because I remember looking down into the lake and seeing logs forty feet, fifty feet down underwater; it was so clear and pristine. We, two buddies and myself, ate fish for a week. Eighteen to twenty-inch goldens and brown trout were not uncommon, and man were they fat. Probably not many of that size left as that was before Kings Canyon became a park and the whole area got such acclaim and esteem. Just another adventure that settled me on wanting an outdoor lifestyle and livelihood. I feel so fortunate to have been able to live a dream at times.

My first adventure at fishing a small creek such as this one, the side of which I sit, was Scott Creek up near Cow Mountain, near Blue Lake in Northern California. Also one of the first times I ever went on a pack trip with my dad (and brothers); I don't remember. I just remember packing several horses with my dad riding Pinky in the lead, us kids walking and holding on to tails as we climbed the mountain. Then a scary moment as a wild boar charged at Pinky as we arrived at a trail side spring. The only other part I remember is that the creek tumbled down the hillside, over and under huge boulders, leaving deep pools of water and logs in that water too. The fishing technique was a bit different those days as well. Kinda reminds me of Huck Finn, as we took leader and hooks out of our pockets, tied it to a willow switch we had cut and dug up some worms for the hooks. All we did was dangle these lures over the boulders and into the pools and caught ten-, twelve-, and fourteen-inch rainbows to put on our stringer. Never more than we could eat, but that was enough. That creek was not more than six to eight feet wide as well. I guess I was a lucky kid to have those kind of experiences, and now look at me. Or better yet, look at m'lady and what she has done and continues to do, making memories all the way.

It's time to move on and experience another day. Things to do and goals to achieve, so I'll be writing you again one of these days when time allows and my mind gets rolling along its mindless path. Do take care and stay with us as we meander along the journey. Goodnight, all, and may peace be with you.

P 'n' R

(Sent from my US cellular smartphone)

Liz gets a 1ˢᵗ hand look at Forester Pass

The team gets a drink and a little nourishment

They have made it through the pass.

The way up and through Glenn Pass

PART

22

July 20, 2015

Howdy, folks!

Well, it's a clear blue sky, with the temperature a mild seventy-two degrees and the sun headed for a lazy setting over the . . . oh hell! The wrong damn mountains. Try as we might, for the last two days, we have been trying to set our wheels a turning towards another horizon. Ain't happenin'! My, oh my! How plans do change when you are havin' fun, or maybe not so much fun, grumbling all the way back to the ol' homestead.

So here I sit in one of our European chairs planted in the gravel outside our barn and wishin' I were somewhere else but happy to have a margarita in one hand and ye ol' telephone in the other. Dammit, all. I have to put the margarita down to type with my one fat finger. Well, hell, now I have to put the whole works down as m'lady delivers chicken quesadillas to my lap at a time when there is only one thought in my head: "Food!" Umm, yum!

So when I last left you, it was a full week ago, and I was stargazin' along Goodale Creek in the Owens Valley of Southern California. To say a lot has happened since then would be kinda trite, so it's better to ramble along with the story. Some of you may already know the crux of the story from viewing and reading Rhonda's blog, but now I will tell you the "rest of the story." Hmm, wonder if that's copy written? Oh well.

About the time I was telling you of the wrath of Mother Nature, she was truly letting it all out, with Rhonda taking the brunt of winter weather in July. On July 8 at 9:15 p.m. Rhonda texted me to let me know that Liz was not doing well. Now 9:15 in this latitude it is pitch dark. It had been raining for several hours. Rhonda said that the following day or day after, she would be heading out by way of Taboose Creek trail, leading from the high country to the valley and my land of repose. Amazing that I was still in the vicinity, having just fished the creek by that name, but I'm sure glad I could respond that I'd be waiting.

Unfortunately, I had to inform Rhonda that according to the weatherman, things were likely to get worse. Snow was predicted for the high country. The following day, I spent several hours trying to get a response from the appropriate government officials regarding the trail conditions and whether or not the Taboose Creek trail was even passable by stock (horses and pack animals). Lucky for me, I finally landed with the right person, and Nancy told me the trail was rated for stock, although not great it would get them down. However, when asking if it was clear of obstructions, she did not know, the last report being in 2014. But bless her heart, she would keep researching.

I passed along this news as Rhonda was packing up a wet camp and preparing to come out. I was able to tell her that the trail was rocky, with a lot of shale and steepness, having to come down four thousand feet in seven-plus miles. At about that time, Rhonda was breaking camp, and I received a message from Nancy that the trail was clear, as reported by a hiker on July 2. Whew! Maybe this can happen after all, and Rhonda was on the move by 11:00 a.m. in the snow, no less. At twelve thirty, I got Rhonda's last message for the morning: "The snow's too deep, and I can't find the trail at the pass. Going back to camp at MP 811 and wait the storm out."

2 days later and camped at S. Fork Kings River

Maybe tomorrow or better yet on Saturday, when the weather is supposed to turn for the better. Damn, damn, damn!

I worried enough for the both of us, sitting in the dark, fretting for what I could not do . . . what a man was supposed to do, protect his woman from harm and the elements. Fortunately, there was a wilderness ranger camped near to Rhonda and would keep an eye on her. That took some of the load off. And then I worried for the venture that was not to be, what with two down horses. But egad, 811 miles under the hooves, up and over Mt. Baden-Powell, through the desert and into the Sierras to rise to the heights of Forester Pass at 13,200 feet above sea level. Do we really have to abandon all that and just go home? Not on your life, but the whole shebang just ain't gonna happen, because if Liz is that bad off, then the only thing that will help is a lot of rest and a lot of food, which means another trip home. Now that makes three trips in five weeks from Southern California to Central Oregon. Definitely, this was not part of the plan and doesn't leave enough time to finish the trek. Oh, what to do? What to do?

Well, I'm not gonna solve that quandary all by my lonesome, but it won't hurt to consider the alternatives. Cheyenne is down due to injury, but an optimistic consideration would put him back in the mix in a few weeks. We'll be headed home soon and can check on his status and recovery rate and balance that with the need for his services. Haven't seen Liz yet, so don't know what it is that Rhonda is so concerned about, but it must be serious to take her off trail. Liz was acting a bit strangely at our stopover on the fourth at Horseshoe Meadow campground, but I can't get my head around just what the problem is at this stage. Rhonda says she'll be able to travel, so we'll just have to wait and see. Still doesn't change the fact that she is off the team for the time being. Back to the planning stage and what to do or where to go from here.

All I really know is that in one or maybe two days, I have to be prepared to receive the gang at the Taboose Creek trailhead, which I've never been to. That alone led me to Goodale Creek campground as there is a camp host at this location, thus I could safely disconnect the Hilton and leave it while Tucker and I drove to the trailhead. I needed to scope it out and see if the Hilton could make it up there, thus eliminating four miles of travel for the horses. The road turned into a jeep road in the first half mile, but we kept on truckin'. Finally, after three miles, I decided I didn't need to see anymore and looked for a place down the hill where I could legitimately get the Hilton, which ended up about one and a half miles from the highway. Rhonda would have to walk the horses out the extra 2.5 miles to where we could camp for the night. Next came a trip to town to get propane so the fridge wouldn't quit and I wouldn't have to chum for bears before Rhonda would arrive. Can you believe $3.75 per gallon? At home, I paid $1.39. No wonder these folks down here don't lavish about in their own Hilton.

The waiting began on Thursday thru Friday, and on Saturday I received the text "I'm comin' out!" Whoopee! Now to get ready and the Hilton up the hill and the truck up to the trailhead and wait for her arrival. The pack gear would go into the truck, and then I would point out to Rhonda that she needed to keep going to that little white spec down in the valley (the Hilton), where we would spend the night. Geez, this sounds so familiar, just like South Lake Tahoe. I hoped Liz could make it as there really wasn't a choice other than pitch the tent. But Liz, as usual, was a real trooper and smelled the trailer two-plus miles away, and off they went. The road was so bad that I barely beat them down the hill.

We undressed the critters, and I was stunned by how much weight Liz had lost over the last week. No wonder she was floundering at ten-thousand-foot elevation, up and down ridgetops and side-hilling down to small meadows of grasses she had never seen but must consume. The miles and miles had taken their toll, and as Rhonda had so aptly put it, "I'm not gonna kill my horse in order for me to keep going. I'm done!" Never thought there were multiple meanings to the word *done*, but it seemed to me that some discussion was in order. Are you like done, done? Or are you just done for now?

The way down from the top of Taboose Pass

A look at Taboose Pass Canyon from the top

A look at Taboose Pass from the valley floor.

You see, in my time of idleness, I had envisioned a number of scenarios that might work for us, and that would allow us to continue in a modified version of the original plan. It just wouldn't be the original plan. After all, we are down two horses and the colt doesn't have the training or stamina to do it on his own. Hell, there are multiple days of packing through these hills that require extra ponies. Plus Rhonda clarified one of her "dones" to simply mean she was done with the Sierras and the incessant rock trails, steep sidehills, and the climb and descent to so many passes. We would pass it up and consider a return to complete this portion—the two of us and three horses in a more leisurely fashion.

Now, out of our discussion that night came a scenario we thought we could carry out with a minimum of fuss, and hopefully, no more heartache.

1. We would return to Oregon and put Lizzy out to pasture (a symbolic mention since we don't have a pasture) so that she can rest and gain much-needed weight and body fat.
2. Cheyenne would stay with Liz and continue with his rehab and rest until such time as we felt he could venture forth once again.
3. And Rio, my poor boy Rio, would be put through the ultimate test of being ridden more than just a little.

We would start at the southern border of Oregon, where the terrain is milder. There is less rock to negotiate, and the elevations are less than the lowest pass in the Sierras. I believe the highest spot on the trail in Oregon is near 7,600 feet. We would see if we could enlist the help of a friend or two to pack us through some wilderness areas and Crater Lake National Park. Hopefully, by that time, Cheyenne will be able to join up and do some packing or reverse roles with Rio. We will plan more rest days for our crew, and maybe, just maybe, we can make it through Oregon and Washington this summer. More than 1,800 miles, total. Whew!

Of course, you have now just witnessed what can happen to a plan. Remember when I mentioned that I believed our success in getting to Walker Pass at about the time we had hoped was all because of our forethought and a well-devised plan? Well, that just jumped right up there and bit me in the butt! How do you plan for a horse falling off the trail? How do you plan for a steady diet for your critters when the dealerships could care less and the manufactures even less than that? Of course, we should have factored in more rest days for our two or three tireless workers and also that two of them are well into middle age at twenty-plus years of age. Shame on us! And we should have realized that Liz would not, would never be a packhorse. A princess being led by a mere laborer! How dare us to even think such a thing.

So back to the scene in front of the barn, eating quesadillas. Rhonda came out on Saturday. We drove all day Sunday and Monday and arrived home Monday evening. How fast do you think we could turn it around and head towards Ashland, Oregon? Tuesday I get my new glasses, pick up my repaired hearing aid, get the truck a welcome oil change, and go shopping at Costco. Wednesday, maybe, but certainly by Thursday, don't you think? Think again! Bluegrass hay is available in Madras, and I commit to an early morning pickup of one load on Wednesday. Well, there goes Wednesday. After unloading, I make a second trip, but unloading another three ton of hay just isn't in this sixty-nine-year-old body, so I tell Rhonda, "Tomorrow!" Bright and early, I unload but with a cell or two of brainpower as I enlist the help of my little tractor that is now available, thanks to Wayne's schlepping it back to our place from the fixit store. Thank you, thank you.

Okay, Thursday morning is only half gone, so where is my bride? I find that she is in some kind of a trance and is glued to the computer and temporarily "out of service." So I guess it is on me to get everything ready. Water into the trailer. Rearrange the horse supplies since only one horse is going this trip. Make sure all the camping gear is dried out and repacked. Finish doing laundry. Do some repairs to the trailer and fill up the water tanks. The list seems never-ending, and as the day goes on, it becomes evident that Thursday is not the day either. Then that evening I discover a nearly flat tire on the trailer. Get out the compressor and check the tire in the morning to see how bad. At least we got the house cleaned up and ready to mothball for our return a few weeks from now.

Friday and we are ready. Once the horse is done eating, we can get out of here, or so I thought. Well, we did make it out by ten-ish, not too bad for us, but with several stops in mind. So, Les Schwab, here we come as it is your tire. Two hours later, we find out it is not the tire, but another cracked wheel. Luckily, they have a replacement in stock and we can be back on the road. Two stops in Bend, and we'll be showing our tail feathers to all the tourists, hehe. After gassing up, I tell Rhonda that it is a no-go because I'm already tired of driving and don't look forward to trying to find a camp spot in the dark, so back to ye ol' farmstead and the waiting margarita. What a week! What was gonna be a Wednesday departure is now a Saturday go, but you know, with this new plan comes a certain amount of "what the hey!" Plans are meant to be broken for the good of the order.

So Rhonda has just finished her first ride in Oregon, going past Mt. Ashland while looking south at Mt. Shasta on the southerly horizon some forty miles to the south. What a view! And now we are camped along the old Highway 99 just east of Callahan lodge near the Siskiyou summit. I found this old one-fourth-acre area of fill material alongside the road this afternoon after searching high and low for a spot to park the Hilton. Easy enough to get to, but I'm sure it is private property and the ol' boot could be coming our way at any time. I took the Hilton back up and over I-5 to pick up Rhonda and then we parked for the night, high-lining Rio behind the rig. To celebrate our restart on the trail, we had a leisurely dinner in the patio at the lodge and then settled into a quiet night of slumber. Awakening the next morning and having completed chores, I encountered an older gentleman working a tractor on the other side of the fill slope. Uh-oh! Time to bite the bullet and ask for forgiveness for our intrusion into his space. The "so sorry" was just waved off, and with the second breath, he asked what we were up to. Settling into one of our chairs and a cup of coffee, he was enthralled by my tale of good and bad but was most happy to host our stay. Come to find out he was the originator, builder of over twenty Shari's restaurants along the West Coast. Having sold his food chain, they came to settle here and buy Callahans. Such was the rest of his story.

But the journey must go on, and Rhonda has a long day planned to get on down the trail some seventeen miles hence, where we will meet again for a pleasant night in the Hilton. Several days later, with a rest day nestled in between, we should be at Highway 140 to await the arrival of our backup team. The next four days after that will be a pack trip to get up to the highway into Crater Lake National Park.

Rio is doing well, handling the time alone just fine and moving along at a pretty good clip. A bundle of energy compared to our two twentysomethings. Heartwarming to see all the efforts we have put into his ground training and riding that are now coming to the forefront as he gains confidence in himself and Rhonda as his passenger. We have done well by him and he by us.

It appears that our plan to cross Oregon, south to north, is workable. While extremely modified from the original. which included three horses, it was never that aggressive to get lots of mileage underfoot. And now we just don't have the urgency going at this stage. We don't need to wear out another horse! And since there are a bunch of lakes in this vicinity, and me with an Oregon fish license, I'll get to practice my fly-fishing techniques. Actually, I should say relearn because it has been so damn long since last used.

So now you have the rest of the story. and I'm hungry for breakfast, and someone needs to get onto the trail. Granola, here I come!

Love you all, and we really love the fact that you are coming along with us. Have a great day and week, and we'll be right back at ya when time allows.

Pat and Rhonda

(Sent from my US cellular smartphone)

PART

23

July 30, 2015

Well, howdy ho and a happy Sunday to all of you!

Jeez, where do I start? I suppose just by telling you . . . we are in Southern Oregon and doing just fine. At this time, we are parked at Summit Snow Park at the summit of whatever mountain group they call this. Mt. McLoughlin is to the north of us and Brown Mountain to the south. Probably the Cascades, as it is still in the string of volcanic action. We are looking to stay here for a day or two as Rhonda will take a "0" day tomorrow and rest up the colt.

Rio is doing magnificent, having covered ninety-one miles in seven days of riding time with m'lady. We are resting him more often and trying to do less mileage on a daily basis so we don't wear him out like we did Lizzy. Now that we have eight hundred less miles to travel, we can do that and still finish. We still feel bad about the Lizzy episode and probably always will, just because she was a trooper and didn't complain until she just didn't have it in her to go another mile. I think of some of the old cowboy movies and how they sometimes rode a mount into the ground. Well, we don't have any emergency and still came close.

Rhonda just rode twenty-seven miles in two days through Crater Lake National Park, but it was boring! They don't let the horses anywhere near the lake, and the park is otherwise made up of pumice clearings and lowlife timber clinging to the lava. Nice trail, though, with soft footing for Rio and Rhonda, as she does walk occasionally. But after a while, you've seen one tree you've seen 'em all. Maybe I should find a bear costume and liven up her life on the next day out. Hehe!

Been a little boring for me too; now that we have radios and cell coverage I can't seem to misplace our rendezvous points. Johnny on the spot every time. I've taken to getting there a little early, and if there is a feeder trail or lack of clarity on where the PCT is, well, I just go out and find it. Pretty simple, huh? This morning was particularly easy as Rhonda was to ride the feeder trail right in to the trailhead we had stayed in overnight. In fact, we all walked out there last night to make sure she wouldn't get lost. And then, Tucker and I, being bored and all, decided to go out there to the junction and wait for her. Tucker is always so cute when he sees her coming, getting down low with his tail spinning like a helicopter rotor and running up to Rio with his toothy grin from ear to ear. Rio has been real tolerant of Tucker as he jumps up to put his paws on the stirrup and get a quick pet. We came to this location (Summit Snow Park) right after the ride, driving sixty some miles and fueling up before settling in for the night.

Why this location, you ask? Yeah, I know you didn't ask, but I'm gonna tell you anyway. See, when we were strategizing our next move way back when, during our return to Oregon, we knew we had some packing days ahead of us if we went to Southern Oregon. So two horses down, and who was going to do the packing? Not me, that's for sure! In theory, Rio could pack while Rhonda walked, but I'm not even sure that option was mentioned. I was in self-protection mode. What I did mention was the opportunity for friends to help us out, since several had said they would like to ride with Rhonda when she came through Oregon. Our first request for assistance was met with welcome arms and a big "SURE!" So our good friends Don and Gerry will be here tomorrow.

Don, like me, will be delivering Gerry and two mules to take the trek from here to Crater Lake National Park. It will be a four-day ride of fifty-some miles, with three overnight campouts planned along the way. Hopefully, there will be plenty of graze for the horse and mules and water for everyone. With the light snowfall this year in the Sierras and the Cascades, the water situation has been iffy and troublesome. The Cascades got around 30 percent of normal, and the Sierras got even less. Topping it off is that the trail is called the crest trail for a reason, staying high on the mountainsides or at the Ranges' summit, leaving the creek and river headwaters considerably lower and "off" trail. The question being "How much mileage are you willing to give up in order to get to water?" With stock, you don't have much choice because they have to have water to keep their digestive system in order. A Hidalgo they are not.

So Rhonda has been planning like crazy on this, her zero day. Oh yeah, it's Monday now! A couple of calls to the local ranger station (USFS) has helped her settle on a course of action, knowing that certain springs or creeks have water and are accessible. Glad the panic-stricken phase is over! It's been a little disconcerting that while we have stayed busy all day, our car alarm keeps going off and then running across the pavement. Of course, I'm talking about a little black furry thing that thinks that wherever the Hilton is parked is where home is, and by golly, I'm just doin' my job. This trailhead / snow park has been a pretty busy place, so the deer in the area have been forewarned and are likely miles away. Except for one wayward deer that was right out front as I opened the door this morning and nearly got knocked down by the ever-incessant hunter. Luckily, the screen door opened as well, or that black furry thing would be wearing it.

So the day has been a fine one and is coming to a close. Rio is fat, dumb, and happy, having stuffed himself with grass and alfalfa and packer pellets, and whiling away his time in the sunshine. Rhonda has planned to her heart's content, written in her log, cleaned herself up, and relaxed. Me, I've just been doing some odds and end chores and wondering what the next few days will bring to this story line. Maybe dinner for the moment, and afterwards, we'll see where it goes.

So yeah, it is another day. We while away the morning, getting our associative chores done, and then Rhonda lays out all her gear on the side of the trailer. Don't want to forget the necessities, like a rope for the high line or a nose bag for the horse in order to feed him his grain and not have it spread all over the ground. I remember that one time it happened, and after about half the grain was spread around, I guess it must have been inedible, because the gelding peed all over it. "If I can't have it, no one can!" or so it seemed to me. So we sit and await the arrival of D and G, signs up at the Y pointing our direction. Don was optimistic that they would be here early, and knowing them, the mules were loaded up before we ate breakfast, but it's a four-hour drive or longer still if you make the wrong turn, which, I'm sorry to say, happened. A little mix-up on directions, but alas, the cell phones came to the rescue once again, and ten minutes later, they were in the parking lot. Whew!

Now they are a little bit later than we had anticipated, but not so much as to cancel the ride out today. But first we needed to discuss our strategy and make sure we understood their commitment and for how long. No twisting arms here, just being clear so that everyone was on the same page.

Now, in case you didn't know, Gerry is a story all by her lonesome. Raised on a ranch in Southern California, not far from where we have already trekked, she has been riding forever. Some of her childhood stories remind me of my time growing up with horses, but my brothers and I were not fanatics as I'm sure this young lady was. We rode, but not every waking moment, and certainly not every day unless we were preparing for a parade or practicing on the drill team. But back to Gerry, I believe marriage and children may have interrupted this passion for a bit, but eventually, she found herself training horses and riding for show on the Arabian horse circuits in Southern California. I can't imagine anything other than ribbons and accolades for many years. Meeting Don along the circuit, they were married some thirty-five years ago, and lo and behold, transported themselves to Sisters, Oregon, some thirty years ago. Now if I've got this all wrong, I'm just gonna fall back onto the old adage of "bad hearing" and "senior moments." Some of you know what I'm talking about.

So anyway, in the year 2000, our riding group association, Oregon Equestrian Trails, decided to celebrate their thirtieth anniversary with a trail ride through Oregon on none other than the Pacific Crest Trail, and guess who was a volunteer to accomplish this feat? You guessed it, Gerry, and at the age of sixty-seven, she completed that 454-mile excursion with at least two others, Becky and Rebecca, if my memory serves me right. Many others joined up for shorter periods to help with the logistics and to participate. But Gerry on Buck, her most trustworthy mount (a buckskin, of course), with Oscar the mule being dragged along at the tender age of four as a pack animal, the scene was complete. Now do the math, because here comes Gerry in 2015, still towing Oscar the mule but now riding Oliver the mule. This lady, so young at heart, has so much "go power," it nearly puts us to shame. Rhonda is in good hands.

Don and I go our separate ways, he to his other mules needing attention at home and me to the Hilton to wait out these four days until we are all together again. By the end of the week, Rhonda will lay claim to having gone one thousand miles on the PCT. Such an incredible accomplishment, but we aren't done yet. The zero day had us mapping out and strategizing the rest of the jaunt thru Oregon, and now we have another plan. By this time next week, I will be back home to pick up Cheyenne and bring him back to the trail. It's time he cowboys up and joins Rio and the team to finish out Oregon. There will still be another 250 miles to do to get to the Columbia River and then comes Washington.

So I am spending my leisure hours at snow parks that obviously don't have any snow. These parking lots serve a dual purpose as trailheads (places to park and embark onto a trail), and they are free and typically have a convenient outhouse, saving me the anguish of finding a place to dump our sewer tank. Quite convenient facilities, and now I'm back to our old haunts we were in nearly a week ago as Rhonda approached the ride through the park. Annie Creek runs by here, and I'm just gonna have to try out my fly-fishing technique once again. The creek runs off the hillsides around the lake and has a magnificent waterfall about ten miles upstream, but I'm hoping that the fish have migrated upstream from Agency Lake or Klamath Lake and are really hungry. The Williamson River and Wood River run into the same lakes and are known for their excellent fish populations, so I'm hopeful. They gotta be hungry because I can assure you I've still got some learning to do on my end so the presentation of the fly is not likely to be enticing. At least I will have a little more room as this creek is fifteen feet wide. I need at least one more fish so as to be able to present one to Gerry as Rhonda, and I scarf up the ones in the freezer.

Did some shopping in K Falls yesterday on the way here, so I would have enough food for three bodies and not just P and R. Gotta be hospitable, especially after what D and G are doing for us. What wonderful folks to have as friends. We are thankful. Tucker is thankful too, as he will now have three and maybe four plates to clean up. Tomorrow afternoon, we shall pick up the ladies after their last day of riding before the zero day, and I'm hoping to talk Don into staying for dinner. Shouldn't be too hard at five in the afternoon. For now, I just need to button this puppy up and fix some breakfast as my energy level is depleted from all this finger poking of my telephone screen. Or maybe it is the six-mile hike I took yesterday to give Tucker something to do other than signal a newcomer to the snow park. At any rate, I'm done.

Love you, one and all! Please take care and have a wonderful weekend.

Pat and my loving mate, Rhonda. Oh, and Tucker too!

(Sent from my US cellular smartphone)

Lots of timber in Oregon. Hope most are standing or cut!

Our dear friend Gerry joins the crew to help pack through the wilderness areas.

A view of Southern Oregon.

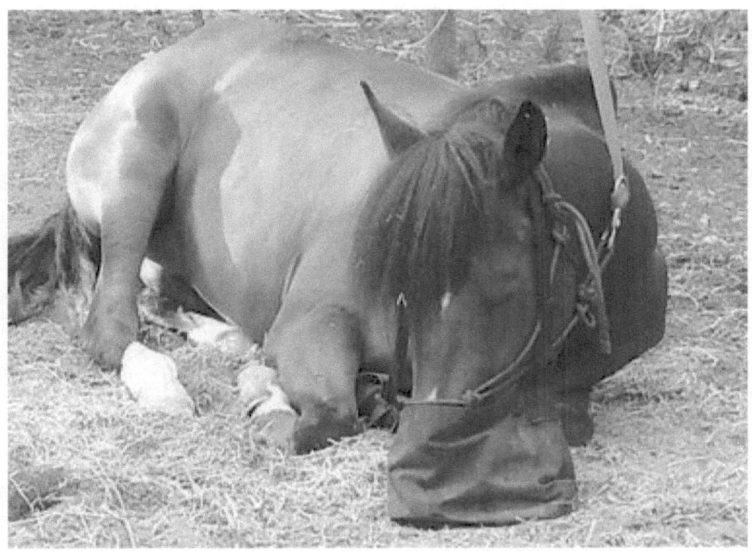

Rio had a long and tough day keeping ahead of the mules.

Oscar is a photogenic old cuss. Thanks for taking us along.

PART
24

August 8, 2015

Good Morning, Vietnam! Whoops, that's wrong.

Good Morning, Central Oregon! Yeah, that's better, and yes, I know most of you don't live in Central Oregon. But it sounds cool, anyway. Really, did you know that these messages are travelling to Alaska, Washington, Florida, maybe Texas, and possibly to some South Sea Island (I don't actually remember where our nephew, niece, and families are residing at the moment)?

I suppose I could figure it out if I could only figure out Facebook. Signed up a couple of months ago and have a slew of you as friends, but I don't have the faintest idea of where to go from there. I need a Facebook primer to guide me into it, as I try to be ever so cautious with this phone, as it seems to be the single thread of communication I have with the outside world as we travel on all these back roads in the vicinity of the PCT. So all you Facebook friends, please forgive me if I have shunted you aside for the time being. Time will come when I will be there. Enough to do for the moment.

So back to the salutation (the first one), does anyone miss Robin Williams as much as I do? He was one remarkable person and actor and comedian. I think my generation needed someone like him and, of course, others such as Eddie Murphy, Chevy Chase, Steve Martin and the folks of *Laugh-In*. After a war and the draft and antiwar and social and political upheaval, comedy was a good thing. It served to lighten the load and allowed us to consider the realities of living without shuddering at the thought of what lay ahead. It was unfortunate that Robin Williams wasn't able to shed some of those demons and survive with the rest of us.

So on the lighter side, we have just completed our trek through Crater Lake Park and are taking a zero day. Rio is flat out on his side, Gerry is on her bunk, and I'm punching away at the keyboard. Rhonda, well, she is in her element as she has encountered hikers here at the trailhead and is settled into an easy chair in the neighbor's motor home as they trade tales and stories of their survival and joys of the trail. It is so good for her to have these opportunities to exchange with others that have been there and done that! Of course, she is the ONLY one on horseback, so the hikers are intrigued by what she has done and endured. They can talk about the drive and the ambition that has brought them this far and what the allure is that will get them up and back onto the trail. Building relationships in this manner has been a big plus and, for me, an unanticipated joy of the trail.

Just the other day, I relished just such an experience. On the day that I moved from Summit to Annie Creek snow park, I had found it necessary to shop in K Falls for a little resupply, part of which was getting ice to go into our freezer. Yeah, I know, if you have a freezer, what do you need ice for? Well, the evening cocktail, of course. You can't drink margaritas without ice! But we are in the Hilton, and the freezer is just not that big.

So after getting settled at the snow park, I set about resolving this dilemma by approaching my neighbors, also parked and settled in like situations, just without horses. The first couple was travelling in a small camper van and had no room for more supplies. The second group was in a large fifth wheel and, lo and behold, had an ice chest in the bed of their pickup. I offered, and they took. They offered a beer right back at me, and you know me, so when I begged off, you can know how out of character that was. Pat turned down a cold beer? What's with that? Well, it was the waiting margarita back at the Hilton is what that was. Had to try out the new ice cubes!

And so back at the Hilton, relaxing after a fulfilling dinner and trying to avoid the ninety-plus degree heat, I was approached by the lady of the house (van) who had come from a riding household and was intrigued by my being housed in a horse trailer. Where are your horses? And that got the conversation going. She and her husband being newly retired and moved from Oakland to Truckee, California, and me being from Santa Rosa led to more conversation. Come to find out that they were just returning from a two-month jaunt thru Alaska in their van, which led to even more stories of yesteryear. I loved it. Being alone for days at a time in strange surrounds gives conversation and casual relationships a whole new meaning.

Common threads entwine us into webs of knowledge and rapport that support and bolster us to keep on treading into the next day and the unknown of what it may deliver. What a joy!

And the next day was certainly that, as the recipients of my ice cubes came by and asked me to join them for a cuppa java. Once again, I had to turn them down as breakfast was done for me, but not the coffee. I asked if I could join them, only with my own coffee, and of course, it was a resounding yes. Travelling with the Hilton just seems to invoke questions galore, and once you get me started after two cups of coffee, well, settle down 'cause I can rattle on for a spell. They were intrigued by our endeavors and somewhat amazed by the complexities of travelling by horseback up the trail. Really nice folks from the middle of Washington, John and Laurie, together with John's in-laws. First time for any of them to be visiting the park so after a couple of hours and another cuppa, I decided I wasn't lonely anymore and should let them go. So glad to have made their acquaintance and to have had some time together. RV'ing could be fun if you don't shut yourself in and watch the boob tube all the time or traffic to spots where everyone is of like kind and bent.

So today we are mixing it up with the parking lot gang at North Crater trailhead, all of whom are active or past PCT trail junkies. Walk, talk, and think the trail. Rhonda is in her element, but some of these guys are just a little too full of themselves for my blood. I'm sometimes grateful for the chores that just have to be done right now. I don't need a following, and this isn't the most exciting event of my life. While my remembrances have certainly glossed over the minuses and focused on the plusses of my sixty-nine years, the grandest part is life itself and ALL that it offers. I can't think of anything that tops the moments that our children were born and their continued presence in our sphere of being. You hear that children? I love you so much!

And today was a day that brought the unknown, which was a real pisser if you don't mind the term. But it was also a day of texting the kids in an abbreviated conversation to keep them informed and to learn of their life happenings. First off were trials of my new truck, which by now you've heard me sing the praises. Well, I guess you gotta take the bad with the good, and today was part of the bad. The new Dodge diesels have an afterburner, but not like fighter jets, as they are using liquid fertilizer, not jet fuel, to burn the emissions of the engine in an afterburner. Well, something is broken in our afterburner, and a smart-ass computer programmer figured out this was a bad thing and sent a message that I had one hundred miles to go and if it wasn't fixed, I couldn't drive the truck. It started a countdown while I was in the middle of Crater Lake Park, 130 miles from anywhere. Now where in the hell do they think people are going to drive one ton, long bed pickup trucks? To go get the groceries? (Don't tell 'em I've done plenty of that lately.) What was I supposed to do?

So today (Sunday) I made a run for it, with some hope that a contingency plan or two would keep me from parking truck and trailer thirty-five miles from town on the side of the highway. Not having cell service in the park did not help my blood pressure much, so when I got service, I contacted the two closest friends or relatives, or let's say I left messages, as they might be able to provide support services, like tow the truck or the trailer off the highway. I kept my fingers crossed and moved on. As the miles piled up and the countdown kept ticking, I kept calling. Nephew John called back but was just headed back from the coast and two hundred miles away. No help there, and our friends Les and Dorleen were likely at church and not available. The countdown continued. Wouldn't be the first time I needed a tow off this highway.

Finally, as the countdown proceeded to one mile and then zero, I was informed on the computer screen that if I turned off the engine, stalled, or sat idle for any length of time, I would be limited to a top speed of 5 mph. I guess that was so that I could drive into the ditch to clear this two-lane highway. Yeah right, and tip my Hilton onto its side. I think I would have been more inclined to just park it in the middle of the lane and let Dodge answer all the questions!

But alas, there are no stop lights until the last half mile and only two stop signs to roll through, so I kept the pedal to the metal and then tried to time the lights just right to roll thru them. Didn't work! But neither did the 5 mph computer command, and so now I am ensconced in the back of the Dodge Dealer's parking lot where Tucker and I will spend the night. What a camping experience! Something I can tell my kids and my grandkids, so are ya listening?

Monday morning and I'm ready to go read the riot act with the dealer. Only then and of course, not having enough pressure on me, Rhonda decides to come into the next port of call a day early, which is tomorrow night. No pressure, just get the truck fixed, go home and pick up another horse, get more horse food, go shopping, do laundry, and then drive 150 miles to be Johnny on the spot when they arrive. And oh yeah, could you figure out how to run that new computer program in your spare time? All this while she saddles up and rides twelve miles while chatting away with our friend Gerry and taking pictures and videos of the highlights of her trip. Tough duty. Now, don't tell her I said that!

And did I tell you what a wonderful thing it has been to have friends that would drop everything and come help us out with packing through these wilderness areas of Southern Oregon? Well, I should have because they have saved the day. Hopefully, Cheyenne will be healed and can take up the slack come Wednesday of this week. I haven't seen him over the past couple of weeks and can only hope that he is mended sufficiently enough to help us out. Keep your fingers crossed, and for those of you that do, we'll take a prayer or two.

So the saga of the truck continued when I was the first one in the door come Monday morning. Oh, you don't have an appointment? Well, we might be able to find a slot tomorrow to get your truck in and take a look. I was having none of that! I explained that the truck is in your parking lot and can't go over 5 mph, and my horse trailer, sans horses, is also out there. I'm living right here. "The fellow I spoke to on Saturday didn't say anything about an appointment, just said to bring it in and they would look at it, so I'm here." That seemed to make a difference, that and the fact I had driven one-hundred-plus miles on his say-so.

About nine thirty, I was paged, and when I looked, the truck was gone. Hallelujah! News at last. Only it wasn't good news . . . seems a rodent had vandalized the truck, and oh yeah, did I remember Tucker tantrums at the snow park? ☆~}۹¿¤! was about all I had to say. "Order parts please, and I'll contact my insurance company." Parts should be in Wednesday, and the insurance gal said I'd have an appraisal in my hands in twenty-four hours. This was Monday morning.

So today is Thursday. The appraisal finally made it to the insurance company, and they authorized Dodge to do the work, but the parts aren't here. Gotta come from back east, they say. I bet they tell everyone that. I'm just hoping it's like an architect or engineer that goes by the adage of "underpromise and overdeliver," but it looks like we have a long wait on our hands.

During this time of my flailing about in the big city, Rhonda, since Tuesday, has been camped out at the trailhead along Highway 58. Now I am ensconced here at the tent to give her a break and a shower and our Tempurpedic bed at home. Gotta babysit Rio and hold down the fort for a night. Since Rio appears to have a sore spot on his back, the additional days of rest might do him some good. Me, they just make me more irritable, so it's a good thing Rhonda has taken leave of me. All I have to do is listen to traffic all night, which, if you remember, I can switch off by taking my hearing aids out. This sure isn't the way I wanted to usher in the month of August, and the delays will make it damn tough to finish this trip out to the Canadian border. At least we won't be worrying about all those fires that have sprung up this past week. Poor folks that are catching the brunt of those episodes. Broken truck doesn't seem nearly so bad in comparison, and we ought to know, having endured our own fire some nine years ago.

So sitting alongside the highway isn't all bad. Just had a conversation with a gentleman headed out onto the trail to make it to a lake and fish for a bit, like three days. Come to find out he has a body shop not far from here (sixty miles isn't far) and was knowledgeable about rodents and the like. MOTHBALLS! He said the critters don't like mothballs and that I need to distribute them around the undercarriage to discourage any further transgression. Yahoo! And another hallelujah! I don't need to stand guard with a shotgun or bazooka. About time something goes our way.

So while at home and like most other times during this traverse of the countryside, I got to thinking about the days ahead of us. Surely, I would like to join m'lady on this ride, if at all possible. The obstacle to us actually doing so is . . . ? Who's going to drive the truck? Well, we will be headed into Washington in the not-too-distant future, and guess who has a residence in that fair state and, hopefully, time to help us out? I'm sure a few of you were able to answer that puzzle as the relation is all too familiar. Rhonda's dad, Rod, lives in Wenatchee, Washington and, after a short phone conversation, agreed that this might be a possible scenario if we can pin down a time and place. Easier said than done, as this week has just shown us. We are losing nearly a week of trail time, so when we get to Central Washington is anyone's guess. We just hope we make it that far. I could ride with Rhonda from Snoqualmie Pass to Stevens Pass! Four days on the trail, whoopee! Gotta have positive thoughts to keep going and create all these memories! Thanks, Dad.

So Tucker has forsaken his blankie and is hunkered down in the crook of a fallen log. Other than a lone deer, there has not been anything to chase but flies and yellow jackets, so he is about as bored as I am. Maybe time for a little lunch and then a short walk. Can't go far because there is a simple fact of a valuable horse tied in our midst and about $1,000 in supplies under the rain fly of our tent. I think I'm going to leave you now and take up on that computer program I was supposed to learn a while back.

Hope your days are more productive, less noisy, or at least more fun over this coming weekend. Be it known that we are thinking of you with love in our hearts and wishing you peace and happiness.

Pat, Rhonda, Rio, and Tucker

(Sent from my US cellular smartphone)

Nearing the end of Gerry's team help.

The boys joke about the trail,
"We don't have to go up there, do we"?

PART

25

August 15, 2015

My Fellow Americans and all you friends and family too!

We are on the road again, yahoo! And on the trail again! Wahoo! The last week and a half has been a severe trial on our patience and perseverance, but persevere we will. Kind of like the hikers, just keep putting one foot in front of the other.

I did manage to get in a couple rounds of nine-hole golf and some much-needed eradication of noxious weeds on our place over the past week. Not the most romantic use of my spare time, but it did make me feel better. Rhonda kept busy paying bills over the internet and then mapping out her course for the remainder of this journey. Particularly in regard to several fires in Washington and some nasty trail go- arounds. You've probably heard a great deal about the fire near Lake Chelan and the town of Stehekin. I'm saddened as I remember visiting this location by travelling on the ferry from the south end of the lake. It was one of the perks I had as a project manager of land survey work for the Federal Highway Administration who had a job for us to accomplish near Stehekin. Poor crews had to stay in the lodge at the north end of the lake, oh darn. I forget how we picked which crews got to go do the work, but it must have been something like a lottery, or fistfight or something.

So back to the PCT, a portion of the trail was being routed onto an existing and parallel trail to avoid an old burn where they were having trouble maintaining the trail and keeping it safe. So now the reroute is involved in the fire, so it is closed. So a new go-around is in use until, so I've heard, a hot-shot crew can reopen one trail or the other. (Boy, that's a lot of *so*s) Not sure if that is a "fire" hot-shot crew or a "trail" crew. As I understand it, the original go-around was not safe for stock use, so we were going around anyway. So be it! (Just had to have another *so*.)

Then there is another section of trail that stock users are being warned off due to the nature of the trail itself and the terrain it passes over. A narrow trail on loose rock along a hog back ridge, with steep side slopes on each side that go for hundreds if not thousands of feet. I'm told the hikers don't like it much either unless you are the mountaineering type that can hang from a rope on the face of Yosemite's half dome and talk to your family on the phone. Just watching the ad on TV sends shudders down my spine. Rhonda will avoid the area called Goat Rocks (aptly named) and be exiting the trail for a thirty-mile drive around as there are not any parallel trails. If this journey had been nearing completion and in whole, then there would be no faltering or choices made, only to go forward, young lady, until it's all done. But it is what it is!

All the foregoing will be prior to meeting up with and hopefully being assisted by Dad (Rhonda's and mine because I adopted him). She and I are hoping to travel together on horseback from Snoqualmie Pass to Stevens Pass while Dad ferries our truck and the Hilton around on the road system. We are both very much looking forward to this episode on the trail. Hopefully, all three horses will be healthy and ready to do this.

Speaking of which, Cheyenne is on the trail today with Rio in the lead with Rhonda on his back. Or at least that's the way they left here. Rhonda ponied (led) Cheyenne yesterday out of our campsite at the snow park on Highway 58 without any gear on his back to see how he could manage the trail. He appeared to do fine, but got really tired or really sore, we don't know which. He didn't like uphill, and luckily, there wasn't much of that between where he started fussing and where the Hilton was. However, he didn't show any severe signs when he arrived, eating and drinking well, walking and standing straight and being alert. We are trying him on a light pack today and a shorter haul with very little uphill involved. More resting and grazing stops also. It's really unfortunate, but if he doesn't go, then we don't go, as Rhonda has several overnights on the trail coming up and including tonight. Rio just can't handle or tote an overnight package along with Rhonda, and like I previously mentioned, Rhonda is not into walking that far. This trip will be interesting as Rio adjusts to leading another horse instead of being the follower. We will keep our fingers crossed that Cheyenne can get himself back into shape and that the muscles will heal while being used in this fashion. His injury is such that he is not rideable. We will know a lot more tomorrow night when Rhonda and the boys trudge (I obviously like that word) down to the Hilton.

Today I am hanging out, parked near the graveled forest road that crosses the crest of the Cascades, and passes very near to Charlton Lake. Tucker and I will take a leisure walk around a portion of the lake and then hitch up the Hilton and move on towards tomorrow's meeting point at the Elk Lake trailhead. While this is a pleasant place amongst the fir trees, I don't have cell service and thence communication with m'lady, should she need my help over the next thirty-six hours. So skip the fishing and the swimming and move on, but wait . . . we are going to what? Why, Elk Lake, and surely they must have fish there too or in one of the other nearby lakes. I can only hope now, can't I? I'm not sure Tucker cares as long as he can get into the shade as it is going to be a scorcher the next few days. Cooler up here in the mountains, but his black coat just absorbs those sunrays and the heat. Right now, he is under the Hilton and loving it. We are just about packed up, so we'll leave you folks for a bit as we hike along the lake front.

Boy, where have I been? Not looking at the forecast, that's for sure. Parked overnight at Six Lakes trailhead, only because it was handy and the timing was right. Pleasant-enough spot, so Tucker and I had a leisurely dinner and sailed off to never-never land at an early time.

Awoke this morning to the sound of a pickup and horse trailer pulling into the lot. I suppose it's time to rise and shine, put on boots, and saunter over to the outhouse. Saunter 'cause I gotta be cool with another horse person in the vicinity. Don't recognize the trailer or the horse and my vision's not good enough to discern if the rider-to-be is man or woman. Hey, it's a chilly thirty-five degrees out, so I didn't spend a lot of time gawking at my new neighbor. Got coffee brewing so I can go offer some and decide then. Only I got short stopped by another early arrival and come to find out by virtue of an introductory question, "You part of the group that's going to pack our gear up the mountain?" The answer was a resounding "No, sir." But I did come to find out that there was a volunteer work party afoot to put up signs at some of the lakes and trail junctions. Right up my alley when I have horses! But alas, not today.

About that time, several more cars show up with worker bees coming from every doorway, and then a familiar sight of a couple of trailers and rigs I recognize. Hey, we are not so far from home after all! Told you I recognize rigs before people, but with Rhonda, it is their mounts first. So being a little starved for human interaction, Lane and Linda and Buck get to hear the latest in our episodes. Sure is nice when folks are willing to listen, and of course, I get to hear all the local gossip and adventures they are into. Buck gets busy packing up all the digging tools, saws, wedges, hammers, and whatever is needed to cut down trees, peel them, place them into the ground, and mount a sign upon them.

Lane and I are chatting when I look over and see Linda outfitting their mules with some periphery gear, horn bags and saddlebags and the like. Now Lane tells me that Linda is the Wrangler and how I can relate, all the while wondering how he coaxed her into that role. Maybe I should get out a mirror. They are not packing any work gear and are basically along for the ride to help with the labor and offer good cheer as the worker bees are all afoot, backpacks and all. Lane will eventually help with 150 pounds of garbage that has been collected from around a few of the wilderness lakes. What makes people think that leaving their garbage in the wilderness is okay? Somebody actually left a deflated float tube, like I want to gaze at it while enjoying the ambiance of a mountain lake. Maybe the same guy that throws his beer cans out the window down the street from our place, but then again, I wouldn't expect him to be in the wilds of the Cascade Range. Ah hell, quit your bitchin' Pat and pick up those cans.

So (aha, another one) this morning, we packed up and left our friends to their likely duties, saying our goodbyes and reminding them to look for Rhonda when they cross the PCT. I have their assurances they will. Tucker and I are off to the Elk Lake trailhead just off the Cascade Lake's highway and only about forty miles from Bend. I expect Rhonda to arrive early this afternoon, so I'd better be there. Hope there is room as I know it's a pretty small trailhead. Rhonda and the boys stretched out yesterday's ride, probably to find graze or water near the trail, leaving a short day today. Good plan, and with a rest day tomorrow, the horses should be in good shape to go forth for the next forty-plus miles, leaving here on Sunday.

While here at the Elk Lake trailhead, I happened across two other young at heart OETers from Central Oregon, leading to lengthy talks about horses, people, and of course, Rhonda's ride. One of the ladies is a staunch supporter of the trail Pacific Crest Trail Association and would have stayed all afternoon I suspect but had other commitments, and it so happened that I did also. Still needed to get the high line up and cleared for easy access by the horses and get the Hilton leveled out and unhooked so I could go get some more water at the lodge across the highway and next to the lake. With that, my chores will be done, and I can rest easy until the crew shows up.

It's been a grey day all day with the temperature hovering around fifty degrees, and with the breeze, it is downright cold. With a sweatshirt on, I was still hunkered down inside the Hilton until Tucker jumped up and stood panting at the door. 'Twas a sure sign that horses were afoot, and sure enough, when we exited and walked to the kiosk, they were on their way out of the woods. Always a good feeling to know they are safe and sound and especially at a time in the day to lie back and relax a bit. Which wasn't very long because our friends had decided to take me up on a request to come visit for a spell.

Lane and Linda pulled that all-too-familiar trailer by our window, and it was time for hugs once again. Come to find out that they had crossed paths with Rhonda when they rode in to get the garbage, had a short chat, and each departed to their own commitments. Took each of them about equal time to get down off the mountain on separate trails. So good to see them again, though the visit was shortened by our newly arrived but unsavory neighbors. I was tending to some of the horse chores to get them settled on the high line and thus missed the excitement, but as the story goes, these new arrivals set up another tent and were about to light up a campfire to cook their dinner. Now, everyone, keep this in mind: the fire danger limit has been in the extreme phase for well over a month, and it doesn't take a rocket scientist to see and hear about all the forest fires in the western states, so Rhonda immediately told them in no uncertain terms that there would be no fire. Hooray for Rhonda! Cops will be called if they persist.

Unfortunately, when they whined that they just had to cook their chicken, Rhonda volunteered, being the nicest human being on this planet. And that was my introduction to the whole melee when I entered the Hilton and saw a pile of chicken on the stove. "Where'd that come from?" I asked, expecting her to say that Lane and Linda had brought it for dinner but instead got the forgoing tale. You could hear cuss words aplenty about that time as Rhonda was not very happy. It seems the young lass from next door, with plenty of sass, had the nerve to bring her veggie burger over for Rhonda to cook with the chicken. Thought it looked a little weird seeing a cardboard package of veggie burgers perched on top the chicken. Rhonda's way to say, "Go to hell." Remind me not to piss her off when cooking dinner.

Remember a few months ago when I introduced our unsavory neighbors along the Whitewater Canyon? Well, Rhonda was getting the same vibes from these folks, meth addicts or whatever, and it only took us fifteen minutes to pack everything up and leave this scene. Rhonda was steaming because of the loss of her quiet evening and a personable chat with our friends, but fortunately, we only had three miles to travel and we were right back in the spot where I had camped the night before. Inconvenient but a whole lot safer than staying where we were. Unfortunate because we will have to go right back there tomorrow morning to get m'lady back onto the trail. I won't be staying either, and if we are the lucky ones, those folks will be gone also.

Such are the highlights of travel these days, but the odds have been on our side with twenty good encounters to everyone that is hinky in some way. I am most thankful for that. Today we are at that "other" trailhead and have a constantly changing scene as young and old folks alike come to hike into the woods. At last count, there were forty cars in the parking lot, some arriving and some leaving, with a great many staying for the weekend. The young outnumber the old 4:1 at least, which I find as a good sign that not all is lost with this generation, equating the longing for the outdoors to be a good thing in this electronic and urbanized world we live in. I just might be a bit biased if you consider the makeup of my career and nature of our families trek through life. Wouldn't trade it for anything.

Well, the day is fast coming to an end, and I need to push Rhonda into getting energized and go to the local lodge and take a shower and on the way out pick up some burgers to go. It's a zero day, and the cook gets to zero out too. Or is that zone out? I'm looking forward to a mellow evening of burgers and wine, but unfortunately, no campfire. I hope you have a wonderful evening as well and a very pleasant Sunday.

Until next time, we wish you the best, with peace and happiness permeating your every moment. Love to you all!

Pat and Rhonda

(Sent from my US cellular smartphone)

Cheyenne gets to munch some breakfast along the trail.

There are many lakes in the high country of the Cascades.

I met Rhonda and we tent camped together at Lava Camp Lake.

PART

26

August 29, 2015

Good afternoon, everyone, from the land of sunshine and bees.

Yellow jackets everywhere, and now Tucker has found a new prey to hunt. I think he hates them from the look on his face and the aggression he shows. Can't say I feel the same way, having grown up with them all around us, especially at Blue Lake, where we spent many a summer month. The location was in Lake County, Northern California, and the family would set up a summer tent camp, with canvas tarps hung from ropes to establish our campsite boundary. 'Twas the place I learned to swim, and I was pretty decent at it, having received a life-saving certificate from the Red Cross but one that I could not use because I was too young. Those were very memorable times, swimming and fishing most days and hanging out at the dance hall at night. I remember there was a family there—the Cantwells, I think—that had three daughters about the same age as my brothers and yours truly. Again, I was young, but I remember the very beginnings of summer romance.

What I remember about the bees was that they would swarm all over your dinner plate, but you didn't want to be too aggressive in shooing them away. Surefire way to get stung. Now Rhonda, being Alaska bred and born, does not have that kind of understanding with these little critters. In fact, I don't really remember seeing one in the fifteen-plus years I was up in Alaska; so I can see why, not having the initiation, Rhonda would have such a lack of tolerance now. Enough competition with two brothers at mealtime to have to put up with mini jets in yellow and black.

So what does this have to do with The Journey? Not much other than to highlight the fact that Tucker and I have been spending many a day and night communing with nature along the trail and campsites we have found to our liking, as well as being home for a few days. I can't say that I am bored because that seldom happens with me, if ever, but I'm not doing a whole heck of a lot either. Such is the plight of the Wrangler and his sidekick as m'lady goes trippin' down the trail. Since getting the truck fixed and leaving Highway 58 in the dust behind us, we have seen Rhonda a total of six nights while she has travelled over 143 miles by trail in twelve days. That's with two "0" days spent with us. Pretty good rate of movement averaging slightly more than fourteen miles per day of riding and also considering that she camped out on the trail seven nights during that span. Gutsy!

One of our friends, Duane, cautioned me to tell Rhonda to be careful along the backside of Three Fingered Jack mountain as the going gets pretty rough. I chose not to say anything because, by now, Rhonda has seen the worst and probably the best in the way of trail conditions. From the video Rhonda took as she crossed over Forester Pass, I don't think any portion of the trail will intimidate her or cause her undue concern unless it is totally unsafe. I spoke about such a place in part 25, and we plan to definitely skip over it. As she said over dinner last night, she can't be alarmed by difficult conditions, or she shouldn't even be out here because by now she has passed over hundreds of miles that the average trail rider would consider difficult or dangerous. She is of the mind-set that she has good mounts, and she trusts them to stay on the trail while she rides them through and over it. She is not one to dismount and travel those intimidating stretches on foot but instead to use her balance and savvy along with the horses' surefootedness to master the trail conditions. Again, why would she wish to tackle this monstrous endeavor if she didn't have that kind of relationship between horse and rider? Besides which, being on foot would most assuredly introduce another element into the mix for the horse, with his limited brainpower, to have to consider with every step, change in direction or obstacle encounter. Why complicate things? For instance, I have been riding Cheyenne for fifteen years on trails, roads, and cross-country for what may total four thousand miles. I have walked in front of him, with him in tow on a lead rope for, what, maybe thirty miles in fifteen years. We are a team with me on his back, and we are two unpredictable individuals with me on the ground. Enough said.

Now the colt Rio was and has been a different story, and Rhonda has taken the necessary precautions because of it. He is five years old and has had someone on his back for only the past fifteen months, and for nine of those months, he and she (Rhonda) were flatlanders, riding in training sessions on our own property. Rio had seen the mountains and some difficult trails, but only in tow behind Liz or Cheyenne as a packhorse hauling some of our gear. Not all of it (gear) because he was still a young colt, and we didn't want to sour him. And you wouldn't recognize him today, a well-muscled young horse. Small in stature but big in heart and go-power.

Mind you, he is still a colt but a well-heeled young horse with sound mind. He is really amazing. We took him with us to Southern California in order to give him some experience whenever possible and naturally because we didn't know what else to do. Rhonda probably rode him a total of sixty to seventy miles in the first six hundred miles it took to get to Walker Pass. She picked the easiest, shortest stretches to see how he would do, and he handled it well. He was used as a packhorse many more miles, as we switched horses around to rest them for various stretches, thus taking fewer zero days and maintaining the fifteen-mile average we considered necessary to complete the journey in a timely fashion.

Each day, whether for Rhonda or myself, is a totally new experience, bringing with it new challenges and new triumphs as she moves up the trail. For me, those experiences can resemble past ones, and I can negotiate the day with some aplomb and assurance that everything will be just fine. For m'lady, the opposite is true because every footfall is upon new ground, every bend in the trail providing a new vista not seen by anyone before in quite the same way and every moment on the trail fret with potential disaster. South Lake Tahoe was one of those moments when, if you had asked me, I would have said that portion of the trail should be relatively safe, with all the attention this area should have been fostering by virtue of its popularity. How wrong I was.

We didn't have Rio at that time because we felt his inexperience could prove to be hazardous on the bulk of hazardous trails. We knew the trail through the Sierras would present a whole new series of challenges and larger-than-life trail obstacles. We opted for experience as in "been there, done that." So much for plans, eh! And so Rio found himself back in the mix, only this time strictly as a packhorse since the princes couldn't engage her brain in that role. He did remarkably well, following the leader over trails I'm not sure I would be willing to hike on, let alone travel astride Cheyenne. Until one day Liz just couldn't go on, and the threesome came out of those mountains to welcoming arms, barks, and the big bad Hilton. M'lady having said, "I'm done!"

I guess now we know what those words meant as Rhonda has meandered over 350 miles of the PCT in Oregon, with only one hundred miles remaining between here and the Columbia River. And she has been aboard Rio the entire time, and he has shown his mettle, stamina, and mental strength to take it all on and in stride. Two days ago, the three of them (Rhonda, Rio, and Cheyenne) crossed Whitewater Creek off the western slopes of Mt. Jefferson, a glacier-fed and silty stream flowing over boulders and between steep banks. After two aborted tries, they made it with a loud "Yahoo!" and kept right on moving to camp out near Russell Lake, where they encountered thru hikers that were aghast that they even attempted, let alone, made it past that obstacle. I don't exactly remember the words, but Rio has been measured and found worthy. Rhonda's trust in him has solidified, and his confidence has soared because of it. While Rhonda still wears the crash helmet whenever riding Rio, she believes he is ready to go almost anywhere, that is if he could leave his colt mentality behind. For those of you that have raised teenagers, the term *space case* comes to mind.

So now you know that Rhonda has ridden 143 miles through Central Oregon while, hmm, what was it that I was doing? Well, I have put another seven hundred miles on our new Dodge because there are no straight lines that parallel the trail. I've been home for three days in order to catch up with various aspects, such as laundry, resupplying us with groceries, getting Liz shod, mapping out our course of action should the fires in Washington still be a threat when we arrive and locating feed stores near our route that can supply us with the horse food in use. Do you realize that we have changed our horse feeding regimen five times during this trip? If there were anything that I could wish for and get a do-over that would be the one. I know I've complained about it, and without having this experience, I'm not sure we could have figured it out from the beginning. Our past experiences just didn't go far enough in preparing us mentally for what we needed to do.

We now know that our horses should have been receiving way more calories for the energy they were expending. All the books tell us what the hikers go thru in order to maintain themselves, but for some reason, this never really registered in our brains, enabling us to extrapolate what that would mean for our horses. We are now feeding a very high-quality feed, and lots of it, meant for competition horses. Hell, we're not competing; we are just trail riding! Yeah, right. Tell that to our three heroes, and they'll probably say that it's about time they get the fat and protein it takes to keep on going, day in and day out. It has taken Liz six weeks to recover from the strenuous work and ups and downs of the Sierras, and while not at peak form, she was brought back to the trail yesterday. She departed camp this morning with Rhonda astride and Rio in tow. Cheyenne gets to rest for a few days, having done his job very well over the past twelve days, packing horse food and camping gear along the trail. His body isn't back to normal after the accident, but he seems to have recovered most of his strength and stamina and definitely likes the new feeding regimen. Hooray for the good guys.

Tomorrow I get to go a hundred miles out of my way to find a tire shop and replace the trailer tire that blew as I was halfway here last night. Went forty miles without a spare because a certain young lady was counting on me—that and all the tire stores were already closed. Last ten miles was a washboard gravel road that didn't help my nerves much, but we made it. Now I have two more days to make it to the next meeting spot, Clackamas Horse Camp. There we hope to meet up with the kids and a couple of friends for an evening of pizza, tall tales, and a glass or two of Merlot. Can't get much better than that!

So it is now tomorrow and yesterday Rhonda arrived a day early to Clackamas Horse Camp. Luckily, I was still on the road, new tire and all, and got the text message that she didn't like the prearranged camp spot, and since it was so early, she wanted to step up the pace and take a day out of the ride by doing it all this day. Sounded good to me, and I agreed to meet her a day early. As I said, luckily, she reached me because I was twenty minutes from being out of cell phone coverage and parked at a totally different location for the night. All's well that ends well.

And tonight, we reverse roles as I get to sleep in a tent and eat freeze-dried food and Rhonda gets to haul two geldings back to the barn to get new shoes put on. My guess is that she might be eating Mexican out and then just enjoying a hot shower, air conditioning, and a comfy bed you don't have to climb into. I think she deserves it. Unfortunately, she has to awaken and get up early because the farrier is arriving at 7:00 a.m. Not her forte! But it gives her time to finish up our shopping list and get back here to entertain our visitors for the evening.

Saturday begins the race to the river, only five more days to go in Oregon and then it's cross over the Bridge of the Gods and arrive in Washington ready to cover some miles. A long ways to go and not much time to do it, but we'll give it the all-American try! For now, it's rest easy and enjoy our family and visitors tomorrow evening and thence each and every day thereafter as it brings new adventure and future memories to nourish.

I hope all of you are having a day to relish and remember, with friends, family, or merely your own thoughts as you move on down the trail. Isn't it a precious time? Our love to all of you wherever you may be and peace be with you.

Pat, Rhonda, Tucker, Liz, Cheyenne, and Rio

(Sent from my US cellular smartphone)

Rhonda had to saw this one. No way around it.

Our guys graze near Mt. Jefferson.

Cheyenne takes a good look. "I don't want to go down there!"

The pair prepare to head to lower ground and in
2 days will be at Clackamas Horse Camp.

PART

27

September 5, 2015

Howdy, howdy!

Boy, that reminds me of when I was a little tyke and couldn't wait for *Howdy Doody Time* to show on TV. Musta been a favorite to have lingered in the recesses of this old mind all this time.

Boy, last night was an eye-opener as I awakened to the sound of drizzle on the tent fly. And of course, at my age, there was something else nagging at my miniscule brain. Damned if I didn't have to get up and go check on Lizzy in her very own quarters, make sure everything was properly covered, and then tighten up that rain fly before hitting the sack once again. I guess Tucker figured I had it covered because he didn't move a muscle off that blanket of his, and of course, he's only two years old!

And a happy good morning to all of you. I hope you are having a wonderful summer of sun and fun, or at least making the best of what comes your way.

This morning, I have a whole new perspective on life and especially life in a tent, sleeping on an eighteen-inch-wide air mattress in a comfy sleeping bag. Now I said the bag was comfy, not necessarily myself. Ten years ago, I awoke one morning and must have said, "Let's go buy a Hilton," and now I know why. I'm six feet and two inches and the mattress is six feet. I forgot my pillow! And the tent is a pup tent, which merely means you've got to be a puppy or you don't fit. I can't even sit up in it without hitting my head, and if any of you have used these nylon tents, hitting the wall or roof when it is raining is not something you want to do, unless you want an early shower. So being a contortionist at sixty-nine years of age is nearly mandatory in order to put a jacket on and climb into shoes you left just outside the doorway in the foyer. Who needs pants at this hour of the night? And a-trippin' we go. The only noise Liz is making is a contented snore, which is a good thing.

Rhonda had asked me if I had or needed a flashlight. To which I had hurriedly noted that no as I typically have several, which I now remember are in the truck. She asked me if I needed batteries, and of course, the answer was asserted the same, as I am always well prepared. I have spare batteries in both my day pack and my lunch bag, double As to fit those flashlights in the truck. Aha, I do find one of the newer LED lights in my lunch box, so I'm all set, that is if you have good night vision because these batteries are shot. All I need are some triple As, which are residing eighty miles from here in the Hilton. I'm starting to understand why Rhonda goes over and over her preparations for each trip away from truck and Hilton. Luckily, I don't have far to go because I know there is a bush just around the corner. Whew! And the rain had stopped!

But my respect for Rhonda's endeavor continues to grow when I awaken in the early morning to a crook in my neck and an ache in my lower back. Oh, do I really have to get up? Reminds me of being a teenager and having the same thought, albeit for different reasons. But YES, you do! As Lizzy is pawing and Tucker is sitting, eyeing the zippered door, letting me know that he is young but not "super dog," and please can I go out now? My first thought is that, egad, Rhonda is doing this all the time, and she has two horses and no fenced-in stall. No wonder she lights up like a Roman candle each time she sees the Hilton! And here I thought it was me. Love is bliss after forty years of marriage.

So up and at 'em, I feed Lizzy her grain and go in search of the outhouse potty, which has become Tucker's signal that we are on the move. He has learned the word and takes off like a bullet in that direction as the early morning hunt is on. What four-legged creature awaits him in them thar woods. Thankfully, we are the only ones in the campground at the moment, or he would have to be on leash. This will become a contentious issue this afternoon as more campers start arriving for the weekend and lay claim to what is already Tucker's turf and hunting grounds. He will lay claim as if it is home, and with the voice of a critter three times his size, he will let each and every one know that they are trespassing. But that's this afternoon, and this is the morning hunt as I take the morning stroll. What I notice and have noticed on prior occasions is that Tucker suffers from a lack of vertical stature. In other words, he's short. So I see the rabbit a hundred feet away, tiptoeing into the tulips, and he is totally unaware. To compensate, Tucker has extraordinary hearing and smell sensors that he must rely upon. But the rabbit knows this, and thus the tiptoe shuffle is in the other direction.

So having nothing else to think about, my mind begins to conjure up an evolutionary hypothesis. See, I'm reading one of James A. Michener's novels, *Centennial*, about the beginnings of earth and time and how many of the evidences of prior epochs in Earth's history are told through the archeological and geological finds of nineteenth, twentieth, and twenty-first centuries in and around the town of Centennial, Colorado. My theory that I can now foist upon you, an unsuspecting reader, is that man evolved to be upright because as a hunter he could thence see further than his brethren on all fours, allowing him to see that prey before they dispersed into hiding. And because of this, he was more successful and lived longer due to his newfound prowess as a hunter. Unfortunately, it also meant that he no longer needed exceptional smell or hearing senses, so they started to atrophy. You could extrapolate this characteristic to include additional brainpower in order to assimilate the knowledge that a critter was there but how to use this knowledge to one's advantage. In other words, he had to strategize the hunt in order to be truly successful. And now you see what a bored hunter who is relegated to seasons and regulatory constraints does with his spare time. It's noon and time for lunch, so I'm gonna go hunt for my lunch box. What are we evolving into now?

How about a wrangler who makes sure that the food is there when needed for all parties? I like to go hunting with my horse as a companion and mount and pack animal. So am I reverting to a historical model in the genetic line, or am I the future? Kind of a regressed Mad Max? Or what was that book series a few years ago that dwelt with a magnetic or electric storm that froze all modern conveniences and society reverted to the sixteenth-century mode of operation and feudal society? Am I the only one that sometimes wonders if I wasn't born in the wrong century? Some of you, young folks, may figure that your century is still to come. Wondering doesn't mean we have to be malcontents, just trying to figure out what's in store for us or what may lie ahead.

On the lighter side, I've been out of the picture for a few days, whiling away my time in some of the remote parts of Oregon where there is no cell service. Who won the baseball game? Has the pro-football regular season started? Is the FedEx Cup in golf determined? Who's traded whom for what? All those really important aspects of the sports world, without even touching upon fantasy football that I know Colin is tuned up for. And then there is the stock market tumbling along its merry way regardless of what you or I may think of our societal and economic pressures that in the past would have been a bell weather of our position. Now it is just another tool for someone to manipulate regardless of the outcome, and we, as participants, are stuck with what others have determined to be in their, not our, best interest. Ooh, I'd better stop.

You could probably guess, if you were a psychologist, that it is pouring down rain out and we are stuck in the Hilton. But not before we had a wonderful evening last night with our children and grandchildren and again this morning as Nicole and family had camped out with us. We are fortunate to have a wonderful extended family that, of course, includes many of you. We love you all.

And the time warp continues as I move on just as Rhonda moves down the trail. We were almost lucky when, as Saturday moved past the farewells to kids and grandkids, the rain subsided, and we grasped the notion that our zero day had ended and it was time to go—north that is. 'Twas nice to have a horse camp with corrals for the beasties and running water (yeah, I had to run for it) together with an outhouse and a level parking pad for the Hilton. Why the outhouse when we have facilities in the Hilton? Well, I found out long ago that a dump station for sewer is not common in the mountains of whichever state we are travelling in, so being conservative of our use of potable water and its outgo was a prudent thing to do. Mind you, we still use the facilities but just not recklessly. Whoa, what got me on this bent? Heaven only knows because now it is a week later and not a word written to you, folks.

I'd apologize, but I'm just too pleased to regress and quibble about the little things. You see, Rhonda has finished the trek across Oregon, and this morning, she left on the first leg of Washington. Wowie-Zowie! Another 450 miles behind us.

Finishing Oregon wasn't on a pleasant note either as she rode her last day in the rain. And I mean pouring-down rain as it can and often does in Oregon. It seems fall has arrived all too early in our book, but we knew it was inevitable. Maybe an Indian summer is in store for us. We can hope, can't we? Anyway, let me digress a bit and tell you all the happenings over this week.

After leaving Clackamas horse camp, it was on to the Frog Lake trailhead next to Highway 26. It was Lizzy's turn to cover some ground, and since they would see me this evening, the load was light. This is the way Rhonda would love to travel all the time, but then where would the challenge be? Me, I just had to clean up the campground and meander the roadways to the next stopping point. Easy-peasy. And while the day stayed cloudy, it was free of rain, and I'm sure it was a pleasant ride, especially with the Hilton, waiting and the high line set up with a hay net hanging for Liz.

Well, good days don't always end with good nights as it pelted us something awful all night long. Felt sorry for the critters standing out in it with no cover, but as many of you know, they'd probably be standing out there even if they had cover. Getting up and out of the covers was a struggle that morning, but the smell of coffee got me reenergized to go out and feed. This was a "go" day, as we or should I say m'lady can't be wasting an opportunity to get miles ahead, not if we hold dear that end goal of the Canadian border. Luck was with us as we found a window of opportunity to saddle up Cheyenne and test him in the riding mode, not just packing. Rhonda was off to Timberline Lodge on the upper slopes of Mt. Hood, where I would pick her up. Originally, I had hoped and planned to park the Hilton up near the lodge, have a luxurious dinner, and possibly even stay the night under a stationary roof, but this was not to be. I was told with no uncertain terms that this could not happen as it would violate the terms of their lease with the Forest Service. It was too late to research this option, so it was onward to find another place to rest our weary bones. Maybe there will be a day when we go there, but it won't be this one. Six miles later, we were back on the highway and searching for a likely parking spot, hopefully legal. And along came another snow park, which is always legal as long as you have a forest pass, which we get gratuitously as a reward for our volunteer work each year. Trilium Lake, here we are.

The next morning showed some clearing sky, and so it was back up to Timberline to let Rhonda and Rio off for another long day ride of seventeen miles. I would be at the end at the trailhead on Lolo Pass, with facilities set up and ready. This stretch has been touted as one of the toughest in Oregon, cruising around the big mountain on steep side slopes with a narrow trail across the scree slopes. Zigzag canyon lays in the middle and a couple of treacherous river crossings as well. Turns out the crossings were a piece of cake as Oregon has had its share of drought and the steep side slopes are just part of the trek. As Rhonda has noted, this trail should be called the Pacific Side Slope Trail! The arrival at Lolo Pass was without incident, unless you count the meeting up with a fellow traveler.

And not a PCTer but another old fart like me with a suburban and cargo trailer. Rick was his name, and he had all sorts of goods in that trailer, including a 200 CC motorcycle geared for travelling the mountain/gravel roads. He was from New Hampshire and had been travelling for months as a newly retired old guy. He had discovered what I and many others have known for a long time, that if you are conservative in where you stay, like in the trailer, and where you eat, like out of the cooler or off the camp stove, you can live pretty cheaply. Gas, food, and an occasional treat while staying in dispersed campsites on federal land and you can just keep going and going, like the Energizer bunny. Rick embraced Rhonda's travels and just had to have a picture to put onto his Facebook page. Now if I only knew how to do Facebook other than to look at stuff.

The next day, after Rhonda had headed into the hinterlands with the intent of camping for a single night on the trail with just Liz, he stopped by to see me. Seems that he had been out riding the motorcycle and gone down the same road I intended to leave on when he encountered a construction site, with a crew building a new bridge. Rick was concerned that I would not be able to negotiate the detour and temporary bridge, so he returned and offered to drive down there and let me see for myself. While I wasn't too worried, it seemed like a prudent quest rather than to be stuck with no turnaround in sight. And while it wasn't a piece of cake, it was doable, and I thanked him profusely upon departing and suggested a few tourists' sightseeing spots along the Columbia River, should he follow our path. We said goodbye to another pleasant encounter.

Wow, the Oregon border is now in my sights as I headed for the historic river highway for the Lewis and Clark expedition that took them to the Pacific. Looks a lot different today, what with all the dams and lakes, but the gorge is still rather a spectacular vista. I would soon see it all, but first, I must find a place to stay. Heavy tourist destinations are not necessarily the most friendly or accommodating to horses and their companions. Didn't think this would be a problem because we knew of a horse camp real close to Cascade Locks, the Bridge of the Gods, and our way across the river and a part of the PCT. But to my dismay, Herman Creek horse camp was closed due to some hazardous trees with some sort of root rot disease. I kinda wanted to pester them into letting us park nearby and just use the corrals, but on second thought, being awakened by crashing trees did not seem like a sensible plan. Further inquiry helped me to find another trailhead / horse camp across the river and eight to nine miles westerly, and the hunt was on. Yahoo! I found it, and while a bit costly, it was far better than being nestled next to the freeway. Been there and done that. Now to figure out where I would find Rhonda and be able to pick her up on the morrow.

Piece of cake as there is a small park on the Oregon side, right at the trail, and I could park the rig, Hilton and all, on the main drag and walk up to greet m'lady. Just what Tucker and I did. It was celebration time.

Celebrate another day of livin'! Celebrate another day of life! And so we did, all the while thinking of Three Dog Night!

Two of our OET club members and now friends asked if they could join us and bring us dinner. Now if you ever hear of me turning down such an offer, just cart me off to the loony bin because I'm surely off my rocker. We enjoyed a wonderful meal brought to us by Barb and Dave and chatted until nearly dark. Not nearly enough time to relate all the stories or to expand upon the realities, but surely a time of enjoyment and friendship making. Barb and Dave, we hope to see you again soon.

So now we only have 507 miles to go, or after today, make that 487 miles. Timing of our travels will determine if we actually traverse all that. As I'm sure you know, the state of Washington is riddled by fires, many of which lay before us and very near the trail. We know of one 15-mile stretch that is closed and coupling that with the treacherous Goat Rocks area, we will bypass nearly 50 miles of trail. Then there is the fire near Lake Chelan that has trail traffic detoured to a trail that is not for stock, and thus another go-around. And lastly, the fire near Twisp has Highway 20 closed, and thus we cannot resupply ourselves as we head for the border. Since that is weeks away, we will just have to wait and see. Rhonda and I still have our hopes up to be able to ride together along the stretch of trail from Snoqualmie Pass on Highway 90 to Stevens Pass, a four-day pack trip. We are keeping our fingers crossed.

And you know, I'd better get along up the roads to the trail junction, or none of the above will happen. Twenty miles makes for a long day, and the thought of a Hilton will keep you going that extra mile, so I'd just better be there. We will be out of touch for several days as we trek around Mt. Adams, so be patient and keep us in your hearts and minds, as we do you.

Please see the attached photo of Rhonda departing Timberline with new snow on the mountain and a glorious day ahead of her. (Look to the upper left between the trees.) Hugs, kisses, and blessings to you all.

Pat and Tucker

(Sent from my US cellular smartphone)

And Rio gets to go around Mt. Hood on some of
the most Treacherous trail in Oregon.

Rhonda and Liz at the Bridge of the Gods.
We are done with Oregon!

M'lady is back on the trail with Rio.
Washington may not be ready but here we come.

We have our sights on Mt. Adams a few days in the future.

PART

28

September 16, 2015

Hiya, all!

This message is coming to you in what seems to me a tardy fashion. Been quite a while since I have written, and I'm not sure why other than I've been in kind of a funk for a bit. Started back awhile, about the time I sent the last part. And so I thought that you might just have to take the bad with the good, and I should continue on. After all, it's part of the tale I'm telling, just maybe not so joyful or enthusiastic as some other parts.

Passing over the Columbia River was a big goal, or so it seemed to me since we had reevaluated our position after Lizzy hit the wall physically and I think mentally. The start in Oregon was full of a lot of different challenges, not least of which was the inauguration of our colt, Rio, as a full-time trail machine. Gad, he has done so in a masterful way, keeping m'lady safe and on the move.

And then there was the incorporation of our dear friends Don and Gerry as partners in the enterprise, if only for seven days. We couldn't have gotten to this point without their assistance, and we will be forever grateful. Rhonda relished having a partner on the trail after nearly ninety days out there alone, and while it wasn't always a piece of cake or without incident, those are often the memories most cherished as you meet the challenge and overcome it.

I guess for me the prospect of traversing Washington State was even more daunting as it was really unknown territory compared to our backyard of Oregon. I've always thought of Washington as wet and cool and kinda grey. Remembering my summer spent in Aberdeen on Grays Harbor at the coast and just a short ways south from the Olympic Peninsula had tainted my view and conception of this wonderful timber-clad state. I think I saw the sun a total of five days that summer. I guess it couldn't have been all that bad as it was the beginning of my surveying career, which lasted nearly fifty more years.

So when I crossed the river, it was to find another place to stay since our first choice horse camp was closed, a negative start right at the get-go. But I did find a suitable location, just not the first choice. And then it was "sit and wait" time, for Rhonda was making camp in the woods. And if the skies were at all telling, it was going to be a wet night. She would be riding into Cascade Locks the following day. And so that night it poured, like buckets were rolled over in the heavens, and everything got instantaneously damp. You ever stay in an eight- by-fourteen-foot living space in those conditions? It wasn't as if I could just hunker down in the cabin and have a hot toddy and wait this thing out. I still had two horses out there to care for. I remember that morning thinking that if Rhonda called the whole thing off after crossing the river, that would be okay with me. You might say I was a little depressed.

Thankfully, the day didn't end that way, and with the sun shining thru broken skies, Rhonda rode into the little park on the Oregon side, all smiles. Four hundred fifty miles of trail riding is certainly something to be proud of and thankful for, and the smile was well-earned. We now had all three horses with us, just as when we started out, so it was a time to turn another page and move on. But not before a little rejoicing with Barb and Dave and taking a zero day to plan and contemplate the challenges ahead of us.

Washington was bringing a whole new set of problems that seemed insurmountable in the time we had allotted as we looked at the maps, and Rhonda perused the water report, and a new one for us was to scope out the northwest fire map. Washington was burning, with twenty-eight fires going all at the same time, and it was nearly impossible to keep up with the fire caused road and trail closures. The empathy we felt for all those affected folks as we remembered our own brush with a wildfire in 2007 that almost burned our home. (Thirty feet close enough?)

And I implore you all to say a prayer or do whatever you do for the many folks that have seen their life dreams go up in smoke in the Middletown conflagration that is currently burning in Northern California. This is dear to my heart as our nephew Jon and wife, Stacey, and their family is smack in the middle of it all. Word is that they were miraculously spared but that 90 percent of the homes on their road are gone. It's hard to just stay here, but helpless we are in our abilities to give aid from afar. So we go on.

Our first few days in Washington went smoothly as Rhonda rode away from the river and then paralleled it as they both ran in a northerly direction. Here it was three days later, and she is less than twenty miles north of the river and the small town of Carson, Washington, but still forty-five miles down the trail. A good start, with decent sky and a good trail. Rhonda is still wearing her raincoat as the brush alongside the trail is still wet, and you can get just as soaked from secondhand wet. Onward and upward.

We finally get to the "crest" of the mountain range, and lo and behold, there is Crest horse camp, except that I drove by it twice without realizing that this is it. Going back to the books and the printed description and it fits, just not what I am expecting. Three campsites with a waterless toilet and somewhat primitive. On close inspection, I find three picnic tables and three fire rings, and of course, the concrete outhouse is hard to miss. It's just that the picnic tables are out in the woods and not next to the single-lane road that dead-ends one hundred yards in. Multiple cars out along the main road in what appears to be a trailhead. The PCT trail runs right next to two of the tables. I'm in luck because none of the parked cars are blocking the entry, and I'm able to back the Hilton to the end of the line. Gettin' pretty good at this backing thing.

So the high line goes up, the horses get strung along it, awaiting their third mate Rio, and I set about leveling up the trailer. We have these stackable blocks that allow us to create a small ramp to raise one side or the back end a bit as we back onto them. Only this time, I look down at a flat tire, ugh! Here we are, thirty-five miles from anywhere on Labor Day weekend, like I'm gonna be able to get this puppy fixed. This is one of the brand-new wheel and tire outfits I have purchased from Les Schwab not too long ago. What to do, what to do? Just had a flat tire less than two weeks ago, so what gives? This is on the Hilton, and I don't dare continue to trudge along on these gravel roads without tire backup, as a spare wheel and tire! In my pondering what to do, I reach for my sweatshirt as the warm summer days seem to be behind us. The little light bulb comes on. Oh hell, I'm not prepared for a cold fall or early winter. Rhonda wants me to ride with her a couple of times towards the end of this gallop, and all I have is short-sleeved shirts and cotton long sleeves. I'm gonna freeze! And the plan is hatched. Get the wheel and tire off, unhook the truck, and prepare to leave shortly after Rhonda arrives. The plan is to drive all the way home tonight (Labor Day) and be at Les Schwab's doorstep in the morning to get the tire fixed. Or will it be the wheel needing to be replaced. Either is fine with me as long as we get mobile early and on the road. I load up more hay, water, and of course, warm clothes upon arriving home, so all I have to do is visit Les's in the morning, or so I thought. Never quite that easy, but it wasn't too bad either. So I was out of town by ten and had three-plus hours to go. Texted Rhonda so she could plan her day's ride and be on the trail by the time I arrived. Slick!

Got the new "fixed" (sharp rock) tire back onto the Hilton, cleaned up camp, and was on the move by 4:00 p.m. Two hours ought to do me, and I would be there waiting for m'lady by six. Just twenty miles of gravel road to traverse. Piece of cake! That is until I come to a sign fifteen miles down the road: Road Closed Ahead. What? Am I on the wrong road? I back up to a trailhead I had just passed (told you I was getting good at this) and asked a couple of hikers if they knew what road this was? No idea! Do they have a map? NO. Now what hiker goes into the wilderness without a map? Well, I guess there are at least two. But aha! There's a map on the kiosk that tells me that the bridge is washed out, and that means that I only have another twenty- five miles to go around the detour to get back to the PCT. Better get movin'.

Well, I just messed up and deleted about an hours' worth of writing, a portion that I was having fun with. Maybe I should be using a Selectrix typewriter. So I'll start again. Ugh!

Twenty-five miles takes an hour and a half when you are on gravel roads, and that's when they are smooth, but luckily, I met pavement for the last ten, and there was a horse and rider waiting in the road as Tucker and I arrived. Now all we had to do was get the Hilton down that narrow driveway to the trailhead. But I told you, I was getting good at this backing-up thing. Piece of cake. A wonderful ridgetop location with huckleberry bushes, small fir and cedar trees interspersed, and some grassy meadows. Just the kind of place I would pick to go hunting but without the PCT trail running through it. It is archery season right now, so we are ever wary.

A sunny and warm evening with two horses onto the outriggers and Rio onto a high line, we run from the back of the trailer to a small tree, and we are all set for the evening. Dinnertime, first for the horses and then for ourselves, and then we bed down for the night. A bit cool, but I have winter clothes now, which I don't need as it ain't that cold. An evening walk is in order to while away the time, let Tucker do his duty, and just check it out to see if my instincts are right and there might be game about. Naw, too much activity in this neighborhood as two young ladies ask if they can settle for the night as our neighbors. Through hikers they are.

We awaken to a sunny morning, glorious it be as I feed the critters. Girls are already gone as I finish breakfast and load hay nets for the ponies. A typical start for us and also for our hiker neighbors. About two hours difference in departure times because of the need to let the horses finish their meal, suck down a bunch of water, and relax before departing. Cleaning hooves, brushing coats to remove burrs and dust, and then we can saddle up and load the bags up that have survival gear, medical supplies, and food cache for the rider and maybe some extra clothes, like a rain slicker. Rhonda is off this morning for the westerly slopes of Mt. Adams on her trusty steed, Rio. Feels great to be able to say that. For the first time, she will be wearing her cowgirl hat instead of the helmet, a showing of trust in this little guy and his sensibilities.

Me, I'm off to the south on a fifty-mile journey around the gorge that separates us from the slopes of Mt. Adams. While there are a few minor gravel roads that cross over, I'm not willing to risk the truck and the Hilton on such a route. The long way around it is, through the small berg of Trout Lake and back up the other side. Good time to get a couple of items for the fridge and gas up once again. Just as I'm leaving the town, it occurs to me that there was a Forest Service District office in Trout Lake and I could check on the latest fire status. A U-turn later, I'm at the counter finding out that the fire closure at Mt. Adams has been lifted. This is texted to Rhonda so she can decide what course she wants to take, and then I'm off to the woods. Or so I thought! Another flat tire on the Hilton in the parking lot of the ranger station. Man, am I getting tired of this scenario! Get out the spare tire and mount it, and I'm off to the service station that just filled me up. An hour later, I find out that I have another cracked wheel. Damn, damn!

So now what? This station is more than helpful as they locate a wheel (Les Schwab they are not) in Portland and can have it here by tomorrow. Steel is all they can offer, and the style will be different, but I don't care if they can just get me back onto the road. It's ordered, and now I must go to get m'lady because she is sans camping gear or food or clothing, so spending the night on the trail is not an option. Tenderly, I drive up the hill on what is welcome macadam pavement to where I find yet another horse and rider standing patiently alongside the road; Rhonda and Rio are happy to see us.

We find a wide spot on the side of a nearby gravel road where we can park nearly level and high line the horses on nearby trees. Gotta do it because I don't want to risk further driving, and I need to disconnect and head back to the station and my waiting wheel tomorrow. So it is that we park in a timber grouse's home turf and suffer the antics of a very disturbed bird. With camp set up, meaning the Hilton is on its blocks and jacks and the horses are munching hay as it hangs in the nets off the high line, we settle down for a bit of respite and an evening cocktail. As we are sitting there, a grouse ambles out of the nearby woods, pecking at gravel or food bits as it meanders towards us. Strange that it seems so unconcerned about our presence, and when it gets to within ten feet, I stand, expecting it to immediately fly off. All this time, Tucker is in the truck because we are next to the road and busy with our activities.

The bird does not fly away but just keeps coming into my circle of influence and personal bubble. Is it a bird raised in captivity and released into the woods? Why isn't it afraid? I throw a few kernels of horse feed out to see if I have a taker, but it doesn't take. By now, Rhonda is videotaping the whole episode as it is so bizarre! He's within five feet now and still coming when I hold out my hand with grain in it. The damn bird attacked me, making a hole in the back of my hand as I jerked away. What the hell? Want to play that way? Let Tucker out!

Tucker was as baffled as we were when he finally spied a bird, a big bird, only five feet away and not on the wing. He froze, and so did the bird. Suddenly, a rush of four feet and the bird stood his ground, if only for a second, and then he turned tail and ran with Tucker on his heels. He had to fly or our boy would have had him, and they were both off into the woods, one in the air and the other wishing he could fly. Minutes later and Tucker was called back, "Give it up. Leave it," and so he did. But you know what? The bird didn't get the message and was back not ten minutes later, only to repeat the scenario. And again, fifteen minutes later, but this time Tucker took some feathers back with him, and the bird disappeared a hundred yards down the road. Now, if any of you know what we just witnessed, other than a cuckoo bird, please let us know. The video is rather hilarious, so we have evidence it really did happen!

Rhonda and I discuss what comes next, and she is adamant; we are not continuing on the trail only to pull off eight or ten miles away. Let's go around this forty-mile stretch and restart northwards. Okay, she's the boss, and doesn't she know it, love it, and use it. I'm okay with that until she steps into my world. Doesn't happen often but . . . why go there.

The next morning, I'm off to purchase a wheel and get us movin' again, which happens but not until 3:00 p.m., and we are excited to be off and on our way to Randle, Washington, where we have made arrangements to visit with Paul and Joice, longtime residents of the area. Paul grew up with Kenna, a dear friend back home, in this very valley and is all welcoming as we knew he would be, just like sis. Kenna suggested this stop, and we are pleased that she did, especially when we get to lay eyes on Joice's prize winning rainbow of dahlias alongside the home and driveway. Unfortunately, we don't have a lot of time because we still want to get to White Pass and settle into a horse camp we have been told about. Paul has offered water for us to tank up the horse and Hilton water supplies, which were badly needed. Thank you, thank you, and after hugs, we are off once again.

That evening, we plant ourselves in the White Pass horse camp, setting up in the dark but without a problem. Just making it here seems like such a major accomplishment, considering where we were this morning. Rhonda will be ready to ride out tomorrow morning headed for Chinook Pass, a twenty-nine-mile jaunt. She will camp along the way at Fish Lake, aptly named as she catches one on camera splashing the water. Lots and lots of water and ample graze for Liz and Cheyenne. And the weather is fine and actually too warm. Believe me, it was too warm, as my T-shirt stuck to my back. Now why did I go all that way for winter gear? Yeah, it's Washington, and I'll find out, hopefully much later. Rhonda left that morning with orders for me to research the area north of Chinook Pass so she would know what she is getting into in the coming week. Sure, Rhonda, sure. Remember what I said about my business? Yeah, you got it.

So I elected to stay at White Pass and watch Rio go airborne with his anxiety of lost companions and soul mates as they hoofed their way northwards. Had never seen a horse dance like that under a high line. Guess there is a first for everything. I busied myself around camp, tidying up the place and getting set for an early departure tomorrow morning. I have cell phone coverage here, so it's time for business, with my first calls going to Back Country Horsemen in the local area to see if we can get info on the trails, such as "Are they cleared?" "Is there water along the way?" etc. I left messages.

Then I called the Forest Service, who was there and quite helpful as I explained what we were about. Her first question was "Which way you going, north or south?" Why, north of course! And her first words were, "But you can't!"

"Huh? Whadaya mean I can't?"

"It's way too dangerous for stock, being very narrow, shale and loose rock and a steep side slope with no trees!"

Like, Rhonda hasn't seen this before? But I'm nice and explain that we have no intention to go onto a dangerous trail and put our stock and rider in jeopardy. She calmed down to a level where we could discuss alternative trails and access points to get us through this stretch, and then we discussed the availability of water for the stock. She confirmed that most of, if not all, the seasonal creeks were dry. Side trails to lakes would be her choice. Now, whoever heard of Washington creeks being dry? We have now!

So then I go on to discuss roads that appear to cross over several passes along this stretch. Can I drive them with my pickup? She confirms my thoughts that they are passable but not for the trailer. Oh yeah! Did I forget to tell you that this is a forty-five-mile stretch that will require Rhonda to camp out for three nights? When I drive up, I will be delivering water and food, but she will be camping on her own as I must return to the third horse. All doable, albeit not very pleasant for either one of us. Just part of the journey that we have accomplished many times before.

Our BCH partners, when calling back, are not very helpful other than to tell me what we already know. None of them ride this stretch of trail, opting for the safer models at lower elevations. Surprise, surprise. I'm really thankful for their calling back and attempting to help . . . maybe next time when we have more time.

On the morrow, I leave the horse camp early, loaded down with all this information and wondering what we will do. It's a trip into Packwood for fuel and groceries and a much-needed shower and then northerly through Rainier National Park and onto Highway 410 and Chinook Pass. What a spectacular pass, with the highway carved out of sheer granite. I'm impressed. Now that very helpful young lady at the Forest Service said there would be trailer parking available on the north side of the highway. In your dreams, as the last day of summer is about to pass us by, this very fine Saturday and the whole city of Seattle has decided to visit the mountains. The temperature keeps rising, and I quit looking as the thermometer passes ninety degrees, and there ain't no shade. Oh, maybe under the truck. I double park alongside a backhoe that has taken my spot, all the while blocking a lane of traffic but leaving ample space for folks to get around. Their problem, not mine. They chose to park in the trailer spaces.

Rhonda arrived later that day, hot but in good spirits. A short time later, Liz and Cheyenne are loaded, and we are on our way, easterly and to where is anyone's guess. No time to scope it out ahead of time. Keep an eye out for any side road that offers promise for us to settle. We go into one trailhead only to find it chock-full of archery hunters, shucks. A little farther along, we spy another campground, and a perusal seems a prudent approach, and we cruise through. Definitely a people camp but worth a look, nevertheless. Rhonda suggests that we ask the camp host if he knows of any horse camps in the area, and when he is confronted with the inquiry, he suggests we camp right there. Wow, how cool! We are on board with that! Another tour and we find a spot away from the river and with trees for high-lining the horses and ground that is durable enough that the horses will not leave a mess. One night only as we find out later because the camp is closing the following day and we must be out by 2:00 p.m. No *problemo*!

And the search continues for a new place to rest the following day. After serious discussion the previous night, I find that my research on trails and roads will not be needed after all. It seems Rhonda is done. Now you know that *done* has many meanings, so what's this one mean? Are we going home? NOPE! Had to ask. This *done* means she is done camping out on her own and all alone. Now I can relate to that and have considered it miraculous that she made it this far. This has to have been the hardest part of the journey, by far. I can relate through my many treks into the woods on my own, all alone, and hoping to land that trophy deer or elk or just some meat. I usually last seven to eight days before I start to question what I'm doing out there, alone and lonesome. Remember, Rhonda has not had the camaraderie of hiker havens to mix it up with fellow travelers. She camps alone to be able to manage the mess horses make. She must be two hundred feet from water and one hundred feet from the trail per the "leave no trace" epithets. The hikers are usually bunched near the water and near the trail, if not on it.

So the decision has been made, and we are headed to Yakima to shop and do other necessary things, but not on a Sunday, when nothing is open. We are again in the mode of scoping out the terrain to find a friendly waypoint to nestle into and, hopefully, have cell coverage at the same time. We check out a game reserve for winter feeding of the elk, but it's no dice and we keep going. Aha, a wide spot on a little dead-end road, and we pounce. No grouse to attack us but am not too sure about snakes, but the trees are sturdy enough to hold three horses. We've found our spot for another night. And would you believe it? 4G and four bars show up on our phones. Boy, have we found our spot!

The long and short of it is that we stayed one night, located a stable where we could house the horses, located all the stores we intended to visit, and then we holed up on the outskirts of Yakima for two nights, with electricity too! The weather has turned cool and cloudy but with little rain, but we can now run the heater in the morning and act like civilized folk. Wonderful!

But all good things must come to an end because m'lady is done but not ALL done. We have a trail ride ahead of us . . . together! As Dad has agreed to ferry the trailer around to the north end of the trail at Stevens Pass. Ought to be fun, and now I have some warm clothes to truly enjoy this trip. We've had to adjust our sights almost daily, and this stretch of trail required yet another switch from our plan. A quick call to the local ranger district and we found out a bridge was out on the PCT and there was no immediate go-around. The only choice was to bypass a section of trail and start elsewhere. Done! We'll start at Cle Elum Lake and ride north to intersect the PCT and then on to our meet up with Dad. Hooray!

We are now off to our new camp spot and likely out of touch. So you, my readers, my friends and my relatives now know that I haven't forgotten you and that you are ever with us, on the trail or wherever we may be.

Love to you all,

Pat, Rhonda, and the Gang

(Sent from my US cellular smartphone)

PART
29

September 27, 2015

Ugh, I should not try to do things until I have had my morning coffee. By now you have received part 29 and realized it was incomplete, which was something I was going to remedy this morning, only it didn't go as planned. I had chores to do and was merely going to save my draft and come back to it, but instead hit Send! No escaping that one or calling it back once it hits the airwaves, so now you have two partials you'll have to muddle through. Just go have your coffee (or tea), and you'll make it, connect it, or whatever. I could cut and paste and resend, but what's the fun in that? And knowing from past experience that cutting and pasting from this itsy-bitsy screen is no picnic, this is what you get. Time has passed, and we need to get on with the journey.

And now I get to include another "Good morning!" to each and every one of you. It is Sunday, and much has happened, so I really should get on with my tale. Backing up to the eighteenth, Rhonda and I decided it was time for a trip into town to shop but mostly to engage our instruments of mass communication for multiple purposes. Dad is due to arrive on the morrow, and we should let him know that everything is a GO and we will be ready to continue down the trail.

NOTE: I said WE!

During our downtime and travels to and thru Yakima this past week, Rhonda was busy sending out smoke signals to multiple parties up ahead of us, closer to the Canadian border, as she is always stressing out how she will get thru the next stretch of trail. Actually, this concern was over the "last" stretch as we had already decided on skipping a bunch beyond Stevens Pass. Due to the many fire "complexes" in Washington and all the reroute of the trail, we just weren't sure how up to date any of the posts on line were. And you must understand that most of the info is for hikers, not equestrians! As far as we know, Rhonda is the only rider still on the trail that attempted a thru ride this year. Hikers tell us that she is the only one they have met or witnessed. For a trail that is touted as being both hiker and equestrian, we have found this lack of information to be a rather appalling shortcoming. Rhonda has been trying to fill in the gaps in any way possible. In this case, she attempted to contact members of the Back Country Horsemen of Washington state to see what they could tell us. We are members of this national organization, only in Oregon, but we're hopeful that locals would have an idea of trail conditions in their vicinity.

Unfortunately, there were no responses to her inquiries. There could be any number of reasons for this, and we couldn't dwell on this as our attention needed to be on more immediate issues. Like where to go for a shower to cleanse our bodies and clear our heads for the endeavors soon to come. As it happens, part of our itinerary for the day included a stop at the local Forest Service, Cle Elum District office. I wanted a map of the area we were about to enter upon, an area outside our existing map sources. What did I say about a couple of hikers going into the wilderness without a map? And here we were, about to embark upon trails of which we had no knowledge. Day trippin' should not be part of the plan! Four days in the Alpine Lakes Wilderness warranted a more stealthy approach if we were to see Dad at Stevens Pass on Tuesday. So with new maps in hand, we were about to leave when it occurred to me that these folks might know of a shower facility nearby. Several came to mind as possibilities, but none for sure!

Not for the first time we were on to the search, with the closest possibility right down the road at a State Park facility. Washington State Parks often have RV hookups and full facilities available, so we were hopeful but very unaware of the kind of facility we were about to enter. The Central Washington Horse Park was fairly amazing for us outsiders, with a myriad of facilities including two arenas with bleachers, twenty to thirty horse stalls with cover, ten to fifteen full hook-up RV parking spaces, and an equal number of parking spots. Not to mention the "day" parking areas and, to our delight, three showers in a small building as we entered the area. The shower facility was donated by a local family with a request for donations to maintain it. Wow! What a find!

Before leaving, we had to go see what all the racket was at the arena we spotted through the trees. What we discovered was a competition of mounted shooting where riders carry two six-shot revolvers and race (singly) through a course of balloons on sticks, which they must pop and all the while being timed through the course. Pretty impressive as I probably would have difficulty popping all twelve balloons if I walked on foot through the course. They did it at a full gallop without missing a pop. Entertaining, as we heard from the announcer that this is the fastest-growing mounted sport in the country. Maybe we should invite one or two to join us in this mountain lion country, or would that take the sport out of it?

Time to move on with still no response on our inquiries, but maybe we should give them a little more time. Just so happens there is a Mexican restaurant down the street, and we've got two hungry pardners with a thirst to quench. Two margaritas later, dinner is served. A shrimp filled enchilada for me and I'm not sure what Rhonda is having. Reminds me of the tale Rhonda loves to tell, with some dismay, about a dinner meal where we ordered separate items with one being delayed in its arrival to the table. Upon arrival, Rhonda finds out that I have nearly devoured her entire meal while she waited. Ugh, not a happily married couple at that moment. But tonight is a different story as two satiated diners rush to get back and care for their trusty buds who will carry them down the trail on the morrow.

And so Saturday brings a day of sunshine and Dad and friend Beth from next door. So good to see them again, and hugs are given all around. For us, the work is just beginning. We thought we had everything in order and ready to go, but it's been raining, and horses don't seem to mind getting down and dirty. Endless minutes of brushing later and we can start saddling, leaving loose cinches on the two to be ridden while we manage to get Cheyenne loaded with the supplies. Except that our intended pack is not going to work, with horse feed inside action packers that are inside soft canvas panniers (bags that hang from the pack saddle). The hard cases are just too bulky, and Rhonda decides to leave them and put the horse feed loose inside black plastic and then inside the panniers. We save about one-fourth size and just enough to make everything work, with a top pack holding our tent and sleeping bags. Finally, with a tarp over the load and all tied down, cinches are tightened, and our goodbye hugs are given, and we mount up. Whew, a late start, but hopefully a short day of riding to Waptus Lake, our first day's destination along the Waptus River Trail.

"Hey, this isn't so bad riding in the lowlands along a river. Rhonda, what's all the complaining been about?" I said as I duck the missiles coming my way. All this talk about the Pacific Crest Sidehill Trail? And the sun is still shining as we meander through the Washington backwoods on a wide and clear dirt trail. It then occurs to me that we are on a well-beaten trail, two to three feet wide, and that we are still very close to the trailhead. Three and a half days to go, and the sky is getting a little grey as I begin to see signs of recent trail maintenance, like loose dirt and new furrows in the slope. Not much longer, and I hear the tingle of steel hitting rock, and just around the bend, we come upon Ranger John, the wilderness ranger for this district. We become very engaged in conversation as we realize he has knowledge we need.

The one hitch to knowledge gathering from the local districts and users is that they are so vested in their knowledge that they talk way above your level and ability to absorb all that they have to give. They talk about places you have never been to, locale that you can't even find on the map, and about issues that you don't care a lick about. Like if a bridge is out . . . We don't care about the 2012 flood; we just want to know if there is a fjord around it and how to find it. On this trip, we are mostly concerned with the locale for finding water and graze along the trail, camping spots and the status of clearing to allow us to get by. Once John got started, we realized he was a wealth of knowledge, and we had better listen closely to what he has to say. Unfortunately for us, we would be out for three more days and just couldn't absorb all of it for all the places over the next forty-plus miles we would cover. So be it, absorb and remember the critical and let the rest fall where it may.

Critical: a portion of the trail is closed ahead, and there is a reroute to get around it. The reroute is a totally different trail system that will eventually take us back to the PCT. Now why didn't this get mentioned by those two ladies in the office yesterday? Ranger John is puzzled by this also. After getting directions to a potential camp spot for this evening and to the river fjord, we are again moving along the trail under further graying skies and the threat of rain. And rain it did, only a sprinkle, but wet it was until just before we found a place to camp. Water available but no grass for the stock, so we waste no time in getting them high-lined and placing the tent in a friendly location. It's going to be a wet night.

And wet it was, but thankfully, it let up enough for us to pack up and get on the move once again. A short ride up a feeder trail to the PCT, a few miles on, and then we intersect the trail for reroute per Ranger John. According to the map, we will climb up the side of the adjoining ridge through a series of switchbacks and then descend through a mirrored image down the other side where we will try to find a decent camp spot before completing the trail down into the adjoining valley and then a whole new ascent to Deception Pass on the PCT. Piece of cake!

Remember my ascent up to the Horseshoe Meadow campground through a series of switchbacks? Only then I was aboard a one-ton truck and not a half ton mare called Liz. I shudder at the prospect. Months ago, looking at maps of our originally proposed trail course, I often had this feeling of dread as well. Now I must consider the prospect that I was actually going to do this. The countryside and mountains are magnificent in their awe-inspiring splendor. Fall colors abound, and mountain lakes are so clear and calm that you can't tell if you are looking at the mountains or their reflections in the mirror like surface. Awesome!

We managed to find one of those lakes on the other side of the ridge, and this one had some friendly grasses on the tail end to the delight of the horses. Still wearing our raincoats, but the weather is starting to turn for the better. We give the critters a chance to fill their bellies before it gets dark. A good campsite and hard ground to put the horses onto and we are set for the night. Tomorrow will be a lengthy day of rising to the pass to reconnect with the PCT, and then we will cross over the ridge to camp at either Deception or Glacier Lake, whichever is reachable.

Leaving the lake the next morning in bright sunshine and high spirits, we continued down to the valley floor and the Hyas Lake trailhead. From there, we started all the hard work of climbing back up to the ridgetop. At least Cheyenne has sixty pounds less to carry as the horses have consumed that much food in two days. We find lots of grass at the trailhead and must take a break to be sure they get their fill. It's a long gradual climb through heavy forest, and I'm liking it a lot until we get to more sidehill on a narrow trail. Per Rhonda's suggestion, I look no more than ten feet ahead of the horse and focus on the trail. Don't look down or to the side! You see, a horse has very sensitive feel for the rider or anything that it comes in touch with, so even a slight look to the side by me may be enough for the horse to sense my very slight shift in weighted position and thus react. That reaction is what I want to avoid because it may be enough for Liz to change her focus and alignment to the trail. Remember a while back when I noted that Rhonda had to have absolute confidence and trust in her mount. Well, now I must apply that to me. Hard to do when you haven't been riding for six months and are now on a horse you've not ridden forever. Thankfully, I had reasonably easy trail for the first twenty miles, which built my trust in Liz and our relationship. She is a remarkable horse.

The sidehills just kept coming, and my nerves were all a jangle. Liz helped me to calm down. That and the prospect of just one last night and a final ride tomorrow, and my heart and nerves will have a chance to settle down. It became obvious as we kept moving that we would never make Glacier Lake, and Deception Lake would provide our home for the night. When we got there, we found signs that directed horse camping up an adjacent trail. However, after climbing the hill for a quarter mile, we gave up on it, not knowing where we would end up and knowing that we couldn't be that far from water. We went back to the lake and climbed the PCT for two hundred feet and found a tent site and solid ground amongst trees to set up the horses on a high line.

Whoopee! Water, grass, and one more day done. Unfortunately, the last day was going to be a long one.

An early start was imperative on Tuesday, so we decided we didn't have time for graze that morning, and we were out of there before 10:00 a.m. Eighteen rugged miles to go, with more than its share of sidehill, ups and downs, and hopefully some graze and water along the way. Cheyenne now had a very light pack, so all we had to do is keep moving. Rhonda was my savior as she agreed to pull Cheyenne and let me focus on keeping Liz on the trail. I know, I know . . . she can do it on her own, but I can't close my eyes! I lead out while we are in the timber, which gives me some reassurance that if I fall I won't go very far. Hey, the idea is not to fall! On the way up, we are climbing a 15 percent grade and having to rest the horses periodically when Rhonda suddenly yells, "BEES!" which means go forward as fast as you can! Gallop if you can, and all this on a very narrow and steep trail. At this point, you don't think, you just GO! Rhonda had to handle a bucking bronco in Rio and still drag Cheyenne up the hill at a bouncy gallop. Thankfully, she was able to keep her seat, and we made it through one more hurdle.

Nearing the ridge line, we found a very rich grassy area to graze the horses on. They needed the respite from the climb and the moisture and energy the grass would provide. Reaching the crest of the ridge, I had to ask Rhonda to go ahead of me and continue to tow the extra horse as we had extensive sidehill to negotiate. My nerves were getting the best of me.

There are times when you have no idea where the trail goes, and this was to be a whole stretch of those moments. Up onto a shelf, switchbacks down and onto the next shelf, across a slope, and then switchbacks across and down a rocky scree slope and onto the valley floor, a spectacular descent. And then traverse for a while and then do it all over again. Glacier Lake came and went, and it wasn't until we crossed a ridge and looked to the north to see a ski lift, still miles away, but a promise of the end of today's journey. By golly, we are going to make it.

And make it we did. With Rhonda on Rio leading, we had made incredibly good time for this 18.2 mile stretch, getting in before

6:00 p.m. Dad was there waiting, whew! I had just completed my second ride of the year (remember I rode the first five miles) and was exhilarated, hugging Rhonda and anyone else willing. Now I needed to get back into my Wrangler role as Rhonda had led me through this with patience and loving care and deserved some peace. She was thankful to have me along, and I was likewise to her having me. It was a time that we shall forever remember. Thank you, Dad, for making it possible by agreeing to ferry the trailer ahead for us.

And to the rest of you, thanks for being with us through these miles, days and months. Stay with us for the finish as we contemplate our final surge to the Canadian border, planning, stressing, and of course, driving the 150 miles to our jump off spot.

See you down the road and trail.

Happy trails,
Pat and Rhonda

(Sent from my US cellular smartphone)

Packing in the rain, ain't it fun! Tucker is finally cool, but not happy.

Finally, some grass to eat.

Cathedral Mtn. is fogged in with the trail in the foreground.

What a beautiful morning!

Rhonda calls it the blue trail. It's a magnificent morning.

Moving down the trail.

More side hill trail.

We find the asphalt and Tucker collapses after 18 miles.
We are DONE!

PART

30

October 1, 2015

Good morning to each and every one of you! I'm sitting down and drinking my coffee this morning, so hopefully, there will be no flub like the last message. Rhonda and I wish that all of you are well and find this day to be a pleasant one, unique in its own way with love and good cheer all abounds.

I feel so grateful to having all of you with us throughout this journey, with your blessings and warm thoughts given to us so freely, nursing us through the trials and bolstering our efforts with encouragement to keep on moving on. Rhonda has done what she set out to do, which was "Ride, partner, ride," and while the miles didn't stack up as we had envisioned or as m'lady had most certainly hoped, they did stack up. As I review my calendar, upon which I scratched out each day's events in a very brief kind of shorthand, I am amazed by what I read and subsequently have so meekly attempted to convey to all of you. What fun this has been, along with the pain, the trepidation, the anguish, and the joy.

By now, you have probably figured out, and those of you that have been following us through Rhonda's blog already know, we are back and enjoying all the comforts of home. Yes, Rhonda is done-done! No more "Maybe this" or "Maybe that" or "What if?" or "What do we do now?" or "Where do we go?" We have finished *the journey*! At least the physical side of things is done, but there seems to be so much more wrapped up in our noggins as remembrances and warm fuzzy feelings about what we just did and what Rhonda accomplished. It gives pleasure every day.

We left home a little over six months ago, on March 17, with the Hilton in tow and three warm bodies housed inside, not completely prepared but as well prepared as our knowledge and the understandings of this journey and all its trials and trappings would take us. Little did I know, some fifteen months ago when Rhonda smacked me across the head with this dream of hers to ride the PCT, just what I was getting into. There may have been some premonitions, as I didn't really respond for well over two months, but finally capitulated as I realized, "What else would I be doing?" Rhonda, as only Rhonda can be, was determined to make the journey! To make it happen! In retrospect, I am so glad she did and that I was along for the ride.

We spent months planning and preparing, and I got pretty grumpy as it seemed to be taking forever. We had purchased maps galore, and we poured over them, viewing and reviewing each (approximately) fifteen-mile stretch of this trail 2,660 miles long, trying to ascertain off the maps just what we were about to encounter. We coupled the maps with a PCT log of trail miles in the form of a book that stipulated all the trail intersections, road intersections, water stops and locale, and the elevation changes of each along the way. We thought we had it all figured out, just average fifteen miles per day for 177 days and we'll be done, high-fiving hikers and each other at the border! Never mind what we didn't know; we had it figured out. After all, we had ridden many trails and gone many miles in cross-country fashion, and our horses were solid mounts with many years of experiences. We can do this!

Maybe our first failing moment is not realizing that with all those years of experience comes an aging process that would deteriorate their abilities to endure such a trial. Cheyenne and Liz are twenty-three and twenty-one years old, respectively. This means they are two-thirds down the trail of life, which for us would be somewhere around sixty years of age. What is in your gas tank today? I'm seventy years of age or nearly so and know I couldn't do what they just did. They are both remarkable, and we are so lucky to have them. And then there is the five-year-old

Rio, who has more energy than good sense but sure learned and proved himself throughout this journey. We are both extremely proud of him and especially Rhonda with all her hours of training him and bringing him this far along to be trusted the way few five-year-olds have ever been trusted. We have gained so much by just trying!

I am the Wrangler, and it was up to me to provide a place to call home and the sustenance to make the trip each day to find it waiting for them. In this, you might say I failed, but it was not through a lack of effort but more through a lack of knowledge. We honed up on so many things in our preparations, but in this instance, we missed the mark. We had researched over the World Wide Web all the likely places we would be able to stop and house two humans, one dog and three horses. Horse camps, county fairgrounds, ranches, and the many national forests throughout our travelling corridor would be likely places for us to stop and catch our breath. Little did I know that each forest management scheme was different, some more hospitable than others, allowing our presence only under their terms. Of course, what they didn't know would not likely hurt them, so we practiced LNT (leave no trace) wherever we went and used whatever camp spot seemed hospitable and some that were entirely nonhospitable but doable. I think I shall remember every one of them and that in itself is remarkable when I usually can't remember where I was yesterday, and these places are now indelibly etched in my mind. Thank you, Rhonda, for taking me along.

And then there was the planning of our sustenance for the duration of the trip. As I have mentioned before, horses do not take well to a sudden change in their diet, so consistency was a high priority in our planning. That and the ability to store and carry with us a volume that would be consumed daily. After all, a thousand-pound animal does not survive on a dinner plate, and we had three of them critters along for the ride. Once again, the World Wide Web proved to be of help as we researched feeds across the western states and found a source that could supply compressed hay bales and had distributorships and dealers up and down the west coast, with a search engine to find one near you. Of course, they didn't tell you that not all these dealers carried all their offerings. My shortcoming was that I didn't realize this until we were well underway, which in and of itself was not impossible to surmount; it just meant I had to travel further to the dealer of choice. So armed with the knowledge of our feed of choice, we stocked up at home and began to switch the horses over to their new feeding regimen. Everything was going as planned, and we had settled into a pattern we thought would hold us for the duration. Only then, a month into the trip, did our trusty steeds tell us that our plan was not to their liking, and they refused to eat the high-protein grain (pellet) we were feeding. Now we are amongst feed stores that we have no knowledge of, and we are carrying grain we have no use for. And now we cannot find a dealership that cares a hoot about our problem. Why should they, as they seem to sell everything they carry? Which isn't anything we want. We do everything we can to make the pellets more delectable and palatable but to no avail. Then we find a nutritionist at a small country feed store who has a product we believe will work. We buy her entire stock of this item. And we line up a delivery of more down the road a piece. This just might work! But alas, we run out of places she can deliver to, because now we are going into the Sierras and the towns are few and far between, and the dealerships she can persuade into carrying her products are even fewer. The horses like it, but we cannot get it.

At this point, we have finished about 20 percent of the ride and are headed home to do our St. Jude's charity event. Before leaving Southern California, we attempt to find other food sources, particularly Packer Pellets, which we feed when travelling off highway and through the woods. They have never heard of them! Purina (the producer) doesn't even list them on their website. We will be needing a feed supplement to carry when Rhonda is packing through the high country or where there isn't graze for the animals and the new feed would fulfill our needs if we can get it. Finally, after many phone calls, our nutritionist returns my call, and we arrange for a dealership in Central California to receive our shipment and we can be on our way. We left Oregon to return south in high spirits. Only the shipment doesn't arrive, and we cannot wait around, so another feed is purchased with fingers crossed. Has anyone ever heard if crossing one's fingers actually provides the magical touch for things to work out? Sure didn't for us! After a short time, they wouldn't eat this stuff either. Damn, damn.

After Cheyenne's injury and the witnessing of our horse's loss of weight, we are home again and inquire with our feed store as to what they can provide to get us over the nutrition hump. With their advice in hand, we leave the newly purchased feed at home, and we take their supplements with us on the road back to the trail. Only Liz doesn't like these either, which finds us trailering her back home, malnourished but alive. Then a contact Rhonda has made with another rider on the trail leads us to our final feed change. High-fat, high-protein feed that the horses love and we wish we had been feeding all along, and should have been. If only. Where would we be now? Heaven only knows, because we are not there, and there isn't a single thing we can do to put us there. We must be satisfied that we did the best we could. It's exasperating, but we have limited knowledge and limited experiences that proved to be insufficient to complete the task, as insurmountable as it was. Hindsight? Always 20/20, isn't it?

Well, I'm not the one to dwell on the past or the negative. It is what it is, so let's move on. And that's exactly what we did, picking up on the positive and the doable and pressing forth with accomplishing all that we could. It was obvious, after bringing Liz home, that our sights needed to be adjusted and the goal altered to the realities of our place in time. We would do what we could, and the remainder would be just that, remaining for some future time and place.

Oregon and Washington now seemed to be within our sights and within our powers to complete. Some adjustments would have to be made, with only one horse available now, but the other two could be transitioned in over the coming months. We got the show on the road, and the days passed turned to weeks, and up the trail Rhonda went. Then the critter broke the truck, and a short backslide was incurred, but we persevered and kept moving with summer beginning to wane. And rain and more rain and our mind-set seemed to be that we just needed to get through each day, and it would lead to the next. Meeting up with the kids and grandkids near Mt. Hood was a fortuitous event that seemed to bolster Rhonda's and my resolve that we could do this, and so she kept moving northward and forward. Mt. Hood and its new mantle of snow should have been foreboding, but its splendor was elegant and inviting and invigorating as Rhonda moved up and over the ridge. Lolo Pass and only two days to the river and another 450 miles could be chalked up and become an annotation on our logs and diary. Washington, here we come.

After 241 miles of traversing the Washington portion of the PCT and after considerable deliberation, Rhonda decided that the journey should come to an end. It was a culmination of many events and a conclusion that was hard to come to, but a welcome respite. It was just meant to be. The Canadian border had always been the goal, and we had planned to make the final distance together. However, having bypassed eight hundred miles of California, it seemed to be somewhat anticlimactic to reach the border. Did we still want to do it? Of course, we did! But at every juncture, there seemed to be an obstacle of some sort, not least of which was my reluctance to subject my horse, Cheyenne, to more endurance and pain. He was still feeling the repercussions of the accident, with a shorter stride on the right rear and swelling of the hock. This was exacerbated by the past four days of being our packhorse as Rhonda and I negotiated the trail to Stevens Pass.

Having completed that portion of the trail, we had already decided to drive around (160 miles) to Rainy Pass to embark on this final leg to the border. There just wasn't enough time to do all 160-plus miles before significant snowfall would cover our tracks. So sitting in the Hilton and with cell coverage at Stevens Pass, we began to inquire with the local ranger district about trail conditions. Our plan had been to trailer to Rainy Pass, camp out, and while Rhonda waited, I would take the truck and ferry supplies up to Hart's Pass. I would leave a stash for us to pick up along the way and then return to Rainy Pass to embark. The supplies would be needed both northwards and on our return south back to Rainy Pass. In other words, up and back. Seven days of riding with six nights of sleeping in a tent and packing all our gear.

Then the rangers informed us that the PCT was closed to stock (horses) between Rainy Pass and Hart's Pass. Since we couldn't trailer the horses (no trailers allowed) to Hart's Pass, we would have to find another route. We found a satisfactory one, only to be told that the trail was closed due to a 2012 flood that washed out the trail. They suggested another route that would add another day and night to the effort. Plus we didn't know anything about the alternate, such as water sources, grazing opportunities, or points of resupply. The unknowns were daunting. I suggested to Rhonda that she make the trip on her own, and I could be at Hart's Pass to resupply her, but her answer was that she was done with camping by herself. Can't blame her. I was not willing to sacrifice Cheyenne to the cause, and suddenly there was only one choice left. Go home.

Can you be sad and glad at the same time? I believe we both were, with our journey called to an end, nearly completed. Tears in my eyes, I hugged Rhonda and told her of my love, which after forty years still seems to be never-ending. A phone call later, we had dinner plans with Rhonda's dad a short hour away. Time to pack up and make tracks with only one more phone call . . . to make arrangements to leave three horses overnight, and then we could park in the subdivision that Dad calls home. And a week ago, we arrived home. Home sweet home. Turtle, the cat, was glad to see us!

So what exactly did Rhonda do? Let me recap this astonishing achievement!

She embarked upon the trail, starting at the Mexican border, in my company for the first five miles and ended in my company for the last fifty-three miles, ending at Stevens Pass Washington.

During the course of her travels, she passed over or onto the Cleveland National Forest, the San Bernadino NF, the Angeles NF, the Sequoia NF, the Inyo NF, the Klamath NF, the Rogue River / Siskiyou NF, the Winema NF, the Umpqua NF, the Willamette NF, the Deschutes NF, the Mt. Hood NF, the Gifford Pinch NF, the Wenatchee NF, and the Mt. Baker-Snoqualmie NF. She entered into and crossed the Sequoia National Park, the Kings Canyon National Park, Crater Lake National Park, and Mt. Rainier National Park, together with the Sequoia National Monument, the Cascade/Siskiyou National Monument, and the Oregon Cascades National Recreation Area, the Olallie Lake National Scenic Area, and the Columbia River Gorge National Scenic Area.

Rhonda and whomever she was riding or towing entered into and traversed along and over the Hauser Wilderness, the San Jacinto Wilderness, the San Gorgonio Wilderness, the Sheep Mountain Wilderness, the San Gabriel Wilderness, the Kiava Wilderness, the Owens Peak Wilderness, the Chimney Peak Wilderness, the Dome Land Wilderness, the Southern Sierra Wilderness, the Golden Trout Wilderness, the John Muir Wilderness, the Sequoia-Kings Canyon Wilderness, the Sky Lakes Wilderness, the Mt. Thielson Wilderness, the Diamond Peak Wilderness, the Waldo Lake Wilderness, the Three Sisters Wilderness, the Mt. Washington Wilderness, the Mt. Jefferson Wilderness, the Mark Hatfield Wilderness, the Mt. Hood Wilderness, and finally in Washington, the Indian Heaven Wilderness, the Alpine Wilderness and the Alpine Lakes Wilderness. One should keep in mind that *wilderness* means there are no motorized vehicles and that access points are few and far between, hampering Rhonda's movement and my resupply efforts.

In the midst of all this mountain wilderness, she managed to cross portions of the Mohave and Anzo-Borrego Deserts, which were squeezed between mountain ranges in the Southern California regions. And speaking of mountains, here is another list of the mountain ranges she followed or crossed over in this monumental ride: the Laguna Mountains, the Volcan Mountains, the San Jacinto Mountains, the San Gabriel Mountains, the Sierra Pelona Mountains, the Tehachapi Mountains, the Piute Mountains, the Scodie Mountains, the Sierra Nevada Mountains, the Scofield Mountains, the Siskiyou Mountains, the Cascade Mountains, and finally the Wenatchee Mountains. Had enough?

Nah, I didn't think so. In total, Rhonda rode for 108 days on the trail. She took twenty-one "0" days to rest and recuperate. Of those 108 days, 96 were days she spent entirely alone on the trail. Thirty days of which, while alone, she made camp and broke camp alongside the trail, high-lined the horse or horses, cleaned up after them and moved on down the trail. Ten additional days, she had the company of Gerry or myself riding with her, helping to set up a remote campsite, high-line horses and or mules, and then break camp to spend another day along the trail.

In 108 days of riding Rhonda amassed a remarkable total of 1,450 miles passed, giving her an average of 13.4 miles per day of travel. How many of us can cover that much in one day of riding, let alone consecutive days? I am truly amazed as I recount these accomplishments and so pleased that I could be a small part of this journey.

Some of you have asked if she plans to return and give it another go. Another year maybe. Last evening we went to see the movie *A Walk in the Woods*. As Bryson said, the trail is a lot like life, you never know what's around the bend or over the next rise. Many of us just sit back and wait for that bend in life's path and see where it takes us. Then there are others, like Rhonda, that don't wait but rush to make it what they wish, still not knowing but anxious to see. What we saw will forever be remembered, and I hope I gave you a peek now and then of that vision.

Thanks again for being there with us. And thank you, Rhonda, for taking us for a ride.

Love you!
Patrick

We make it home in one piece.
Sure love the Central Oregon sun.

Time to dry things out and settle back to enjoy a job well done.

About the Author

The author, Pat Marquis, a.k.a. the Wrangler as he was known on the Pacific Crest Trail, was born and raised in Northern California in a rural setting with horses in the fields of their twenty-acre ranch. He learned about horses and riding at a young age, participating on a local drill team and performing in parades and venues such as the Cow Palace in San Francisco. Pat's father was an avid hunter and fisherman and taught his young family how to enjoy and survive in the back country of California, hiking or riding horseback into the Coast Range and Sierra Nevada mountains.

What Pat knew and learned he would later teach to his new bride, Rhonda, as they settled onto acreage on the Kenai Peninsula of Alaska in the 1970s, shortly after marrying in 1975. There they raised a family and spent many outdoor moments in the Caribou Hills, travelling on horseback to their wilderness cabin and hunting the elusive moose and avoiding the brown bears this area was known for.

When the economy faltered in the late 1980s, Pat's business as a professional land surveyor also crashed, and Rhonda's comment was "Let's go south so that I can ride more than three months a year," and Oregon is where they landed and have lived for the past thirty years.

Now living in Central Oregon on the edge of the high desert and at the foothills of the Cascade Mountains, a horseback ride is right out the back door or the mountain trails are only an hour's drive away. Now retired, horses and mules are the staple of their pursuits, and their focus of many hours of volunteer work for government agencies in support of the trails they so love and cherish.

This book is about a hope and a dream, and the efforts and love it took to bring *The Journey* into focus and become a reality for two hardworking people. I hope you enjoy it.